Spirit Unleashed

Spirit Unleashed

Reimagining Human-Animal Relations

Anne Benvenuti

 CASCADE *Books* · Eugene, Oregon

SPIRIT UNLEASHED
Reimagining Human-Animal Relations

Cascade Books
An Imprint of Wipf and Stock Publishers
199 W. 8th Ave., Suite 3
Eugene, OR 97401

www.wipfandstock.com

ISBN 13: 978-1-62564-187-8

Cataloging-in-Publication data:

Benvenuti, Anne.

Spirit unleashed : reimagining human-animal relations / Anne Benvenuti.

xvi + 204 p. ; 23 cm. — Includes bibliographical references.

ISBN 13: 978-1-62564-187-8

1. Human-animal relationships. 2. Ethics, Evolutionary. 3. Animal welfare. I. Title.

HV4708 .B46 2014

Manufactured in the U.S.A.

Molly Brown, Spiritual Teacher Extraordinaire
Truly this is a Labor of Love

My questioning was my attentive spirit; their beauty, their reply.

—AUGUSTINE

Table of Contents

Preface

THE DAZED BRAZILIAN CRESTED cardinal stood up in my hand and gave what psychologists call a pressured telling of her story. She looked up at my face, and "spoke" rapidly for some seconds. Just prior to this soliloquy, she had appeared to be on the verge of losing consciousness. At that moment I did not know her breed or sex; I only knew that I had taken her out of the role of football for two rather obnoxious myna birds who appeared to enjoy tormenting her.

I took her back to my room at the guesthouse. Once there, Elizabeth offered to go to the store for some syrupy food and a dropper. I sat on the bed with the little bird cupped in my hands and the lights dimmed; she quieted and slept. When Elizabeth returned we made a t-shirt nest for the bird in my bed, and I tucked in for the night. In the morning there was an aborted egg in the nest and so we knew she was a female. We named her Emma for the Hawaiian Queen Emma.

After three days, Emma was only able to walk around the bed without falling off; she had not made a great deal of progress in her recovery from what appeared to be neurological symptoms, probably caused by flying into the window of a high-rise. Because we were leaving Hawaii the next day, we stopped at the local bird sanctuary on our way back from the beach; and there we learned that euthanasia was the only thing they could offer. As we drove to fetch Emma to her death, the scent of flowers on the trade winds wafting through our open convertible was not enough to drive away our sadness.

When we opened the door of the semi-dark bedroom, we could not see her, though we searched the space. Then, looking up, we saw that she was perched atop a curtain rod. What relief! I got a chair and gathered her into my hands. Elizabeth opened doors for us, and when she opened the door to the garden, Emma darted from my hands into a nearby tree, where she sat barely moving, seeming very unsure of herself. Within minutes, two new Brazilian cardinals arrived, though we had seen none near to our house prior to that moment. They chattered, the three of them. We decided to think of these new birds as her husband and son, though of course this detail is pure embellishment. But after some time of hopping around on branches and chattering, Emma still clung to the branch where she first perched. The larger of her guys finally flew at her and pushed her off the branch. She and they flew to the peak of the house next door, and then off toward the south where we had first found her.

✧

The core concept of this book is that to change our thinking and our way of relating to other animals has tremendous potential to increase the happiness of all beings on Earth, and further that it is a spiritual necessity to make this change. We do not hold the place that exists in our imaginations, often unarticulated, of being somewhere outside of life looking in from outside, or down from above it. Rather, we are smack in the middle of the messiness of life; any image that denies this truth cannot serve us well. To understand ourselves accurately, we have to see ourselves in our real context of being related to everything else. It is perhaps less elevated than we would like, but it is true. Our relatedness is our essence and not a superficial consideration, and it means that, while we have to surrender godlike notions of ourselves, we get to say that we are home here with our family.

Rapidly accumulating evidence from the biological and social sciences points to the fact that we humans have a great vulnerability in being relatively cut off from our emotions and from the information of our own bodies as a result of having highly programmable brains. I suggest that attention to and companionship with other sentient and feeling animals might help us to get beneath the stream of cultural concepts, ideologies, and the wordy thinking that keeps us ignorant of our own selves.

In the first chapter I make the case that there is a pervasive incorrect meme or assumed concept that is widely accepted by people across time and culture, the idea that humans are separate from all the other animals and that we are superior in our distinctness while all the other animals share something that makes them inferior to us. Embedded in this meme are three distinct ideas—that we are unlike other animals, that we are superior to all other animals, and that they share something that causes them to be inferior to us. I examine a bit of the history by which this meme has maintained its hold on human psyches and suggest that it is time for a new meme of natural spirituality based upon our kinship within the whole universe, but with particular focus on the extended family of life on Earth.

In the second chapter I reference several animal studies to show the great variety of sentience in the animal world, and I examine in greater depth some of the issues that may either cloud or clear our thinking in relation to other animals. Anthropomorphism in particular is a term used most often to keep other animals in their conceptual place, so that, if a person responds emotionally to an animal or considers the animal intelligent, he or she is said to be projecting human qualities onto "mere" animals. However, I make the case that anthropomorphism is more complex and goes much deeper than that, that it infuses everything we do because we cannot escape a human perspective. In a similar way, stories about encounters with animals have often been dismissed as anecdotal and therefore lacking sufficient evidence for interpretation. However, collections of anecdotes lead to hypothesis generation, and so stories are important parts of the scientific process, not to mention that they reflect the meaning humans find in living. Also considered is the fact that all animal behavior, including that of *Homo sapiens*, is complex in its motivation; the simple explanations of the past are incorrect.

If we have been wrong in creating and maintaining a conceptual great divide between humans and other animals, this implies that we have been wrong about them, but also wrong about ourselves. Chapters three and four turn the spotlight directly onto *Homo sapiens*. Chapter three is dedicated to the question, "What kind of animal are we humans?" My intention is to look at humanity in terms of our evolution, our anatomy and physiology, including our brains, in order to take the perspective of seeing our everyday selves as evolved animals, like the others.

In chapter four, the stories are necessarily sad and the material necessarily dense as I make the case that our programmable brains bring with them particular vulnerabilities, especially that of being literally lost in thought. Practically and collectively speaking, this contributes to widely distributed depression and epidemic violence, both at heart spiritual ills of a collective kind. Though it may be more challenging material, it is at the heart of my case for actively and intentionally including animals in our human lives.

Chapter five throws open the doors to full consideration of animal souls, and also to the importance for us and for other animals in our coming to terms with their soulfulness. It was my favorite chapter to write because it is where all the ideas come together in suggesting a surprisingly happy picture. Though this happy picture is far from where we are now, it is not difficult to attain from where we are.

Finally, in chapter six, I attempt to "connect all the dots" by describing a natural spirituality of kinship and belonging, and the importance of other animals to us in finding our way home. I describe what I see as cultural evidence that points to ways in which this is already happening, and to the way that these ideas can be solidly and orthodoxly placed within historical streams of philosophy and theology.

"The best disposition for living is to approach everything with a tough mind and a soft heart." That has been my advice to students over decades of teaching college courses in areas related to this book, and it is advice I have endeavored to take as well as to give. I hope that such disposition is evident to readers. On this point, I would like to insert here a hearty recommendation that readers of this book indulge in some YouTube surfing along the way because a video is worth a thousand words. In the course of writing, I lost an entire afternoon of research on interspecies empathy, viewing videos of wild hippos rescuing other animals from the jaws of alligators.

My hope for the book as a whole is that it will provide fresh perspectives, stimulate conversation, and support people who love the natural world, and especially the animals. When I began the work, I intended that it would be provocative because I felt it past time to discuss the spiritual lives of animals and humans in relation to one another; I had already been a scholarly advocate of natural spirituality. However, challenged at a level I did not anticipate, I quickly found that I was the first one provoked to grow into a new sense of living a life not defined by human beings. I had initially thought that I would have to talk of imagining animal souls until there was more scientific evidence upon which to base the notion of animal spirituality, but new work is coming out at a rapid pace, work that allows us to fully emerge onto the stage of an earthly spirituality that is shared by other animals.

As I hope to stimulate conversation about animals as beings, I also must thank those people whose careers and research have engaged me in my own thinking about animals and in spirited conversation over many decades. These are people to whom I have turned with my scientific and ethical questions over decades, even as I increasingly turned my questions to the animals themselves. First, not surprisingly, I want to recognize Jane Goodall, a field scientist who dared to name what she actually observed, insisting that giving names to the Gombe chimpanzees as individuals and family members was the scientifically correct approach to the reality she observed. Not only did Goodall insist on calling her chimpanzee subjects by name and so change the way the science was done, but she established the model of the scientist-advocate, and many animal scientists have followed in her footsteps. I can attest to her continued dedication, having driven her back to her Chicago hotel after a long day that culminated with her attending to the last person in a line of hundreds of people who hoped to have photos taken and books signed into the wee hours of the morning.

Continuing in Jane Goodall's lineage and in collaboration with her, Marc Bekoff has dedicated his career to a carefully articulated critique of the assumptions about animals in the world of mechanistic science, and has courageously advocated for ethical treatments of animals in science.

I would also like to give special recognition to Jaak Panksepp, a lab scientist whose persistence in the face of both professional opposition and personal calamity cleared a path for understanding the connections amongst all earthly animals. I recall that I nearly flew out of my chair with excitement at his Santa Fe seminar, hearing as I did a set of scientific facts, woven theoretically in a way that genuinely allowed my own thinking to move forward on its long trajectory toward this book. As he noted in a recent interview, the times are catching up with him.

The problem with naming individuals is, of course, that too many are left unnamed, but I would like to say that my use of references is intended to reflect a spirit of conversation and to recognize many scholars who have awakened me in their variety of ways. Even so, many remain unnamed. None of us alone holds the single best perspective, but we together make a rich conversation, to which I hope this book contributes.

⟶

Were the two cardinals who came to Emma her family or friends? If so, how in the world did they know she had lighted in our tree? Had they followed us when we took her to our house? Was it coincidence that they were hanging around at that moment? We will never know, but they were there for her as soon as she was free and they helped her to find the courage to fly again. Perhaps our relatives know something about us, and perhaps they will be there to help us too.

Acknowledgements

WITHOUT DOUBT, THE FIRST of my personal thanks must go to Elizabeth Davenport, the sine qua non of this book's production. She has been generous in her review, unstinting in her critique, and meticulous in her copyediting.

I want to express my deep appreciation for the Zygon Center for Religion and Science, where I have been for several years an associated scholar and fellow. My special thanks go to Lea Schweitz, director of the Zygon Center, and to Philip Hefner, former director, for their support and spirited conversation over several years. I have been stimulated and challenged with every piece of work presented to my colleagues there, especially John and Carol Albright, Mel Gray, Paul Heltne, Charles Payne, and Mladen Turk. The Zygon Center is an amazingly rich nexus for scholars working at the intersection of science and religion.

I am indebted to Richard Rosengarten, former Dean of the Divinity School at University of Chicago, for his encouragement and support while I was an affiliated scholar there. I recall with particular fondness the question from him that stands out in my mind. When I was chasing one or another intellectual butterfly, he asked, "And how is *your* work going?" Here it is, Rick.

The Chicago Group is a salon that began in Chicago's Hyde Park under the direction of Ralph Burhoe in the 1970s, but I have known it in its current form, meeting under the support and "direction" of Carol and John Albright who took the lead in 1992. I am most grateful for the stimulating presentations and intense discussion afforded to all of the members by that group of independent and interdisciplinary thinkers, and for the generous hospitality of the Albrights.

I am grateful to primatologist Amy Parish for providing me an eye-opening behind-the-scenes tour of the primate area of the San Diego Zoo, and for a rich discussion of the inner lives of animals, and particularly of their spiritual potential.

Finally, I thank my professional colleagues Barbara Maria Stafford, professor emerita, University of Chicago, and James Giordano, chief of the Neuroethics Studies Program at Georgetown University, for inviting me into the deep end of the pool of interdisciplinary work centered in the neuroscience revolution. After a fortuitous meeting at Oxford, James hosted me as visiting scholar at the Center for Clinical Bioethics at Georgetown University. My work there is reflected here. Barbara Stafford invited Elizabeth and me to write a chapter for her collaborative project, *A Field Guide to a New Meta-Field: Bridging the Humanities-Neuroscience Divide,* and to participate in her Neuro-Humanities Entanglement Salon at Georgia Tech. Words simply cannot describe Barbara's capacity to create a rich and complex meeting of minds.

In addition to the opportunities presented by professional colleagues and groups, this book has been informed by personal conversations over many years. For the long conversations, I thank Carol Albright, Corinne Benvenuti, Theresa Benvenuti, Liza Cerroni-Long, Elizabeth Davenport, Sue Espinosa, Thom Espinosa, Diane Koditek, Lisa McCann, Corinne Mian, and Jane Turner. And I thank Mary Trollope, whose quirky, brilliant, and compassionate perspectives I miss.

My gratitude to the Ruthless Readers is boundless: Barbara Lieberman, Corinne Benvenuti, and Eugenia Oglesby, I thank you.

As might be expected, I have had the loving support of canine companions, Lexi and Bunny, whom the reader will meet, and of many animal Others, not least of them Jessica, Samadhi, Cody, Bronwyn, Auggie, Jiminy, Modo, Jouée . . . and my beloved Molly Brown. Thank you for bringing me the work.

CHAPTER 1

The Great Western Divide, Multiplied

Before I built a wall I'd ask to know
What I was walling in or walling out.
—ROBERT FROST, *THE MENDING WALL.*[1]

Encounters with the Very Other

EVERY SUMMER MORNING I take my dogs out early, before the heat sets in, to hike up a nearby mountain into wilderness, not a nature preserve but wilderness. The dogs, Bunny and Lexi, rescued Jack Russell terriers, are trained to the command, "On the trail," or just "Trail." This morning's walk was so interesting as to call for understatement. I met up with both death and danger in two separate events within thirty minutes and one mile of each other. Those last few steps back down the mountain, my dogs alive and with me, my heart didn't know whether to sink down in quiet despair or to beat wildly in fear and joy and the clean, clear desire to live.

Death. I first noticed the beautiful lush gray fur, unusual in our dry scrabble summer heat, and then I noticed the deadness of the animal and the fact that this beautifully furred dead thing was lying in the middle of the trail. This was most unusual because if a coyote or bobcat had killed this little one, it would have been carried off as dinner, and not dumped in the middle of the trail. Just as I processed this thought, I wondered about

1. Frost, *Collected Poems*, 33.

1

sickness and noticed that the little rodent was likely a rat, notoriously disease carrying and so perhaps disease killed. My curiosity aroused, I came in for a closer look, first noticing the exquisite round ears; then I saw the puncture on the back of the head, just at the neck juncture. But why would a hunted rat be left to die on the trail? It should have been carried off and quickly munched. I picked it up by the very tip of its long sleek tail to look for other bite marks. There were none. The puncture wound was round and clean and single. Had this little wood rat, of whom the field guide extols its virtue of cleanliness, been shot in the back of the head, executioner style, as the journalists say, for the entertainment of a human? I tossed its dead body into the tall grasses to feed the bellies of other creatures; the ants would probably have done with it before coyotes began their nightly hunt and forage. My heart sank that someone thought this was both fun and his right to do, and worse, that such a thing is considered normal by a great many people, even virtuous given that the victim was a rat.

I could not help but think about this as I walked up and up the steep part of the trail towards the mountain pass with its "singing gate" that the afternoon winds play like a flute. The temperature was in the low seventies, cool for the middle of July in the southern Sierras. I tried not to obsess about the rat and the human, so as to be there for the rest of the show, ridge upon ridge as I looked up towards the mountains, a hawk soaring in the blue bowl of sky, and at eye level oak trees and boulders and tall oat grasses gone dry weeks ago in this very dry year, some blue jays and chickadees darting from tree to tree; and at foot level, cottontail bunnies and quail in abundance, along with a variety of ground squirrels.

I was thinking to have another look at the rat on my way down, so that I could examine that wound again. It seemed so preposterous that anyone would execute a rat. I was thinking so much about that little rat that I did not notice when I reached the singing gate, when I turned back down the mountain. And I was thinking about the rat when I came around the bend to see a rattlesnake, somewhere between four and five feet in length, fat and sleek, sprawled across the trail. I watched my dog Bunny run right over the big snake, and then stop curious on the other side, looking back at me, even as my smaller dog Lexi ran towards the snake from behind me.

The snake began to coil. I had to get Bunny contained. I did not want her in a prolonged dance with this snake. She would certainly not survive multiple strikes. I had to get to her. But the snake was between us.

As Lexi catches up to me, I scoop her up into my right arm, looking, assessing, strategizing, thinking fast. A steeply descending drainage to the right of the trail, a steeply ascending boulder field to the left. There is no way around the snake. Bunny is looking from the snake to me, from me to the snake, trying to decide if she should hunt it. In an instant, I make the decision and I call to her as sharply as I can. "Bunny! Come! Bunny! Come!" Yes, I call her right back over the snake who has not yet rattled but who has moved his head into the air, tongue flicking. I know his little heat sensors will make his aim precise. I know he can move a distance the length of his body in a flash of scales and teeth and venom. I know he is a diamond backed western rattlesnake, responsible for more deaths than any other snake in America, easily agitated and very aggressive. Bunny comes running to me, here she comes flying in the air as the snake's tongue flicks. I am thinking that I will have to get her past the snake again to get her to the vet immediately, knowing she has been vaccinated for just this moment, wondering if she will survive it.

I watch my dog catapult through the air. The snake is alert, head up and tongue flicking, the several rattles on his tail telling me that he has lived years enough to shed that many skins. My heart is pounding in my chest like the desperate pump that it is, sending adrenaline out to every capillary. But the snake does not strike. He senses the heat of her body as she flies overhead, smells me as I scoop her up with my free arm.

Now I have a dog in each arm and am backing away, heart pounding, thinking, thinking. The snake appears healthy and normal. I have seen enough of his motion to know that he does not have a broken spine, but he is not striking, nor rattling, nor going anywhere, just watching and flicking, still half coiled and half looped across the trail. He is alert and ready, but not agitated, just the boss. And the boss is stretched across my only way out. One thing I know about rattlesnakes is that they like to be shown a little respect, make that a lot. I attempt to go through the high grasses and over the boulders on my left, but quickly see that it will be an impossible climb with a dog in each arm, and I will lose sight of the snake while still being very near to it, not to mention that there might well be more snakes in those rocks, given that snakes like to den together. I return to the trail, assessing, waiting. I finally decide that I have to walk on the trail, even though it is not wide enough to bypass sir snake. I move slowly toward him, telling him that I have no choice, asking him to make a way for us. I am desperately but calmly and intently thinking, and saying, "Come on, let us through, snake; mister snake, I need you *to let us through.*"

He reaches his head higher, flicks that tongue one more time, and then slowly glides off towards the boulders, not leaving the trail entirely but giving us leave to pass. Yes, the snake gave us leave to pass; and pass we did, respectfully.

For a two full minutes I was 100 percent engaged with the world around me, mindfully present indeed, gift of a snake. Go ahead: try now to stay mindfully present for two full minutes. You see? It is no small gift.

The Great Western Divide

Going beneath the surface of what happened to the four of us, the encounter leads me to a simple but far from easy question: how shall we conceptualize it? Was it a story of a human controlling three animals? Was it a human, two domesticated mammals, and a reptile? How about one western diamond backed rattlesnake, two Jack Russell terriers, and me? Was it four animals who inhabit the same world yet are utterly alien to one another? Or four sets of mechanical operations, with preset instructions? The questions each represent common ways of conceptualizing what happened on the trail, some of them more common than others.

At first glance, the cognitive framing may not seem to matter so long as I get out alive, with my living dogs. However, I think that the cognitive framing makes all the difference in the world, both to me in that specific situation, and to us as humans who share the planet with other animals, and of course it makes a difference to those other animals.

I have gradually come to see that almost everything I was taught about animals, and a great deal of what I was taught about humans, is wrong: wrong as in incorrect, and wrong as in morally wrong, having deleterious consequences for the animals and for the humans. Another thing I have learned is how easy it is to be wrong. A human did not execute that exceptionally pretty and very clean wood rat that I had found a mile before the rattlesnake on the way up; the punctured rat was the abandoned breakfast of the first snake I might have encountered but did not. I did not understand this until after I got home, then it was the light bulb with the "Aha!" sign. I was relieved to have been wrong.

I live in the Sierra Nevada mountains of California, home of the famous giant Sequoia trees. Very near to the magnificent Sequoia groves is another magnificent feature, enhanced for tourists with pull-over stations and signs that point them to the view: the Great Western Divide, a sub-range of 13,000-foot peaks that separate the river drainages and cause the waters to flow in opposite directions.

These peaks come to mind as I consider the conceptual great divide between humans and other animals in the Western world. It is a pun, of course, a kind of mental Great Western Divide; but it too has causal effects, channeling the waters of thought and behavior in culturally specific directions. From the earliest writings of Western civilization onward is found the idea that humans are the apex of creation, different from and superior to all the other animals, and that all the other animals are somehow like each other in their difference from us and also in their inferiority to humans. The idea is there in the book of Genesis, thought to have been completed in the sixth century BCE from the much earlier oral tradition, and it is there in the writings of Aristotle in the fourth century BCE.[2] It is a concept that has more than stood the test of time, seeming to increase the psychological distance between humans and other animals with the passing millennia.

Even as I have become convinced of its incorrectness, on the basis of both scientific evidence and personal experience, I am fascinated by the way this fundamental concept continues on so broadly unquestioned. It seems to emerge again and again over the centuries. It is expressed in several distinct lines of philosophic and religious metaphysics and the lines all seem to converge on this one idea about the distinctiveness and superiority of humans compared to other animals, while disregarding all the supporting details of the context and lineage from whence the ideas came. It is as though we need to get to this conclusion, regardless of the path by which it is achieved. It appears, in other words, to be a meme.

Richard Dawkins first proposed the concept of meme, in his 1976 classic *The Selfish Gene,* to suggest a kind of cultural version of a gene, some bit of culture that gets imitated, generation after generation, because of its psychological appeal: "Examples of memes are tunes, ideas, catch-phrases, clothes fashions, ways of making pots or building arches."[3] Dawkins goes on to discuss the question of whether memes must have biological value, or whether psychological appeal is sufficient to make their repetition sufficiently compelling; he asserts that psychological appeal

2. Aristotle, *On the Soul*, Part II, paragraph 2.
3. Dawkins, *Selfish Gene*, 192.

alone is sufficient to explain the success of a meme. In this he perhaps unwittingly pointed to the tremendous importance of the psychological dimension in human living.

The psychological appeal of the idea that humans are superior and entitled to "use" all other animals is immediately apparent. It allows us to feel good about ourselves by way of downward social comparison, a term used by social psychologists to describe a cognitive strategy commonly used to boost self-esteem.[4] A downward social comparison is some version of this kind of reasoning: "I may be bad off, but at least I am not as bad off as this other, who. . . in the case of animals, is not as smart as me, doesn't use language like I do, is not God's favorite, as I am; doesn't have moral sensibility, or technology, as I do." In the case of the idea that humans are on the superior and entitled side of a biological great divide and all the other animals together on the inferior and unentitled side, the meme also has biological value because it works to allow us to use animals as we like; and using other animals for food, clothing, shelter, research, and entertainment has been a basic building block of the human habitation of this planet. Further, we return to an obvious psychological value of this particular meme: we do not have to feel the pain of these alien others when we use them in ways that cause them to suffer if we believe that such is our destiny, and theirs. Given our dependence upon other animals and the vulnerability we might feel in empathizing with them, a capacity for which we are biologically wired, the psychological appeal cannot be overstated, even as the biological value cannot be denied. It is no wonder the idea has satisfied the three criteria that Dawkins established for high survival value in a meme: longevity, fecundity, and copying-fidelity.[5] The idea is old, it is virtually everywhere, and it is virtually the same in its content everywhere.

In fact, Dawkins himself seems possessed of this meme, dressed in its scientific garments, in his suggestion at the end of the chapter on cultural replication: "One unique feature of man, which may or may not have evolved memically, is his capacity for conscious foresight. . . . It is possible that yet another unique quality of man is a capacity for genuine, disinterested, true altruism."[6] He of the decidedly mechanistic and reductionistic selfish gene model seems compelled to searching for

4. Taylor and Lobel, "Social Comparison Activity Under Threat"; cf. Benvenuti, "Self Esteem."

5. Dawkins, *Selfish Gene*, 194.

6. Ibid., 200.

that necessary elevation of humans above all the others, though we all be equally the product of those selfish genes. Of course, a great deal of the scientific evidence about the mental and emotional lives of animals has been amassed since Dawkins wrote those words. We did not know then that chimpanzees sit and think about how to solve a problem, nor that hippopotami altruistically rescue members of other species, much less that even rats put aside their own self-interest for the well-being of others.[7]

Dawkins further suggests that, while memes are transmitted through imitation, they are especially likely to be imitated when they are co-adapted to a stable set of mutually assisting memes. He uses the example of a church with its associated architecture, music, art, ritual, laws, and traditions as such a set of mutually assisting memes.[8] In the case of the idea of human superiority over other animals, it has been deeply incorporated into religion with its complex structure, and into the broadly influential structures of philosophy and science, all three cultural institutions with co-adapted mutually assisting memes.

The Meme of Interest

In the world of philosophy, the concept of the human/animal divide goes back almost two and a half millennia. We find its most significant philosophical origin in Aristotle's systematic description of the nature of reality and the hierarchical organization of beings within that reality, his metaphysics and ontology respectively. Aristotle observed that the human being is the only creature endowed with the capacity for abstract thought and for this reason is most like the completely abstract and non-material God. Because the human mind transcends the bonds of time and space, that mind bears likeness to God. Yet humans are also material beings whose bodies are bound by time and space, and so humans have the highest placement of any material being within Aristotle's ontological framework.[9]

Aristotle's set of propositions is one that most of us accept today, a series of interlinked ideas that still operates as a foundation for thought and decision making in everyday life. The primary building block is the

7. Bartal et al., "Empathy and Prosocial Behavior in Rats."
8. Dawkins, *Selfish Gene*, 197.
9. Aristotle, *On the Soul*, Part II, paragraph 2.

idea that we can divide the world into living and non-living things. We do this routinely and perhaps would have difficulty imagining a world not divided into living and non-living categories. Without such a division, we would conceivably think of everything as living, as in animist belief systems. In this case, I would have to greet my coffee cup in the morning, and thank the coffee maker too. Alternatively, we could recognize intentional liveliness in nothing. In this scenario I might use operant conditioning on my spouse by incrementally rewarding what I like and ignoring or punishing what I do not like: a cold clean analysis is all that is called for, one smart machine to another (and while this idea may be even more difficult to imagine than the animist worldview, it is the undergirding of much of twentieth-century psychological science).[10] In reality, we tend to assume, most often unconsciously, that we can use things but must interactively engage persons. This guideline for behavior is perhaps the most practical implication of the distinction between persons and things.

Even in writing this chapter, I find myself on the wrong side of this person and thing "divide." That snake on the trail, where does he fit? I will give you a hint by sharing that the grammar correction function on my word processor and I disagree; every time I say "he," I am prompted to change that word to "it." When this happens, I recall that Jane Goodall often speaks of a similar clash of practice with her professors at Cambridge who disapproved her giving names to her research subjects rather than numbers.[11] She insisted that the chimpanzees demonstrated personality and lived in family groups, and that giving them names was a way of designating as much. Goodall prevailed and changed a whole scientific norm by doing so. In fact, I believe this to have been a pivotal moment in bringing about a paradigm change in the biological sciences. But can I make that "person" case for a snake, a reptile? For the moment, let us live with the question and return to it later.

There are certain qualities that we simply think of as "alive." In his essay *On the Soul,* Aristotle wrote "what has soul in it differs from what has not, in that the former displays life."[12] For him, "soul" is the word that describes the quality of being alive. Most of us also accept the way that Aristotle organized living things by the qualities of their souls, even if we no longer think of living things, even ourselves, as having souls. But

10. Cf. Skinner, *Walden II* and *Beyond Freedom and Dignity.*

11. Robin McKie, "Chimps with Everything: Jane Goodall's 50 Years in the Jungle," *The Observer,* June 26, 2010.

12. Aristotle, *On the Soul,* Part II, paragraph 2.

without the word *soul*, there is broad acceptance for the related ideas that plants are alive but not as alive as animals, and that animals are alive but not as alive as human beings. This "alive and more alive" is the essence of Aristotle's definition of the word "soul" and of his hierarchical distinctions amongst kinds of souls.

Aristotle described the most elemental souls, those of plants, this way: "Hence we think of plants also as living, for they are observed to possess in themselves an originative power through which they increase or decrease in spatial directions . . . and continue to live so long as they can absorb nutriment."[13] He concludes that the power to self-organize and to grow into a unique set of potentials through absorbing nutrients is the definitive quality of plant souls, and the most basic quality of all embodied souls. We may not typically think of plants as souls, but we do think of them as being alive. For Aristotle, aliveness is the same as soulfulness.

We move easily from plants to Aristotle's next category of souled beings, that of animals. Of animals he wrote: "for even those beings which possess no power of local movement but do possess the power of sensation we call animals and not merely living things." Aristotle further developed his description of animal sensation in the direction of motivation, saying that all animals share what he perceived to be the most basic sense, that of touch. He described the relationship amongst the capacities of animal souls in this way, that "where there is sensation, there is also pleasure and pain, and where these, necessarily also desire," or what we today might call motivation.[14] His formulation of ethics begins with the notion that natural self-interest serves to organize the capacity of living things to realize their potential. This realizing of one's unique potential by staying alive and fed and by reproducing is the most basic value or good of living things. Thus all animals, including humans, move toward that which will enhance their lives.

These complex qualities of animal soul are built upon that more elemental quality of plants, the capacity to obtain nutriment. Of animal souls, Aristotle says further: "it is the soul which is the actuality of a certain kind of body."[15] He means two things by this, that both body and soul are inseparable *and* that soul is the unique expression of a type of body's

13. Ibid.
14. Ibid., Part II, paragraph 6.
15. Ibid., Part II, paragraph 8.

potential. I might translate it as: "This turtle is a unique animal soul of the turtle type." Aristotle attributes internal experience and intention to animals as the definition of what makes an animal an animal, with the understanding that when the animal dies, its soul, which is the organizing principle of its body, dies too.

While we may not protest what Aristotle describes as obvious and observable by anyone, and we often do use his system of organization, most often without realizing that we do, we also may not protest ideas that are counter to it. A common example of this would be to think that it is permissible to do things to animals that it would not be permissible to do to humans because animals do not have internal experiences, such as pleasure and pain, in the ways that we do. The latter reasoning is often expressed in terms of the conditioned or programmed behavior of the animal; "it" is acting according to its experience of reward and punishment on automatic pilot, if you will, or according to its genetic mandate, another kind of automatic pilot. It is, in other words, a mechanism or series of mechanisms, and therefore does not act in response to its thoughts, feelings, or desires. But Aristotle would have said of my drama on the mountain trail that there was a human soul and three animal souls in the encounter, all having internal experience of emotions, all seeking to realize their potential, all motivated by natural self-interest, but only one of them a thinker.

Moving toward the qualitatively distinct human soul, Aristotle wrote: "We have no evidence yet about the mind or the power to think; it seems a widely different kind of soul, differing as what is eternal from what is perishable; it alone is capable of existence in isolation from all other psychic powers."[16] And it is the power of thinking that he attributes to humanity that causes him to place humans in their unique and superior category, having all the qualities of other living souls: self-organizing and nutritive capacity, like plants; and like animals, sensation and the experience of pleasure and pain from whence comes desire or motivation, and the capacity to move towards that which we desire. "Certain kinds of animals possess in addition the power of locomotion, and still another order of animate beings, i.e., man, and possible another order like man or superior to him, the power or thinking, or mind."[17]

16. Ibid., Part II, paragraph 7.
17. Ibid., Part III, paragraph 1.

Imagine an illustration of the suggested hierarchy of beings that informs our thinking and behavior in everyday life, a triangle enclosing four levels of earthly matter. The lowest level has the greatest volume and represents inert matter. The next level up is the second greatest in volume and contains the plants. A third level up from the base is smaller yet in volume and contains all the animals, and the top segment is the smallest, reserved for humans alone. Outside the triangle may be non-material beings and, according to Aristotle, must be God, the transcendent cause. First there is the distinction between living and non-living, then the plants, then the animals, and then those with mind, humans, and perhaps angels existing outside the realm of the material forms entirely.

I recommend to the reader a simple thought experiment: select another species, learn something about it, and then construct a hierarchy of beings as it might be expressed by a bright and creative member of that species. What reason might the elephant give to support the conviction that his way of being is superior to that of all other creatures? Perhaps it would be the infamous big-heartedness or long memory of elephants. Might the whales invoke their planetary awareness as creatures who migrate thousands of miles in the great oceans every year, or their ancient lineage as a species that is at least fifty million years old? It is easy to see the potential for exercising that self-serving bias that allows us individually and collectively to take credit for the good things that happen and to place blame for bad things outside of ourselves. It might well determine who is at the top from any species' point of view, were that species to be found to share in what is for humans a pervasive cognitive bias.[18]

Though he elevated humans above all other animals, Aristotle did not in fact conclude that we are the highest order of beings, but only the highest order of beings in the material domain. Not only did he suggest that there might be another order of beings even superior to humanity, but he asserted that that there must be a God whose transcendence was complete, the rationally necessary Uncaused Cause.[19] Aristotle reasoned that something had to be self-existent at the start of the world and that something started everything else in a great series of cause and effect interactions, that something being God. But well before Aristotle's careful philosophical analysis, religious systems had already attributed authority to God and human knowledge to God's revelations to humans. I am

18. Sheppard et al., "Self-serving Bias."
19. Aristotle, *Physics*, Book VIII, 1.

compelled to wonder whether Aristotle did not begin with the conviction of God, if a God meme was already established, and then make the analysis to prove that conviction.

The creation stories of the biblical book of Genesis suggest that the notion of God making humans as the supreme act of creation lies somewhere in our human consciousness from a date long before that of Aristotle. In the first of the two creation stories that appear in the first two chapters of Genesis, it is explicitly stated that God gave humans rule over all the varieties of the other animals, and in the second that God gave humans the power to name all other creatures. For the purpose of grounding this popular image in its sources, I offer the two quotations. From the first account: "Then God said, 'Let us make man in our image, in our likeness, and let them rule over the fish of the sea and the birds of the air, over the livestock, over all the earth, and over all the creatures that move along the ground.'"[20] And from the second: "Now the Lord God had formed out of the ground all the beasts of the field and all the birds of the air. He brought them to the man to see what he would name them; and whatever the man called each living creature, that was its name."[21]

In fact, these passages are broadly descriptive of two facts about humans: first, that humans have acquired (and thus had the capacity to acquire) power over nature, power sufficient to alter planetary systems, such as the weather; and second, that humans categorize and name things, equating this activity with knowledge and power.[22] My point is not to grant authority to these verses but to acknowledge them as one of the key sources of the widely held Western notion that by divine design humans are distinctive, superior, and even godlike compared to all other animals. Historian Lynn White cites this biblical conception of "right relationships" as a core influence related to ecological degradation due to its underlying suggestion of divinely mandated human disregard for the ecological well-being of other creatures and subsequently of the earth.[23]

But there are other biblical passages that give quite a different picture of the relationships amongst God, humans, and the other animals, perhaps most notably Psalm 104, with its list of the glories of the created world, each kind of thing having a special relationship with the Creator.[24]

20. Gen 1:26.

21. Gen 2:19.

22. Vitousek et al., "Human Domination of Earth's Ecosystems."

23. Cf. White, "Historical Roots of Our Ecological Crisis."

24. Ps 104.

Culminating the list of creatures is Leviathan, who was created for the purpose not of serving humanity but for sporting in the ocean. And the psalmist concludes by drawing an image of every kind of animal having a unique and special relationship to a creator whose creative (and destructive) power is ongoing: "These all look to you to give them their food in due season; when you give it to them, they gather it up; when you open your hand, they are filled with good things. When you hide your face, they are dismayed; when you take away their breath, they die and return to their dust. When you send forth your spirit, they are created; and you renew the face of the ground."[25]

The quotations from Genesis and from Psalm 104 represent two very different ways of conceptualizing the biblical relationship between God, humans, and other animals. One might suppose that believers consider each to be divine revelation. Why then has one of them been "selected" into popular thought and the other left virtually unknown? I suggest that the interpretation selected and replicated is the one that has both the psychological appeal and biological value to repeat and maintain a powerful meme. So pervasive is the religious form of the meme, rooted in these verses from Genesis, that Lynn White described modern science itself with its intention to name and to control nature as an "extrapolation of natural theology," and modern technology in terms of its "realization of the Christian dogma of man's transcendence of, and rightful mastery over, nature."[26]

While these ancient philosophical and religious notions persist into contemporary times in their own right, a third version of the meme, based on a combination of both ancient philosophical and religious streams of thought but with a new mathematical element added, was developed by the seventeenth century French philosopher René Descartes. Descartes proposed a creative, profoundly influential, and more modern form of the "great divide" between humans and other animals.[27] Almost 2,000 years after Aristotle devised his hierarchy of souls, Descartes imagined a mechanical universe in which humans alone have internal experience as evidenced by capacity for rational thought expressed in language.[28] He removed "souls" from everything except humans, and defined the quality

25. Ps 104:27–30.

26. White, "Historical Roots of Our Ecological Crisis," 1206.

27. Descartes, *Meditation VI.*

28. Descartes, *Discourse on Method*, 22.

of human soul by abstract rationality alone. Notably, he also took the heart, that is, the emotions or "passions," out of human souls, leaving unfeeling minds somehow to inhabit mechanical human bodies. Everything in the universe except for these rational human minds he conceived of as one great machine operating on a few universal laws.

Because he was unable to articulate an explanation of the relationship between the rational minds and mechanical bodies of humans, Descartes's description of the nature of reality is generally considered a metaphysical failure. Despite this, however, the image of a measurable mechanical universe has infused and suffused the scientific project for centuries.

Descartes was of course thoroughly familiar with Aristotle's concept of the soul and of his categorization of types of soul. Indeed, Christian scholastic theology, a "baptized" version of Aristotelian philosophy, was the established model of metaphysics taught in the universities of his day (and Descartes studied law at the University of Poitiers, a Catholic university). But Descartes's desire was to describe the universe and its functions in mathematical terms. To accomplish this, he sought to explain the functions that Aristotle attributed to soul in terms of mechanical operations, devoid of intention or interior life except in the case of humans, for whom abstract thought, bound by neither space nor time, was definitive.

Descartes, most famous for the singular quotation *Cogito ergo sum*, commonly translated as "I think therefore I am," argued that we can rationally doubt the existence of our bodies, but that we cannot doubt the existence of the doubting mind.[29] The basis for his separation of humans from all the other animals was our use of language; and language became his criteria for determining rationality and the presence of mind. This is of course a somewhat circular justification of the relationship of reason and language. Not only is it circular but it also presumes that the utterances of other animals, not to mention their gestures, are not language. But we now know that the animal world is full of language: that even honeybees have true language, and that prairie dogs have a sophisticated vocabulary for communicating knowledge about their environment.[30] Suffice it for now to say that in Descartes's time people did not think animals used language, an assumption that might easily be driven by the meme of interest, that meme that requires evidence of human superiority.

29. Ibid., 14–18.
30. Slobodchikoff, *Language of Animals*, 52–62; Balcombe, *Second Nature*, 89–91.

Despite Descartes's complete separation of minds and bodies, and despite his method of doubt, or the requirement that every proposition that cannot be logically proved must be doubted, he asserted that human sensation and knowledge are accurate because God created humans and endowed them with minds, and "God is not a deceiver."[31] As for the animals, Descartes described them as machines, incapable of language and therefore incapable also of internal experience. He further asserted that animal cries of pain or distress were mere mechanical warning sirens and not true expressions of the felt experience of pain.[32]

Descartes's separation of bodies and minds into completely different kinds of things incapable of interacting with one another is problematic on multiple grounds, but especially for neuroscientists, the very essence of whose work is in describing how the brain (a bodily structure) is related to thought and feeling (functions of mind or soul).[33] But his equation of language with rationality has persisted and it has been used to bolster the great divide between humans and all other animals, despite accumulating evidence to the contrary.[34] Descartes's definition of animals as machine has, by default, placed them in the category of things to be used. Whether or not he intended to grant permission to hurt animals in the name of science is the subject of debate.[35] But it is certainly fair to attribute to him that he expressed the ideas upon which the maltreatment of animals and all of "inert" nature came to be rationalized in modern scientific thought.

Having looked at three different pervasive culture systems in which the meme of the great divide between humans and all other animals is supported in complex systems of the kind described by Dawkins, let me now revisit the configuration of beings that encountered one another up on my mountain trail. We have already established that Aristotle would say that there was a meeting of one human and three animals, all motivated by natural self-interest. The book of Genesis, compendium of religious understanding that underlies so much Western thought, says clearly that the animals are intended by God to be under human dominion, no explanation beyond divine revelation needed. The dogs in my scenario are as God intended, putatively under the control of the human. The human is

31. Descartes, *Meditation IV.*

32. Descartes, *Discourse on Method,* 22.

33. Damasio, *Descartes' Error,* xi–xix.

34. Slobodchikoff, *Language of Animals,* 9.

35. Cottingham, *Descartes' Treatment of Animals,* 551–59.

God's agent. As for the indomitable snake, he becomes the living symbol of all that might undermine humanity's place as God's favorite. No mention of souls or machines, only favorites and villains. From Descartes's perspective, the whole point is to create a certain stark simplicity, if not clarity: the group interacting on my mountain included one disembodied soul and four machines.

Animal behavior scientists and animal activists cite Cartesian dualism, particularly Descartes's assertion that animals are machines that lack true internal experience, as the broadly accepted basis for the commonly held idea that non-human animals, because they do not think, are things to be used, as contrasted with the category of persons who require ethical consideration.[36] Indeed, a United States court recently heard a challenge to this with regard to the keeping of orca whales in captivity for purposes of human entertainment: "For the first time in our nation's history, a federal court heard arguments as to whether living, breathing, feeling beings have rights and can be enslaved simply because they happen to not have been born human."[37] The judge's ruling cited the fact that animals are not persons under the law: "The only reasonable interpretation of the 13th amendment's plain language is that it applies to persons and not to non-persons such as orcas. . . . Both historic and contemporary sources reveal that the terms 'slavery' and 'involuntary servitude' refer only to persons."[38]

Following Descartes, then, we ask: if the judge denies the orcas' personhood, does he then think of them as things? It is certainly implied in the reaffirmed human right to capture and own them. Yet the category of thing remains deeply unsatisfying in this context. Surely, whatever their legal status in human courts, these beings are not things. And I note that one of the whales in question had been implicated in the deaths of humans on three separate occasions and so his "in between" status, neither person nor thing, is probably to his benefit in that he cannot be tried for murder. While the possibility of trying a whale for murder may seem far-fetched to contemporary minds, it was only a little more than a century ago that elephants were executed for murdering humans.[39]

36. Balcombe, *Second Nature*, 44.

37. BBC News, "SeaWorld sued over 'enslaved' killer whales."

38. *The Guardian*, "Whales not slaves."

39. Peterson, *Moral Lives of Animals*, 8–11.

Whatever the legal status of orcas in captivity, the machine model of animals has been widely disputed and roundly disproved by contemporary animal scientists in both natural and laboratory settings. The scientific study of animals has repeatedly demonstrated not only the interiority but also the intentionally communicated and acted upon interiority of many species of animals.[40] Simultaneously, Aristotle's hierarchical organization of beings has been replaced in the scientific world by the "tree of life" image that illustrates the relationship of every living thing to every other living thing, growing out of the earth in a branching configuration, organic and changing, rather than a solid pyramid suspended eternally in abstract space. This tree of life image suggests a more contemporary scientific understanding of the relationships amongst animals (including humans): that of kin who exist in a context of evolutionary continuity.[41]

The explosion of knowledge in the biological sciences since James D. Watson and Francis Crick's 1953 discovery of the structure of DNA, and especially in animal studies since Jane Goodall's first published reports in 1963 on the chimpanzees at Gombe, has overturned the long held assumption that there is a great divide between humans and other animals.[42] The new model in the biological sciences is one of evolutionary continuity and it calls for a new way of thinking about and relating to non-human animals.[43] However, despite powerful scientific evidence that overturns the meme of the divide between humans and other animals, belief in human distinctness and superiority persists. Perhaps it is the case that the categories of persons and things cannot do justice to a reality as multifaceted as animal life on earth. If this is the case, we will need to cast our intellectual nets more broadly to find a way of thinking that can work meaningfully with the complexity we have discovered.

A Natural Spirituality

Rather than taking the traditional route of analytic philosophy, that of trying to redefine "person," I will make the case in this book that there is a broad category of natural spirituality, essentially seen in the

40. Cf. Bekoff, *Emotional Lives of Animals*; Peterson, *Moral Lives of Animals*; Balcombe, *Second Nature*.

41. Bekoff, *Emotional Lives of Animals*, 36–37.

42. Goodall, "My Life Among Wild Chimpanzees."

43. Cf. Shubin, *Inner Fish*.

intersubjective nature of life and the evolutionary quality of Life itself, in the context of which both humans and non-human animals can be better understood. I will suggest that animal "spirituality" on earth is an evolutionary emergent based in the emotional lives of animals, and is especially evidenced in their capacities to perceive the "insides" of self and others, or to use the more limited terminology of cognitive science, to have a "theory of mind," meaning that they have an understanding that knowing the mind of other animals is important for living.

There is neuroscientific evidence that to understand the inner experience of others does not necessarily require us to have a theory of mind, but only mirror neurons and the capacity for subtle muscle mimicry whereby we create in our own bodies the feeling that is in the other's body.[44] It is this intersubjective space in which the thoughts and feelings, intentions, and desires of beings are shared in a variety of ways that is the location of natural spirituality: the bees' dance, the human symphony or mathematical equation, pheromones, facial expressions, mating displays, gestures, sounds that represent semantic content (or words). Natural spirituality, then, might be defined as the creative "conversation" that occurs within the psychological or "soul" space in which all the lives on earth share the experience of living, albeit by way of myriad kinds of experience. And this creative conversation is not abstract but embodied, so I would prefer to say that all animal bodies are in this Soul, rather than to say each body "has a soul." Each body participates in the intersubjective space of life on earth and this interactive participation, especially the capacity to receive and to reflect the insides of self and others in ongoing conversation, is the natural spirituality that I propose. Further, I suggest that we humans can benefit from reimagining both animal others and ourselves in light of such natural spirituality.

While it may at first seem a bold or even a wild claim to say that animals are spiritual beings, it may not be so intellectually bold as it first appears, and its wildness (or being "out of bounds") may be explained by its defiance of a powerful meme. The human-animal meme, however, is one whose death knoll is already sounding because the bigger idea of which it is a subset, that of conflict between of "man" and "nature" has run its course and left us deposited in a field of ecological collapse brought about by our very successes. Describing this human domination of earth's ecosystems, Peter Vitousek states that "Even on the grandest

---

44. Rizzolatti and Craighero, "The Mirror-Neuron System"; and Neal and Chartrand, "Embodied Emotion Perception."

scale, most aspects of the structure and functioning of Earth's ecosystems cannot be understood without accounting for the strong, often dominant influence of humanity."[45]

Even in the context of powerful, natural, and legitimate self-interest, our easy acceptance of the divide between humans and all other animals is cracking under pressures from several directions. New information about animal experience from the biological sciences calls for a new theoretical framework for human and non-human animal relations. At the same time, rapid extinction of animal species and loss of biodiversity threatens the health of planetary ecosystems. Vitousek cites this as one of the two large-scale consequences of human domination, saying of it, "These relatively well documented changes in turn entrain further alterations to the functioning of the earth system, most notably by driving global climate change and causing irreversible losses of biological diversity."[46] I interpret this to mean that we must at the bare minimum change our thinking to see animals as renewable resources rather than simple "materials" for our immediate human purposes. However, established facts of evolution, especially the generalization that all life on earth is related, go much further in suggesting a kind of earthly ethos that necessarily moves us beyond that minimum with its suggestion of kinship as the basis for natural spirituality. Finally, at the level of day-to-day experience, many people feel discomfort with the discrepancy between what they have been taught about animals and their own experiences and perceptions, most poignantly seen in the common human experience of longing for and being delighted by communion with other animals as companions or pets.

Social neuroscientist John Cacioppo holds that human attachment to animals is a "better than nothing" substitute for human attachments, but I think it more likely that our attachment to animals fulfills different needs than do human attachments.[47] The common experience of longing for and taking pleasure in animal companionship is, I believe, indicative of natural spiritual kinship, and not necessarily an indicator of social alienation from other humans. It may well be that attachment to animals allows us to connect to our own bodies in a more immediate way. Supporting this idea is one study that showed the presence of a pet to have

45. Vitousek et al., "Human domination of Earth's ecosystems," 494.
46. Ibid.
47. Cacioppo and Patrick, *Loneliness*, 256.

a more calming influence than the presence of a spouse.[48] Industrialized nations have large populations in which most people no longer have regular contact with farm animals, much less wild animals; and pets may fill this absence rather than the absence of human company.

The intellectual credibility of the claim that there exists a kind of natural spirituality that is continuous amongst humans and other animals also may not be quite so bold as it first appears. Two different broad areas of interdisciplinary scholarship have been moving steadily towards such a claim, if from very different directions. The fields of religious studies, cognitive sciences, and theology have in recent years developed a strong tradition of naturalism, rejecting supernatural explanations while claiming the vital and adaptive qualities of religion and spirituality.[49] As a general interpretation, the intent of these scholars is to unpack the heavy baggage of religious traditions, so that a vision of the natural framework of spirituality might be both more contemporary in its easy embrace of scientific knowledge, and less encumbered with the weight of cultural conflicts embedded in religions.

Approaching the possibility of a natural spirituality from a different direction are the biological sciences. Ethological studies of animals in natural settings and animal behavior studies in laboratories, along with molecular biology, neuroscience, and evolutionary theory have now established a strong model for animal interiority, defined as the thinking, feeling, "personally" motivated, and intentionally communicated space driving at least some of the behaviors of many species of non-human animals.[50]

Each of these areas of study has been developed through intensive interdisciplinary effort. As a consequence, I am attempting here a vastly integrative endeavor, and as such it will be necessarily exploratory in nature. My thoughts on natural spirituality grow out of work in the fields of evolutionary biology, neuroscience, scientific and clinical psychology, animal behavioral sciences, and philosophy and religious studies, and I will refer to these throughout this work, attempting to bring together the implications of one field of endeavor for others.

The death of the powerful old meme calls for the birth of a new one, and I suggest that the new meme is already forming in a sense of

48. Allen et al., "Cardiovascular reactivity and the presence of pets."
49. Cf. Benvenuti and Davenport, "New Archaic," 204–9.
50. Balcombe, *Second Nature*, 13–44.

biospiritual kinship that can allow us to find new ways of relating to other animals and with them to "nature," our shared origin and context for living. The biospiritual kinship to which I refer is likely not only a human experience but like other features of animal life, naturally distributed and continuous amongst animals, with variations by species and individuals within species. The experience of spirituality then is likely not only human but includes other animals in their various ways.

So far, I have presented an overview of the argument that recent decades of scientific research in various disciplines have together overturned the multi-millennial meme that humans are an entirely distinct kind of being. Conversely, and at least as mistaken, is the idea that all other animals together are alike in their differences from us and inferior with respect to that difference.

To say that we are distinctive from other animals is a fact, as is also the fact that each species is by definition distinct from every other species. The questions, then, are not about our distinctness but about our superiority over all the other animals, and about their similarities to one another in being different from us. With reference to these two ideas, that each species is distinct yet related, I would like to suggest that a better grasp of the distinctions amongst us animals is likely to annul the question of superiority by placing it in the context of each species' specialization within its niche. To paraphrase J. M. Coetzee, why should the crucial test always be intelligence of the kind that enables one to construct machines or philosophical theories?[51] Why should it not be any number of specialized capacities, such as the ability to smell the presence of cancer or explosives, a capacity that dogs whose capacity for smell is measured in parts per trillions possess.[52]

In a collection of Jacques Derrida's reflections on the deconstruction of classical philosophy with regard to animals, Marie-Louise Mallet asserts that Derrida's first objection is, not surprisingly, to the word "animal" itself because it represents a false separation of humans from other animals and the lumping of other animals into an other, "as though everything from earthworms to the chimpanzee constituted a homogeneous set to which the human could be radically opposed."[53] She further suggests, referencing Derrida, that the solution is not in restoring to

51. Coetzee, in Balcombe, *Second Nature*, xi.
52. *Science Daily*, "Dogs Smell Cancer," and "Dogs' ability to detect explosives."
53. Mallet, Preface to Derrida, *The Animal That Therefore I Am*, x.

animals all those presumed human traits, like thought and feeling and
language that were conceptually taken from them, so as to make them
more like us. The point is not to restore them to their humanity but to
restore them to themselves: "Far from substituting for the classical opposition the confusion of a no less deceptive failure to differentiate, such
a deconstruction patiently multiplies the differences."[54] It is as though we
must surrender the feeling of knowledge we attain when we categorize
and then recognize the categories we have created, and in place of that
experience awaken our actual sentient awareness of specifics, all the way
from species to individuals. In order to be more truthful, we have to be
willing to replace the classical division between ourselves and all other
animals, and instead do the multiplication, allowing all the forms of animal life to have their own conceptual space even as they have their own
biological spaces.

Jonathan Balcombe begins his book *Second Nature: The Inner Lives
of Animals* by introducing the term *umwelt*, coined by early-twentieth-
century ethologist Jakob von Uexkull, to signify the inner world of a
species: "The idea is that variations in brains, sensory equipment, and
lifestyles of different kinds of animals likely result in their having different mental and perceptual experiences."[55] My dogs have a "smell brain"
that causes them to run to the backyard every morning and to sit holding
their noses in the air, sniffing the morning news. In this way, they know
more than I ever will about what happened overnight in my yard. The
snake has poor vision but exquisite smell and extremely sensitive heat
sensors that allow him to locate prey with precision, and his moods are
even more influenced by the weather than are mine. The dogs and the
snake smell each other and me, including our immediate emotions, better than I smell any of them. I stand on two legs and look at what is on
the other side of the snake. We inhabit the same few yards of dusty trail
very differently.

The classical philosophy that comes down as culturally received
"fact" puts me on one side of a great divide and the dogs and the snake
together on the other. I am the one who learns, thinks, develops strategies, makes plans (and tools), achieves goals, and is so self-aware that I
anticipate how badly I will feel if I fail to resolve this dangerous situation.
And I have a story about who I am, and this "narrative self" guides my

54. Ibid.
55. Balcombe, *Second Nature*, 18.

perceptions and actions. Some psychologists consider this narrative self to be the apex of animal life, but I find it problematic in a species-specific way; our self-stories *are stories*, stories that require us to be unconscious of competing information that might tell a different story. I suggest that keeping attentive company with other animals may help to mitigate the problems of human narrative.[56]

Of the options I listed for conceptualizing the encounter on the trail, I choose multiplication, the option that is constituted as "me, two Jack Russell terriers (Bunny and Lexi, to be even more precise), and a western diamond back rattlesnake," this particular snake in fact. Paying attention to the specifics matters because it is paying attention to the real material world and not just to ideas about the world. For example, I understand that a rattlesnake can be dangerous, and I also understand that this is because they are incredibly fragile creatures. Anyone who has ever seen a snake with broken vertebrae knows how pathetic is that stepped-on snake.

It was evident that this particular snake had lived a while and was more confident and relaxed than a younger or smaller snake might have been. This breed enjoys a lazy sunning in seventy degree weather but becomes very excitable as temperatures go up, so his choosing not to strike was related to his pleasure in the mild sunny weather. No doubt, the snake's "happy" mood was an important factor in the social negotiations that took place on the trail. This particular human has encountered rattlesnakes before and is less excitable and more knowledgeable than she was on her first encounter with one. She knows, for example, to express respect to the snake by taking him seriously, backing away while maintaining contact. Lexi is a wizened terrier who, having gotten into serious trouble in her youth, adheres to me at the slightest sign of danger, is completely cooperative when she needs to be, and knows by my demeanor when that is. Bunny is younger and more impulsive and only partially voice-trained; the more excited she is, the less attention she pays. In fact, she has been gaining confidence by trying more and more new things, and each confidence makes her bolder and more willing to try the next thing, so there is a good chance she will try to engage the snake. Each of us varies by species and by individual history and by context, and yet all four of us have sensory impressions of the same world, and an amygdala in our brains that alerts us to danger. Additionally, the three mammals

56. McAdams, "Redemptive Self," xiii.

share the neuroarchitecture for attachment to each other. We are alike and we are different each from the other, and therein is the frontier to be explored.

The long reign of the great divide meme is understandable in that it expresses natural human self-interest by justifying the use of other animals without requiring complicated consideration in every instance. Rather than vilify humans for such self-interest, and also rather than glibly use natural self-interest as an excuse to adopt convenient but incorrect concepts, I recognize that self-interest is a common feature of animal life. In fact, our self-interest is no longer served by the old meme and any new meme that would be successful had best serve our self-interest. It is in our interest, for example, to refrain from dominating the planet to such an extent that it is thrown hopelessly out of ecological balance. And I think it is in our self-interest to develop the capacity to escape from our abstract thought and verbal constructions enough to experience directly the motivations that are expressed moment by moment in our body states and also to experience directly our sentience of the actual material world around us.

Not only do we humans think but we think to the detriment of our selves and our kind. Our uniquely human problem may lie in the rational justifications that hide from us our real motives and in the abstract thought that minimally interrupts and more commonly cuts us off from our immediate sentience, our awareness of the material world that we inhabit. Part of the human *umwelt*, I think, is that our capacity for abstract thought creates layers of unconsciousness of a particularly human kind, causing us to be confused by deception or literally lost in thought when, for example, our actual perceptions and experiences are in conflict with our preconceptions, or with the particular conditioning of our familial and cultural context.

Keeping company with animals may help us to understand ourselves at vital levels below abstract thought. More than one generation of Westerners has now been exposed to Disney's animated film in which Bambi's mother espouses human moral lessons: "If you can't say anything nice, don't say anything at all." I have to admit that I might first be startled and then both saddened and dismayed to receive little lessons in human social mores from a doe. But this is not to say that I would not expect the possibility of a very real connection with a doe. I have sung to mule deer in the Sierra Nevada mountains of California, to white-tailed deer in the Illinois forest, even to springboks in South Africa. They stop, and turn their ears like satellite dishes, and most often they stay still and attentive until I have finished singing. I interpret this as pleasure, but perhaps they are only being polite.

Am I anthropomorphizing to say that the deer like to be the audience to my song? Yes, I am; but it turns out that, when paired with awareness, to anthropomorphize can be a good tool for understanding other animals because we share so much in common with them.[57] We share with many of them not only sensory information about the real and shared world but neurological mechanisms for understanding the internal experience of others. This is social intelligence, and it routinely operates amongst members of a species.[58]

When I first began to think about animal spirituality, having worked substantially to understand human spirituality as an evolutionary and natural occurrence, I prepared myself to meet with ridicule.[59] However, not only has the idea most often been met with great enthusiasm, but I have experienced responses of the kind that psychologists call "pressured." There is the feeling of a pressing need to talk about it. When I begin to explain that I am thinking about the possibility of animal spirituality, whether in lecture halls or at dinner parties, among scientists and among students, I find that people need to tell stories about things that they have seen and heard and experienced with animals. In telling their stories, there seems to be a need to have their experience affirmed so that they can legitimately change their beliefs.

Why is it so compelling for us to want to talk about relating with non-human animals? We are in relationship with animals, and we are often in wonder about the simple fact that we sense mutuality of connection, inside of us to inside of them. Our confoundedness about sharing our insides with other animals results from having been taught that animals are prohibitively other, that we cannot communicate with them, nor them with us because we are so vastly different, and different in a vastly superior way. It should be like trying to pour the ocean into a thimble, our capacities into their much smaller capacities. But this does not fit what we experience when our pets calm us more than do our partners.

We need animals as companions and teachers because they are both like us and different from us. They are like us because they think,

57. Bekoff, *Emotional Lives of Animals*, 131.

58. Peterson, *Moral Lives of Animals*, 59.

59. Cf. Benvenuti and Davenport, "New Archaic," 209.

and feel, and have fundamental moral and even political concern.[60] But they are different in that they have no need to navigate their days literally or metaphorically by the global positioning system on some hand-held device. They know where they are, not in an abstract conceptual way, but in a sensory and embodied way. Non-human animals are frequently more aware than we are of the material world, and amongst that large group of beings lumped under the heading of "animal" are myriad ways of experiencing the physical reality of the world. In spite of our much-glorified capacity for abstract reason, the material world retains its reality and sustains us, despite our lack of awareness of our dependence upon it. And the other animals seem to be more attuned to their own bodies and the emotions that flow from those bodies than we are of our own bodies and basic emotions; perhaps our capacity to occupy abstract space hinders our capacity to occupy material space.

I have many times been in the company of people who hear about Descartes's description of animals as machines without internal experience, and invariably someone interjects: "Obviously, he didn't have a dog!" But Descartes did have a canid companion, a small dog, Monsieur Grat, who often accompanied him.[61] It was not lack of exposure to dogs that prevented his making the same observational conclusions that most of us make about their insides and intentions, even their profound love for us. Perhaps it was that Descartes was quite literally lost in thought, so busy trying to make his mental model of a universe composed of two entirely distinct kinds of things, machines and minds, that he lost contact with what was soft and warm and right before his material eyes. He lost contact too with what was apparent in his actual behavior. As a clinical psychologist and trained observer of human behavior, I conjecture that Descartes's behavior indicates that he was emotionally dependent upon his dog. There is a hint of the deep tragedy of human unconsciousness in the image of Descartes going around with his dog as companion, yet insisting that animals are machines. This dissociation between mind and body, thought and sensation, emotion and motivation is, I have suggested elsewhere, a dangerous and distinctly human dilemma.[62] This species-specific dilemma of ours might be improved by spending time communing with other animals who, though they think, do not generally

---

60. Peterson, *Moral Lives of Animals*, 7; and de Waal, *Chimpanzee Politics*, xiv.

61. Harrison, "Descartes on Animals," 219–27.

62. Benvenuti and Davenport, "New Archaic," 215.

become dissociated from sensation and emotion because of that thinking. Indeed, I might restate Descartes's *Cogito ergo sum* to something like this: "I think so much that I am utterly lost in thought, lost to myself and to you." Maybe he too would have benefited from the wake-up call of a sudden encounter with a rattlesnake.

But even if Descartes had merely let the dog take him for a walk into the dog's world, if he had awakened to the dog in his company, we today might not be quite so lost these several centuries later to our own bodies, emotions, and souls. For the fact is that we are not simply abstract thinking things, convenient though it may be to dis-identify with the mortal body, but that we are beings of body, feeling, mind, relationship, and spirit, all thoroughly entangled within us, and entangling us thoroughly within the world. This is home. Waking up to our thoroughly entangled lives is the natural spirituality in which we can reconsider what it means to be human.

Even now, if we let our dogs take us for a walk, perhaps they can help us find a way home. And that is the walk on which I propose that we go: a walk in which we both examine our assumptions and stretch our imaginations to listen to other animals about their experience of living in relationship to the greater wholes of which they, and we, are a part.

Now where did I put the leash?

CHAPTER 2

Other Nations:
Thinking in terms of Multiplicity of Being

Remote from universal nature, and living by complicated artifice, man in civilization surveys the creature through the glass of his knowledge and sees thereby a feather magnified and the whole image in distortion. We patronize them for their incompleteness, for their tragic fate of having taken form so far below ourselves. And therein we err, and greatly err. For the animal shall not be measured by man. In a world older and more complete than ours, they move finished and complete, gifted with extensions of the senses we have lost or never attained, living by voices we shall never hear. They are not brethren, they are not underlings; they are other nations, caught with ourselves in the net of life and time, fellow prisoners of the splendor and travail of the earth.

—HENRY BESTON, "THE OUTERMOST HOUSE"[1]

Incorrect Belief, Mistaken Perception

IT WAS ONE OF those hot California days, and I was glad to escape the radiating heat of the asphalt parking lot. As I approached the welcome green of sculpted horticultural wonders, I saw at a quick glance that Amy was there, her long blonde hair her signature flag in the ticket line. I had

---

1. Beston, "The Outermost House," 394.

asked years before if she might introduce me to a celebrity friend of hers. Now, as she led me to the private area where we were to meet, she assured me that we were expected and that all except the minutest details would go according to plan.

Stepping out onto the VIP platform, Amy said with some excitement, "Look, there's Lana!" Lana for her part jumped up on to a high curb and, when she saw Amy, began to wave, hopping in place and blowing kisses. She was visibly happy to see her old friend. She looked in my direction, still waving. The energy was so contagious that I began to wave back and even blew a kiss to Lana, who refused it, crossing her arms over her chest and pointedly looking the other way. I realized, with some embarrassment, that I had misread the situation; another of Lana's old friends, Mike, was standing behind me and she was happy to see him, not me. I was the rude party-crasher. Chastised, I stepped back, allowing Mike and Amy to converse with Lana, as I waited to be introduced, feeling more than a little humiliated by my own enthusiasm of a just a few minutes before. Lana climbed a tree and continued to wave vigorously and to blow kisses to Mike and Amy.

The only behavior that was out of place in this much-anticipated meeting was my own. I had presumed a familiarity that did not exist. I grew up in Southern California and, having had movies made on the streets around me, have never made much of celebrity but also have learned not to presume relationship with stars just because they were visible. Why had I made such a presumption about Lana?

The answer was simple. I misbehaved because I know that I am "good with animals." What this means in reality is that I generally listen to them as I would a human, attempting to discern their comfort with me and their general interests before attempting to interact. My excitement and my desire to connect, and my presumptions based upon my being in Lana's company with Amy Parish, a primatologist at the San Diego Zoo who has worked for decades with the bonobos, had caused me to forget basic manners. Lana responded to me as my mother might when she says under her breath of someone who exhibits bad manners, "Were you born in a barn?" I had perceived Lana as welcoming me because I believed that she would welcome me, but I had forgotten the conditions that generally warrant a welcome in the animal, including the human, world.

The Complexity of "Being Good with Animals"

We have learned much from scientists about the insides of animals, not only about their organs and cells and observable behaviors, but also about their minds and hearts. While much research remains to be done, the weight of evidence is now solidly on the side of evolutionary continuity of mind, a concept and term advanced by Donald Griffin, professor of animal physiology and behavior, in his 1981 book addressing animal awareness. Well before the "decade of the brain" that went so far to prove him right, he reflected, "The flexibility and appropriateness of animal behavior suggest both that complex processes occur within their brains, and that these events may have much in common with our own conscious mental experiences. To the extent that this proves to be true, many of our ideas and opinions about the relationship between animals and men will require modification."[2]

Over the three decades that have passed since Griffin wrote that prescient statement, biological scientists of various sub-specialties have together established the principle of continuity of mind. Consider these summary words from affective neuroscientist Jaak Panksepp, whose research subjects over decades have been non-human animals: "This book has outlined evidence for ancient emotional feelings in other animals. Why the weight of scientific evidence remains to be accepted by most neuroscientists is a cultural-historical issue, not a scientific one. By sharing a neural platform for diverse affective experiences, the core SELF can be considered to be a *'nomothetic'* (universal) brain function."[3]

The 2012 Cambridge University Symposium on Consciousness, a gathering of neuroscientists in company with scientists from related fields, concluded that the weight of evidence indicates that "humans are not unique in possessing the neural substrates that generate consciousness."[4] The ground has shifted in the direction of broad acceptance of the impli-

2. Griffin, *Question of Animal Awareness*, 1.

3. Panksepp and Biven, *Archaeology of Mind*, 391–92.

4. The Cambridge Declaration on Consciousness was written by Philip Low and edited by Jaak Panksepp, Diana Reiss, David Edelman, Bruno VanSwinderen, Philip Low, and Christof Koch. The Declaration was publicly proclaimed in Cambridge, UK, on July 7, 2012, at the Francis Crick Memorial Conference on Consciousness in Human and non-Human Animals, at Churchill College, University of Cambridge, by Low, Edelman, and Koch. The Declaration was signed by the conference participants that very evening, in the presence of Stephen Hawking, in the Balfour Room at the Hotel du Vin in Cambridge.

cations of that evidence; and of the long struggle to let it speak, Panksepp notes: "Simply saying that animals have emotional feelings puts you into the radical camp where no one wants to be . . . but the times are moving with me."[5]

Panksepp's work shows consistently that core functions of consciousness and motivation are located not in the neocortex (thinking cap) of the brain, but in older and more primitive structures that all mammals share. This unexpected turn in neuroscientific findings points toward the shared depths of animal life that arise from a shared evolutionary history. Indeed, I think it may point all the way to what I might call shared animal spirituality. Contemporary science not only does not rule out animal participation in what we would broadly call spiritual experience, but may support it as a fundamental function of animal minds. I quote Kevin Nelson, neurologist and neuroscientist: "We have strong indications that much of our spirituality arises from arousal, limbic, and reward systems that evolved long before the structures that made the brain capable of language and reasoning. Neurologically, mystical feelings may not be so much beyond language as *before* language. . . . Given that we share many of the structures and systems in our brains with other creatures, we may not be the only ones with spiritual feelings."[6] It seems to me time to try to think in a comprehensive way about how the science of animal consciousness, cognition, and feeling relates to our human experiences, from the personal to the ecological, and also time to frame both the personal and the ecological in a context of spiritual meaning. Though large segments of the population do not know it, science has left behind an old set of questions about whether or not animals have internal experience, and even left behind the paradigm that generated those questions. There is a new paradigm for understanding animal behavior and interiority, that of evolutionary continuity and the social nature of intelligence generally. In the new paradigm we understand that all animals are related to each other, that all animals have inner experience, and that virtually all animals have the capacity to grasp that other animals also have inner experience. By the standards of even twenty years ago, these might seem overreaching statements, but, as Panksepp noted, the times have recently changed: science has substantially moved in the direction of comparing

5. Sorensen, "Animal Mind Reader," 21, 26.
6. Nelson, *Spiritual Doorway*, 258.

and contrasting the inner experience and the behavior of various animals, including humans.

Getting Personal

My dog Molly was smart. When the other dogs had a toy or a treat that she wanted, she would dash to the front door and start barking; all the other dogs would dash after her to create that special canine cacophony that takes on a life of its own. When the sound was intense enough to raise the rafters, Molly would slip away and, snatching the object of her intentions, would take it under the bed where she could enjoy it, free from intrusion by the bigger dogs.

This is a true story of a repeated action by a real dog, Molly Brown, who weighed only fifteen pounds and was the unquestioned boss of three other dogs who each weighed between fifty and sixty pounds. She took her job of commanding the pack very seriously, especially in enforcing human behavioral requirements (not allowing the other dogs to chew furniture, for example). There are many people who, though they might be entertained by my story, even sympathetic to it, would not be willing to take my interpretations of Molly's action seriously. I seem to imply that Molly thinks, strategizes, intends, can predict the behavior of other dogs and manipulate them accurately, and perhaps feel emotional satisfaction in her own cunning, in addition to the pleasure of the chew. Other people might note the way that I identify with the canine heroine, taking pleasure in her action and in her success. Of course, there are also many people who think it obvious that dogs intentionally engage such clever behavior, and that people take pleasure in these things, especially when it is their dog doing the successful deed. This group of people is comprised of those who have experience with dogs and with taking pleasure in their antics.

Others would say that I am anthropomorphizing, or inserting human qualities into a dog's being, where they do not belong. This group includes some who are known to have had their own canine companions, most notably Descartes. He and they might see my story as a kind of sentimental indulgence that describes my own emotional state of vicarious pride and competence, but not accept it as a realistic description of the dog's mind. Even if they allowed for the truthfulness of my story and for Molly's particular genius, they would say that it is, after all, just one story, and that we cannot generalize about dogs, and certainly not about animals more broadly, on the basis of a single anecdote; this is a fair warning in terms of demonstrating the factuality of claims.

These critical thinkers might encourage me to analyze the situation more carefully: to see, for example, whether Molly was acting on some kind of conditioning rather than developing an intentional strategy to achieve her personal preferences. Perhaps there was some trigger in her environment that caused her to run to the door and bark, and then, having been pushed out of the way by bigger dogs, perhaps she had one day discovered that they had left their possessions in their wake as they ran to the door. Indeed, that might well be how it started, but Molly did this repeatedly. It may have been accidental learning the first time, but not the second, third, and fourth times. So, they might point to me and say that I emanate pride and pleasure in her "achievement," lavishing her with praise for this deed and thus causing her to repeat it.

"But," I might reply, "she does not do it in some regular and predictable way so that the other dogs cease to react as she intends. Not only that, she clearly does it to please herself, not to please me."

She does not, after all, run to me to be cossetted, but takes her purloined treasure under the bed to enjoy in solitude. No, I insist, Molly was crafty and intentional.

And it turns out that Molly Brown is not the only smart animal to use a faked distress call in order to get advantageous access to food while the others, distracted by that call, momentarily lose interest in it. In his book on animal languages, Con Slobodchikoff reports that great white tits use the "seet" distress call to distract the more aggressive sparrows, who understand the meaning of the tit's "seet." He describes the response in this way: "These calls cause the sparrows to leave the seeds and to fly into a bush where they freeze, allowing the great tits to pick up as many seeds as possible before the sparrows realize that that there isn't any predator in sight and come back to feed."[7] It is an artful strategy that cannot be done too frequently or with accompanying predictable cues. Whether you are a human, a dog, or a bird, it takes cunning to use an alarm call to personal advantage. Crying wolf one time too often serves to desensitize the intended receiver to the one who seems to perceive danger always and everywhere. But my anecdote about Molly has been

7. Slobodchikoff, *Language of Animals*, 68.

confirmed by research into animal languages to be a strategy used, with intelligent sparseness, by smart animals.

It is a story I love to tell, full of doggy cleverness and artful design. And it is a genre of story I hear over and over, every time I mention that I am writing about animals. I notice too that cocktail party conversation wakes up when pets are the focus. I have received letters from people of all kinds who want to tell me about their experiences of animals because, I believe, they want to be affirmed in knowing what they think they know. After a talk I gave in Chicago while writing this book, I received a letter from a physician and medical researcher who had quit the research and practice of medicine in order to train hospice dogs. She had told me after the talk that she questions whether this is the best use of her time and her education. In her letter she told me how one of her dogs had been the only being who could connect with a particular autistic boy, a boy who was otherwise completely alone in his own world. Overall, she concludes that the work of training hospice dogs is the best use of her time and her training.

After another talk, I received a letter from a retired Texas cattle rancher who told me about the friendships amongst his cows, and about their attempts to communicate with him and his slow-witted learning how to listen, and he described their funerals. His were not delusional stories but careful reflections from someone who raised these cows not to bond with but to eat, and who yet had the courage to consider their inner experience of life, their desires, their problems, their capacity to connect with others. Such are the stories many of us long to tell about the person-alities and accomplishments, about the loves and losses, in the lives of animals we know, and more personally about how moved we have been by moments of deep understanding across species boundaries. These are also the kinds of stories that are considered idiosyncratic, personal (like dreams are personal), and not about the commonly shared version of reality that is intellectually acceptable.

The idea that animals are person-like, while evident to many people who spend time with animals, is still broadly taboo in Western thinking. The notion of animal personality is thought by many—especially those whose perspective is framed by a mechanistic model of science—to be childlike, naïve, a matter of mere private emotion, lacking in critical reflection. Those who believe that animals do not think, feel, have inten-tions, communicate with each other, or desire to accomplish goals, often point to the fact that people who like to tell animal anecdotes are animal lovers in the first place, and thus biased to project their own emotions onto beings unable to correct them.

Challenges in Thinking about Animals

There is much to unpack in my little dog story, and my description of typical reactions to it. First, there is the very real and complex issue of anthropomorphism. This refers to the inescapable ways that being human causes us to see the world as human-centric. It is so fundamental to everything we do, and especially to the ways in which we perceive other animals, that I will return to explore it in depth.

Second, there is the issue of valuing a story because it is personal and meaningful, and devaluing it for the same reason at the same time, as though personal and meaningful is a necessary but embarrassing thing. At a cocktail reception at an academic conference, I witnessed the joyous animation of a "celebrity" research scientist as he described the way in which the dogs were the emotional center of his home and witnessed, too, the change in him as he reentered the conference hall, resuming a persona that does not allow for animals to be other than genetically driven machinery. He is not so unusual in his ability to make this disconnection between his daily living and his thinking about life. Our twinned positive and negative response to animal stories, one part of us excited to engage the world of animal minds and another part of us supposing that they cannot really have minds (much less relational hearts, and personalities) may be more about how we think and feel about being feeling beings than it is about how accurately we can perceive dogs or birds. The matter of emotional bias is important, but it goes well beyond the issue of whether animals have minds, and into issues of the way we inhabit our human minds. Again, I will discuss it in greater depth in the next two chapters as "something about us, not something about them."

There is, too, an important issue of evaluating anecdotal evidence. We really cannot infer from a reported single observation any general truth about the capacity of dogs. To know about dogs with certainty, we need many dogs, many instances of a particular behavior, and many measurements of it. But that doesn't mean that anecdotal evidence can have no scientific merit, as has been demonstrated in the case of elephants knowing about events at a distance simultaneously with the occurrence of those events, and the discovery of an explanation in the form of Pacinian corpuscles, specialized sensory mechanisms of a kind that we do not have.[8] In this case, a collection of anecdotes pointed to more than one testable hypothesis. In a similar way, a hypothesis I might derive from the Molly Brown story is, "Some animals use distress calls as intentionally deceptive distractors in order to gain some advantage."

My smart dog story also contains the complex issue of the many ways in which differing biological motivations are expressed in a whole range of cognitions and behaviors: genetically driven instinct, like recoiling from contact with a burning substance; unconscious conditioning, like moving closer to the fire grate when the weather is cold; conscious learning, like paying attention to the optimal distance from the heated grate; and creative innovation, like making a safety barrier through which warmth can pass at that optimal distance. It used to be thought that animals were "driven" by instincts, while humans made free and rational behavioral choices based upon learning, reflection, and acquired wisdom. Neither of these opinions is accurate. Instead, we know that all animals, including humans, dwell in complex motivational and behavioral structures that include genetic tendencies, conditioned responses, conscious and unconscious learning, and socially and environmentally mediated decisions.

There is too the question of validating the folk wisdom that seems obvious to people who spend time with animals. But is their "common sense" correct? Can we legitimately say that, by knowing three or ten or a thousand people who say that their dogs have personalities, we can reasonably conclude that dogs have personalities? No, we need the science. It is folk wisdom that the sun rises and sets; and, while this never ceases to be a source of poetic and romantic possibility, it is proverbially not a factual description of reality.

The Value of Experience, and Limitations to the Value of Experience

In an advanced seminar for graduate students and professors at the intersection of science and religion, after I had presented on the question of animal souls, one doctoral student told with reverence a story that had come down to him about the family dog of his grandmother's childhood. He related that his grandmother had been playing alone in the farmyard

8. Peterson, *Moral Lives of Animals*, 5.

as a five-year-old when Blackie jumped between her and a rattlesnake, saving her life at the cost of his own. The dog came to be considered a saint in the family, and the story of his self-sacrifice had been told at Thanksgiving dinners over generations. On the other side of the room another man spoke out with equally evident emotion, that of disdain. He, a Christian minister of scientific bent, responded with "Pshaw! That dog didn't sacrifice himself; that was conditioned behavior based on thousands of years of breeding." But was it? A genetically driven behavior implies a reaction rather than a choice. Was Blackie born into the world in such a manner that, given the conditions of a poisonous snake and a human child, he could not have done otherwise than to throw himself between them? If this were so, then indeed we should call it a genetically conditioned response rather than a self-offering. But if anything in Blackie's experience of life influenced what he did in that fatal moment, then we cannot call it a genetically conditioned response. Though the dog's response might legitimately still be called a conditioned behavior, we must consider it in a more complex way. After all, most human heroes act instantaneously according to years of conditioning undergone to bring about just such instantaneous response when it is called for by environmental conditions.

The different perspectives voiced by the two men in that seminar seem to contrast the gullible and sentimental on one hand with the scientifically skeptical and sophisticated on the other. Even more interesting is the way that the incident illustrates that the fundamental beliefs we hold (as individuals or as subculture groups) about the nature of reality filter both what we see and how we interpret what we see. In the case of considering the nature of humans and animals, religious believers and scientific skeptics historically share commitment to a worldview that does not permit for any creatures other than humans to have intelligent insides and meaningful participation in their own lives. The Western religious worldview and the scientific worldview that once sought to replace it share an assumption that only humans have the capacity to live their lives intentionally, while life is something that mechanically happens to other animals, poor brutes. But decades of animal science, conducted by pioneers including Jane Goodall, Marc Bekoff, Franz de Waal, Roger Payne, Cynthia Moss, and Irene Pepperberg, present us with a solid general conclusion. The weight of cumulative evidence, they demonstrate, supports a broad understanding that animals have interior worlds, not identical to those of humans, but like us in the essential components of thought and feeling, selfhood, intention, and relationship to others in their worlds.[9] In the words of Virginia Morell, animal science journalist, "Animals have minds. They have brains, and use them, as we do; for experiencing the world, for thinking and feeling, and for solving the problems of life every creature faces."[10] The efforts of scientists have moved the consensus decidedly away from the generic idea that animals are a homogeneous group of beings somewhere below us on both the IQ scale and food chain and in the general direction of selfhood and complex interior life.

Of course, there are still scientists who believe in a mechanical world to which humans are somehow the exception, and they continue to speak in mechanical terms, even though such terms cannot explain the complexity of biological life as we now know it. This is not to make light of the importance of the mechanics of reality, the way that cause and effect can be known and predicted of both humans and other animals, not to mention protein chains and chemical elements. But it is to say that the assumption that humans are the only exception in an otherwise mechanical universe is patently incorrect and insufficiently explanatory. Those who maintain this stance do so on the basis of what I call a premature cognitive commitment, or a strongly held and emotionally charged belief that causes them to dismiss evidence that might lead where they are unwilling to go. It is, in other words, an expression of ideology. A name has been invented among cognitive psychologists for this common phenomenon of human rationality: it is called the "myside bias," and it functions to keep us confirmed in what we already think through various cognitive strategies.[11]

By way of contrast with the interpretations given to Blackie the dog's self-sacrificing behavior, I share a recent conversation that I had with someone I might call a militantly rational academic friend. In an elegant hotel lounge, far above the earth that lay supportively beneath its tower, I sat with Liza in decadently large leather wingback chairs, enjoying the view of the Chicago skyline and talking animatedly. Liza is an anthropologist and I am a psychologist, and we share Italian ancestry. This combination makes for intense conversations with lots of hand gestures, a scenario that others may interpret as heated argument, though these exchanges delight the two of us. That day, we dove straight into the

9. Balcombe, *Second Nature*, 4.

10. Morell, *Animal Wise*, 1.

11. Stanovich et al., "Myside Bias," 259.

deep end of a discussion in which I queried her about the ways in which humans use abstract thoughts and culturally conditioned learning to override their own fundamental experiences of sensation and emotion.

After spending some hours in intense conversation over sophisticated snacks, we decided that we had picked one another's brains more voraciously than the goat cheese croutons. I took the moment to offer an observation that I had made several years ago, namely that people do not love their pets like they love their favorite ice cream, but they love them like their children, or like dear friends. And people believe that their animals love them in return. I told Liza the story of how I had come to see that depth of love across the boundary between humans and other species is not rare at all, but that it is both common and hidden, suggesting of course the presence of a cultural taboo.

I added an illustrative story. When my dog Molly Brown died, I had taken her small body to the place where vets send pet corpses that they might be returned to their owners as cremains. The crematorium had stopped doing pick-ups in our little mountain valley, so if I wanted Molly dust, I would have to go and get it myself. This was in fact good news to me because I wanted to be sure that I had Molly dust, and not Fido dust. After checking in at the office, I carried Molly's body across the pet cemetery, passing row upon row of little headstones. I made great effort to be matter of fact as I met with the crematorium worker and watched him slide out the heavy metal shelf, put Molly's body on it, slide it back in, pull down the oven door and set the timer. It was going to take a while, even for a little dog, and so I wandered as I waited.

Weeping at first, I stumbled along the rows of little memorials. Gradually I began to read the headstones: "Sweet Pea, my best friend." "Teddy Bear, I'll meet you on the rainbow bridge." "Sammy, my best friend." On and on, the markers bore witness, one after another, declarations of love, and especially of best friendship. Were these declarations made elsewhere with such passionate abandon? I thought it unlikely. Such declarations were taboo; to utter them is to admit to being softheaded, if not perverse (undying love shared with a cat?). But these hundreds of people, maybe thousands, all these people had voiced the love that was for them as love is for each of us, longing to be spoken, to be acknowledged, to be celebrated and served, and wanting somehow to be preserved, to be the one thing that death cannot consume.

I did not get to overindulge this kind of rhapsody about interspecies love with Liza. She waved her Italian hand in the air and said, "Yah, yah, but it's not the animals. We do that; we do that to them."

"You mean like Wilson, the volleyball befriended by Tom Hanks in *Castaway*?"

Yes, she replied, we project our emotional needs on to these furry recipients of our dubious affections. I could see her summoning visions of dogs in a variety of human dress.

"No," I said, "it isn't just that; and besides, how is that different from human love?" We project the satisfaction of our various desires outward on to some ideal person and we are delighted, we are in love. Then we experience something contrary to our desires: perhaps the ideal person begins to tell us that we are not as perfect or as beautiful as we first appeared, and we are disappointed again, maybe even enraged with them. Why is the human to human form of love the sacred stuff of life, and the human to animal form a silly projection?

"Besides, it's not just that we love them. What about the fact that they love us?"

"They don't love us; they need to be fed."

Liza has not experienced being bonded to animal companions, but she is keenly tuned to human forms of clarity and deception alike. She despises "ideology" and espouses science and reason as the royal roads out of ideological deceptions and into the spare lines of intellectual clarity. This, I have asserted, *is* an ideology and it shares in the chief vice of all ideologies, that of premature cognitive commitment that might keep one from considering the evidence. She responds that, as ideologies go, it is a good one in its fundamental attitude of willingness to consider the possibility of error, especially as contrasted with other approaches; chief among these for her is religious doctrine. Research psychologists have found that it is possible but actually fairly rare that any of us awakens to something that challenges our habitual worldview or behavior.[12] The norm is that we easily go along, interacting with the world as we believe it to be, seeking social experiences that confirm our worldview, and often finding ways to explain contrasting experiences in terms of our beliefs or to ignore aspects of life that run counter to them. Occasionally something happens that causes us to question our convictions, however. Let

---

12. Tavris and Aaronson, *Mistakes Were Made*, 1–10.

me recount an "over the backyard fence" report of my old friend and neighbor Diane's encounter with a blue jay.

The blue jay had pestered Diane until she paid attention, in order to solicit her help. At least that is what Diane thinks happened. Maybe. Diane grew up on acreage in the north of Wisconsin, with a grandfather who rescued little animals. He once brought home an orphaned baby raccoon, for instance, and raised him with the family. But let me note that Diane is a cognitive behavioral therapist who uses the tools of critical thinking to bring both herself and others out of confusion and unnecessary suffering. Standing in her yard that morning, Diane had heard the blue jay calling in a more insistent way than its typical punctuated squawk. Wanting to know if the jay really sounded different from the usual wank-wanking, I made my clumsy rendition of that more typical sound for her and asked if that was what it had sounded like.

"No," she replied, "it was different."

"Hey! Hey! Hey!" I suggested, in my best blue jay accent.

"Yes! Like that."

The jay's alarm sound drew Diane to look for the bird, and when she saw that it was a female she wondered if there was a nest nearby. As she approached, the jay came closer to her rather than darting away and vocalized more insistently, looking up at her face and then down at the ground. Diane engaged the very typical animal communication behavior of joining in a directed mutual gaze, whereby one looks pointedly at something, then looks back to the other animal, then back at the some-thing, until the other animal also gazes at the something.[13] So directed by madame bird, Diane looked at the ground in order to see what the bird apparently wanted her to see. The vision she then shared was that of a very large garter snake. Of course, as Diane moved closer, the snake flowed away like water, presumably without its breakfast of eggs or baby blue jays. The mother jay relaxed and quieted.

Diane felt that the jay had clearly and intentionally drawn her attention to the snake. Then she doubted her own reading of the situation, asking herself if it could (or indeed should) have been so. I was delighted with the story because Diane, retired chief executive of a large public healthcare system and a scientist by training, thought it obvious that the blue jay was specifically trying to communicate the snake's presence to her, but also wondered if that was truly possible. Could a jay intentionally

13. Peterson, *Moral Lives of Animals*, 181.

tell her about a snake? She was in conflict between her own felt experience of the situation and what she had been taught was likely or even possible. Diane chose to consider various sets of possibilities, and to be interested in the space of conflict between her preconceptions and her perceptions. Cognitive conflict is often the beginnings of wisdom, and I find it is more likely to happen if we have actual experience of a thing than if we have just heard, read, and thought about the thing. But experience alone is not sufficient; we need some way to analyze the experience in order to evaluate our own interpretations of it.

Current Science of Animal Cognition and Behavior

The scientific study of animals is one way that some people actually— and very carefully—experience animals directly rather than "explaining them" by way of some larger ideology. Ideologies, however, are often subtly present, even when they are actively disavowed. In discussing animal languages, Con Slobodchikoff addresses the conundrum of a supposedly scientific worldview that does not allow for study of a phenomenon preemptively declared not to exist. With reference to commonly accepted ideas about the impossibility of animal language he writes:

> Most of these arguments are built on two fundamental points that pretty much sum up the position of many scientists. One is the stimulus-response theory that insists animals can only do one genetically determined, hardwired thing in response to a stimulus; they don't have a choice. The other is the position that animals do not have any intentions and are not conscious of what they do. By espousing these two basic beliefs about animals, most scientists conclude that animal signals cannot possibly be language. As a result, they are highly unlikely to ever set up an experiment to explore the possibility that animals have language.[14]

Nonetheless, a large body of scientific evidence since the 1960s has served to topple a long list of human capacities that were once thought to distinguish humans from all other animals, with evidence drawn from ethology, comparative psychology, the neurosciences, genetics, and comparative anatomy and physiology. On the anatomical axis, the fallen members include opposable thumbs, big complex bihemispheric

14. Slobodchikoff, *Language of Animals*, 27–28.

brains, dedicated language areas within the brain, and perhaps most recently VEN neurons, thought to be specialized for social cognition.[15] As recently as 2004, noted researcher in human cognition Jean Decety hypothesized that VEN neurons might well distinguish humans from other animals in the domain of empathy.[16] But since that date, VEN neurons have been found to exist in the brains of a wide range of mammals, including humans, great apes, macaque monkeys, elephants, cetaceans, hippos, and zebras.

As for the older and simpler idea that opposable thumbs set humans apart from other beings, orangutans—not known to be tool users in the wild—have proved to be mechanical geniuses in human settings, continually challenging zoo designers to create the orang-proofed enclosure. Consider the case of Fu Man Chu, a resident of the Omaha Zoo, who not only repeatedly escaped but also took his female companion and their three offspring on outings with him. Needless to say, zoo staff had carefully checked barriers and locks after the first escape. After setting up a watch, they discovered his strategy: "In the wall of the moat was a door that led into a furnace room. On the other side of the room was a set of stairs and another [locked] door that led to freedom." After navigating the maze to get to that final door in the series, Fu Man Chu applied both his brute strength and his technological know-how. "Drawing on his great strength . . . Fu Man Chu pulled the door back from its frame. Taking a piece of wire from his cheek, he then tripped the latch, much the way a thief might slip a credit card between a door and its frame."[17] Orangutans do not use their hands for the detail work; they use their mouths because their mouths have a flexibility that their enormous powerful hands lack. I was at the orangutan enclosure of the San Diego Zoo when the dominant male placidly delivered a series of grommets from his cheek to the zookeeper who was staring mystified at the remains of a huge tarp that had come down, not blown by wind but dismantled intentionally. Unless, of course, there is only one behavior available to an orangutan in the presence of a tarp secured by grommets, then we could not say it was only a conditioned response rather than an intentional act based upon personal motives. So much for anatomical differences defining capacities; opposable thumbs are one way but far from the only way to manipulate objects.

15. I use the abbreviation VEN for Von Economo (or spindle) neurons.

16. Decety and Jackson, "Human Empathy," 82.

17. Linden, *Parrot's Lament*, 6.

Behaviors once thought to distinguish humans from other animals include tool making and use, the capacity for abstract thought, use of language, mathematical reasoning, self-awareness, social cognition, humor, creative play, complex emotional bonds, empathy, altruism, awareness of death (and grieving), moral sensibility, social learning and culture, political affiliation, and the capacity to know what is in the mind of the other, known in the research as theory of mind.[18] Each of these capacities has been found in other animals. In a review of thirty years' worth of studies on theory of mind in chimpanzees, Joseph Call and Michael Tomasello concluded that the evidence shows that chimpanzees do indeed anticipate goals and intentions in the minds of others, and that they also use their grasp of the others' perceptions to create deception. However, they are unable to know when another being is operating from notions that are in conflict with reality; they do not recognize the operation of a false belief.[19] We can reasonably conclude that behavior driven by ideology is foreign to chimpanzees, who would be most unlikely to make the interpretation that other animals are "really" machines.

When Jane Goodall first observed the chimpanzees at Gombe shaping grass into fishing poles for termites, Louis Leakey famously responded to her report with the terse statement, "Now we must redefine tool, redefine Man, or accept chimpanzees as humans."[20] His statement was prescient in that we must now approach this issue of redefinition in a serious way, for tool use was just the beginning of questions about the real differences between "man" and "animals."

Anthropomorphisms

The capacity to deceive is considered to be a particularly complex and demanding form of cognition because it involves self-awareness, other-awareness, the capacity to plan ahead to achieve one's purpose, and the ability to know what is in the mind of the other so accurately that one can manipulate that mind by creating a false impression for it to perceive. It has been demonstrated by scientific experiment in many animals, but perhaps the most unexpected results have been found in studies of the food caching behavior of scrub jays, birds who behave quite differently

18. Cf. Balcombe, *Second Nature* for an overview of animal interiority.
19. Call and Tomasello, "Does the Chimpanzee Have a Theory of Mind?"
20. Goodall Institute, *Toolmaking*.

according to who (amongst scrub jays) is observing them, and how, and from where.[21] If a scrub jay is hiding food for future consumption, and he sees that a known thief is observing where he caches his food, he proceeds with his work but will return later and, unobserved, move his stored food to a new and secret location.

This finding about the social intelligence of scrub jays raises questions about who is most like us amongst the animals. The natural assumption has been that those who look most like us, the great apes, are indeed most like us. In fact, we share 99.9 percent of our DNA with other *Homo sapiens* and 98.8 percent with bonobos and chimpanzees, making us *one* of the great ape species.[22] And yet we find language like ours, a trait we consider definitive of our very nature as a species, not amongst other apes, but amongst birds, who possess "vocal abilities eerily akin to those of humans."[23]

Despite accumulating evidence that would lead to the conclusion that there is no singular divide between humans and other animals, I continue to read almost daily of some anatomical detail or behavioral capacity, now usually a neuroanatomical detail or subtle cognitive capacity, that is the new candidate for setting humans apart from the rest of nature. The apparent underlying need to show that humans are distinct and superior remains stubbornly persistent. I have already referred to the suggestion once made by Jean Decety that VEN neurons might define human superiority in social cognition and empathy; and that same research article includes repeated references to belief in and hope of demonstrating the unique and special qualities of human empathy. While providing an excellent overview and discussion of a complex model for understanding and studying empathy in humans, Decety and his colleagues persistently reflected a seemingly unrelated agenda for affirming the notion that we are indeed distinct from and superior to all other animals. One of the explicit statements of this objectively unrelated theme reads: "We believe that self-other awareness and self-regulation of emotions are vital components of human empathy. These components may well steer us toward a clear distinction between humans and other mammals when referring to empathy."[24] Perhaps, though, what sets us apart is our need to

21. Penn, "Scrub Jays," 255.
22. Smithsonian Institute, "Genetics."
23. Morell, *Animal Wise*, 89.
24. Decety and Jackson, "Human Empathy," 72.

be special, but I seriously doubt that there is no other kind of animal who shares in our special needs.

Derek Penn, a comparative cognitive psychologist, writing in a recent volume on issues in comparative cognition, explores what I consider a core problem in comparative psychology, namely that anthropomorphism is necessarily pervasive in human thought because we can only experience the world as humans.[25] The anthropomorphism might be summarized in saying that we often do not get it right about who is like us and who is different from us, and in what specific ways, particularly because we are not always conscious of our comparative process. Reflecting on anthropomorphic interpretations of scientific data, Penn says: "Hardly an issue of *Current Biology* or *Animal Cognition* goes by without some new effigy of human cognitive uniqueness being torn down and dragged through the mud. . . . From tool use to metacognition, from deception to death, much of comparative psychology over the last 35 years has been driven by the single-minded goal of demonstrating that non-human animals are capable of 'human-like' cognition." Then, turning to scrub jays, Penn remarks that "[they] have turned out to be mavens of social interactions within the context of food caching. They also have the inimitable advantage of looking nothing like cute human children."[26] I would say that the advantage is to the scientist who might be less tempted to project his humanity on to the feathered and beaked animal he studies, and perhaps therefore to see more accurately what it is to be a scrub jay.

An illustrative example of the challenges of interpreting who is like us and who is not can be found in the study of the linguistic capacities of apes, our genetically and morphically similar relatives, whom we have assumed to be most likely to be able to use language in a manner similar to our own. It turns out that, while some great apes have acquired vocabulary and even taught it spontaneously to others, there are more likely candidates for study of language acquisition and use in the animal world. Among these are whales, dolphins, elephants, seals, bats, parrots, and songbirds, who share a great deal of our capacity for language. Infant parrots have a signature call, their name, that their parents give them, to which they must learn to respond as an early and necessary step in their behavioral repertoire, as is the case for human babies.[27] Likewise,

25. Penn, "Scrub Jays," 255.

26. Ibid.

27. Morell, *Animal Wise*, 90.

recent research has demonstrated that dolphins also know each other by individual names in the form of "signature whistles." And comparable to the human capacity to identify someone by his or her voice on the phone, dolphins remember each other by unique voice timbre over decades.[28]

On the challenging side, our anthropomorphic assumptions, usually unconsciously applied to situations we encounter, produce anthropomorphic questions.

"Can they think (like us)?"

"Do they feel (like us)?"

"Do they make tools (like us)?"

When we ask such questions with the unspoken, and difficult to avoid, comparison to ourselves, it makes it hard for us to comprehend other ways of doing life, such as that represented in the technological proficiency of humpback whales who, in focusing and directing their breath, create bubble nets in which they corral large numbers of small fish who make up their diet.[29] To make matters even more complex, the particulars of their use of this technology vary by location and culture.

Our anthropomorphic questions tend naturally to anthropomorphic answers, along the lines of "Why, see, they're just like us!" This has the (to my mind) unfortunate consequence of inviting skeptics of the mechanist kind to respond derisively, as did a member of a scientific audience when a scientist said of a female bird that she wanted her offspring to survive.

"Do you mean to say that natural selection has shaped the female's actions to make it seem to us like she wants her offspring to survive?"[30]

And how, I might ask, has natural selection shaped the behavior of this respondent so that he appears to us as he does? As is demonstrated here, a skewering response may feel clever, but it may not signify much: the point remains that we are all animals who are shaped by evolution, including he who would hold himself above the fray of life on earth.

In spite of facile dismissals of suggestions about intelligence and intention being part of the insides of other animals, the issues of anthropomorphism are real and much more complex than simply asserting that we should avoid projecting our humanness onto non-humans when we interpret them as like us. It is quite natural that we bring to our study of

28. King and Janik, "Bottlenose Dolphins"; and Bruck, "Social Memory."
29. Wiley et al., "Feeding Behavior."
30. Slobodchikoff, *Language of Animals*, 28.

other animals a humanizing perspective; research in human cognition has demonstrated that a general feature of human cognition is a default mode of egocentric bias when reasoning about others.[31] We see the world as we are; how else can we see it? And how the mole smells the world, or how the whale hears the world, is not how we see it.

In spite of the ways in which anthropomorphism can interfere with accuracy of perception and interpretation, it is also true that projecting our own experience onto members of other species may sometimes be a good source of accurate information. There is a kind of reliable implicit knowledge that we can have of the other, to the extent and in the manner that we actually are similar to each other and can accurately perceive the similarity. When I see any mother mammal care for her infant and I feel tenderness (perhaps exclaiming, "Look, she loves her baby!"), it is likely a somewhat accurate understanding of the mother-infant bond that all mammals share. There are neural mechanisms, such as mirror neurons, that allow mammals to know directly what the other feels by the automatic reproduction of a "dialed down" version of that experience in our own brains.[32] And in spite of the fact that anthropomorphism can cause us to reach false conclusions, it can also lead us to an accurate understanding of some aspects of the experience of the other. To the extent that we are alike, we can know a great deal implicitly.

But the uses of such derived reasoning are limited. Philosopher Thomas Nagel wrote a now famous essay on the experience of life as a bat in which he makes the case that we cannot and will never be able to penetrate subjective experience.[33] He illustrates this by demonstrating that, whatever we learn about bat life, we cannot know what it is to be in a body that is guided by echolocation. His point that science cannot, by definition, respond fully to the question, "What is it like to be you?" is well taken.

While it is difficult to detach from our own egocentric perspective when thinking about very different others, and while there is real value in being able to extend implicit knowledge of self to the other, it is also necessary for accuracy that we attempt to understand our fellow beings in the context of their own ecological niches, the specific context in which

31. Royzman, "Epistemic Egocentrism," 38.
32. Rizzolatti and Sinigaglia, *Mirrors in the Brain*, 173.
33. Nagel, *Mortal Questions*, 165.

their body-minds make sense, rather than trying to make sense of them in our ecological context.

It is telling that much of the first animal behavior research was conducted with great apes, a fact that underlines the anthropomorphic intent of the early scientific studies. Indeed, Jane Goodall's chimpanzee studies were finally funded (after many rejected proposals) because Goodall's mentor Louis Leakey suggested that chimps might provide insight into our favorite animals, *Homo sapiens*. We cannot fault Jane Goodall, or her science, for the ways in which humans are self-interested. In fact, I was delighted to learn that, as a little girl, she had to be instructed by her mother to take the fascinating and very "other" earthworms from under her pillow and put them back in the dirt, else they would die overnight![34] But the fact remains that the world of science first chose those animals who look most like us to ask questions about their capacity to do what we can do, and we also assumed these apes to be the most advanced of the non-human animals.

This set of assumptions is a reflection of the folk model of evolutionary theory that is driven by emotion, not by science: I refer to the popular notion that the evolutionary process pushed progressively more advanced and superior models until it reached the perfection of humanity. You can no doubt picture the almost ubiquitous cartoon image of a monkey followed by an ape dragging his knuckles, followed by a more upright ape, followed by an upright man, who is followed by the next best thing (sometimes a woman). But this is a projection of our feelings of being the best product of evolution. It is not an image of real evolutionary biology, which would show a vast and ancient tree, with us modern humans as one small and recent, though perhaps very bright, twig on a branch of great apes, many now extinct, including at least two human species, Neanderthals and *Homo floresciensis*.

Contemporary Animal Studies

As my anthropologist friend Liza frequently points out, one of the great beauties of science is that it is essentially self-correcting; and this has been true in the scientific study of animals. In recent decades, questions asked and the data gathering techniques and experimental methods used to test hypotheses about animal behavior and sentience have become ever more

34. Goodall, Foreword to Bekoff, *Animals Matter*, viii.

sophisticated, and the range of animals studied has expanded greatly. Indeed, the cognitive, emotional, and communicative capacities of other animals have been affirmed in hundreds of studies. Further, the results of the research into mechanisms of the behavior of other species have often been surprising in the way that they demonstrate not only the capacities of our fellow animals to be like us, but also our own naive ignorance of the possibilities contained in their very different bodies.

The work of bioacoustics researcher Katy Payne is instructive in this regard. Payne had been studying the songs of humpback whales, and became interested in the question of long distance sound amongst land animals. After departing from a scientific conference on whales, she arranged to spend a week sitting at the elephant enclosure of a zoo so that she might listen for evidence that would indicate that large land animals communicate over long distances. Day after day she got nothing, except that she noticed an occasional feeling of a kind of pulsing pressure in her ears. By her report, it felt like the odd uncomfortable sensation we get when car windows are not correctly sealed shut. She did not think it amounted to much, but after later analyzing the recordings of the environment, she discovered that indeed, a male in musth (male breeding season) and a female, separated by a concrete wall, were having quite a private conversation.[35] Elephants, it transpires, make high-pressure utterances on a frequency (20 hertz) too low to be heard by most human ears.[36] In a related study, atmospheric scientists traveled with Payne to the Elephant Listening Project in Africa. They discovered that the evening atmospheric inversion layer typical in that forest environment created an air channel especially good for carrying sound waves long distance. These evening elephant news reports could be heard by their conspecifics up to six miles away.

Payne's discovery of the means of elephant long distance communication began to solve the mystery that had been reported over and over in anecdotal stories by those who observed elephants in the wild, that elephants seemed to know things that they could not possibly know about distant events. Often the stories involved different groups of elephants from more than one long distance location showing up for the same event at the same time, such as for a very recent death. We now understand that elephants easily could know these things because they

35. Payne, "Listening to Elephants."
36. Poole et al., "African Elephants," 385.

have ways of knowing that we had not imagined. Payne's research caused scientists to think differently about animals and what they might be doing, and to bring to the field and the lab the kinds of sensory equipment that might allow us to understand them on their own terms and in their own environments, and not only with reference to how they are like us.

It turns out that the ways in which other animals are not like us are sometimes remarkable and certainly fascinating to our imaginations. In addition to their capacity to speak and to hear over several miles by way of sound waves, elephants also send and receive communication over even longer distances using their feet.[37] Their stomping and rumbling creates seismic waves in the ground that travel up to twenty miles. While listening to these seismic messages, elephants seem to freeze, leaning forward with their weight on the pads of their larger front feet, pads equipped with anatomical features of cartilage nodules that transmit seismic sound up their leg and shoulder bones to their ears. This freezing behavior is something we generally associate with "deer in the headlights" fear in animals, but we also know it in humans as concentration, as when we are mentally trying to solve a problem or recall a sequence while holding very still and gazing into the distance. It was the striking appearance of concentration while poised leaning forward that first led elephant researcher Caitlin O'Connell to wonder if indeed they were somehow engaged in listening with their feet.

Whales too are able to communicate over long distances, using low frequency utterances that travel far and fast through water, reaching distances of sometimes thousands of miles at a speed about five times faster than that of sound waves traveling through the air.[38] Additionally, as elephants seem to use the atmospheric pressure changes to the advantage of their long distance communications, whales use the ocean sound channel, diving down to sing their songs into this horizontal band in the ocean that can carry sound for vast distances. In the brains of whales, the areas dedicated to hearing are much larger than those for seeing, and it is fair to say that whales hear with their whole bodies, as sound waves amplified by the conduction of water wash through them. A related anatomical feature of toothed cetaceans (baleen whales do not share this feature) is the "melon," composed of specialized fat cells, an organ that is thought to be involved in hearing for the purposes of echolocation.

37. O'Connell, *Elephant's Secret Sense*, 5; O'Connell and Rodwell, "Seismic Communication"; O'Connell et al., "Asian Elephant Vocalizations."

38. Russell, *Eye of the Whale*, 203.

Given what we have learned about hearing in whales and elephants, is it any wonder that these species have been found to try to protect themselves from intrusive and destructive sounds produced by human technologies? The effects of introduced noise on Pacific gray whales offers an example. Marilyn Dalheim, while still a doctoral student at the University of British Columbia, investigated the effects of introduced noise on these whales in their Baja Mexico birthing lagoons because there had been some suggestion that they had abandoned San Diego Bay as a nursery due to the sound of boat traffic. She submerged sound transducers capable of directing underwater sound towards the whales and observed their behavioral responses. "I'd heard about whales hiding behind islands or icebergs to avoid increased levels of sound in their environment, but I never knew whether to believe it," she said. "But when I played oil-drilling sounds, not even at a very high decibel level, I found clusters of whales in the Middle Lagoon behind those sandbars, where there are what I call 'sound shadows' and the noise wasn't as intense." In continued research, she established that mechanical noise caused the mothers and calves to depart the lagoons early, leaving the shelter of the nursery before they were fully ready to do so.[39]

Research such as this underlines the problem of military sonar testing in relation to decades of mysterious beaching and death of cetaceans. In 2000, for instance, soon after the United States Navy began conducting sonar tests in the Bahamas, seventeen whales from four species beached themselves and several died from the mysterious bleeding now understood to be a symptom of underwater sound trauma. Though Navy researchers declaimed any responsibility, the National Marine Fisheries Service found that six whales had suffered hemorrhages around their ears, hypothetically caused by a "distant explosion or intense acoustic event."[40] It is well established that underwater sonar tests of this kind injure and kill large numbers of cetaceans; yet the testing continues, though to increasingly well informed public protest.

We, naturally, had been thinking of hearing in terms of ears, an anthropomorphic assumption that caused us to miss the fact that each of these species lives in large bodies evolved to communicate with low frequency sound waves over very long distances. And, of course, in our curiosity to learn and in our excitement about new technologies, we did

39. Ibid., 204.
40. Ibid., 209.

not anticipate how very destructive underwater research using sound would be for creatures who are virtually all ears.

The realization that different bodies give rise to different kinds of minds can also be seen in the fact that the visual and auditory regions of dolphin brains are highly integrated, allowing them to construct stunningly specific visual images on the basis of echoes. And a recent study published in the Proceedings of the Royal Society for the Biological Sciences announced the finding that dolphins also sense electrical pulses expressed by the organs of other animals, concluding: "Our results show that electroreceptors can evolve from a mechanosensory organ that nearly all mammals possess and suggest the discovery of this kind of electroreception in more species, especially those with an aquatic or semi-aquatic lifestyle."[41] I mention this study because it typifies the way that science is demonstrating not only that other animals inhabit complex bodies and minds, but also that an astonishing array of sensory and communicative capacities exist amongst animals, and that we have missed these while looking for human-like qualities.

Animal Languages and What They Tell Us

From the viewpoint of considering auditory foot pads and songs sung into the ocean sound channel, it is hard to imagine the depth of the conviction with which many smart people still hold the opinion that only humans have language, or "true" language if you will. It is rather like showing up at a performance venue, watching a crew set up amplifiers and microphones and a stage full of musical instruments and being given the explanation that there really are no musicians, only people who make meaningless noises. Then, as the band begins to play the instruments and the vocalists sing in time, you are told that what you are hearing is not really music. Some composers and musicians might agree with this statement, but this puts us on the turf of fine definitions about what comprises music, not to mention who is privileged to define it.

In a similar way, communications specialists have put forward an ever expanding and fine tuned list of requirements that animal utterances must meet in order to qualify as language.[42] The list is, of course, very valuable in allowing us to analyze the nature and functions of language,

41. Czech-Damal et al., "Electroreception in the Guiana Dolphin."
42. Slobodchikoff, *Language of Animals*, 20–22.

but by definition linguists have studied human language and defined the structure of language accordingly. In fact, as has been the case with other presumed "only human" activities, the list of requirements expands every time its conditions have been met somewhere else in the animal world. If this sounds familiar, it is one more case of that now familiar set of anthropomorphic problems. Linguists study and understand the structure of human language, and non-human languages may include other possibilities.

I can recall to this day the classroom in which I sat when I first read about Slobodchikoff's early work in discovering the semantic content, or meaningful "words," in the utterances that serve to represent an idea in prairie dog "speech." I feel too the pleasure I felt twenty years ago when scientists confirmed that the rodents are talking about us. A subtitle in his chapter on warning calls will give you some idea of the amount of content in what sounds to us like brief bird-chirping: *tall, thin human wearing a blue shirt!*[43]

In a natural prairie dog environment, by prairie dog design a confined space and so a good science "lab," Slobodchikoff made visual and acoustic recordings of events and analyzed the correlations between them. Analysis of events such as the arrival of different kinds of predators combined with acoustic recordings demonstrated that prairie dog chirpings have semantic content, including distinctions that refer to coyotes, to domestic dogs, to hawks, to humans, to poisonous snakes. Slobodchikoff then developed a series of experiments, conducted in the field, that confirmed his hypothesis that prairie dogs are actually talking to each other. By flexible (as opposed to programmed) manipulation of their vocal repertoire, prairie dogs make utterances that meet many of the criteria established by linguists, and they condense into a brief utterance a great deal of specific information, such as the fact that the human who is coming through is tall and thin and wearing a blue shirt.

Rather than chase the red herring of trying to prove that prairie dogs and other animals meet the criteria of linguists, Slobodchikoff has suggested that language, like mind, is an evolutionary adaptation that is broadly distributed, and that it should exhibit species-specific expressions of the more general purposes of communication. He refers to this broadly distributed feature of animal life, essential to achieving individual biological fitness, as the discourse system. The discourse system is

43. Ibid., 54.

defined by a set of criteria equivalent to other biological systems (diges-
tion, respiration, reproduction, among others). Among the features that
Slobodchikoff describes as necessary to a discourse system are bodily
structures for sending and receiving messages, a brain area dedicated to
the sending and receiving of messages, these being attached to the central nervous system, possession of a number of signals that can be used
with flexibility, and the capacity to be influenced by context.[44] One of
the things that this evolutionary approach predicts is that there should
be one or more broadly distributed genes that control the expression of
language. When the FoxP2 gene was discovered, it was thought to be (can
you guess?) evidence that humans have a unique gene for language that
no other animals have. But FoxP2 is pervasive in the animal world. When
it is abnormally expressed, animals cannot perform their vocalizations in
the manner of their species.

Animals have specialized sound niches too. In fact, the whole bio-
sphere or the covering of the planet with animal and plant life is an acoustic
environment in time, as niches are areas in geological space. Each species
has its particular way of creating a private temporal and acoustic space
in which to talk with others of its kind. Recall those elephants stomping
to their long distance friends of an evening in the jungle? Those whales
singing their mating songs into the ocean sound channel, those prairie
dogs with their high-pitched chirps, those stranded dolphins? As I am
learning to listen to the world as a series of temporal acoustical spaces,
it is changing me by opening up a living understanding of the way life
works. I understand now that when I hear the dawn chorus of birdsong,
it is that they have found this time of day to make their own, a temporal
space in which they can speak freely, and be heard. Recall the sound of
evening frog chorus, or night crickets, not to mention the din of cicadas
who do not have time for niceties in their short time above ground, so
they simply must drown out everyone else in their search for each other.

One final note about the discourse system: it need not be acoustic. Bees have chemical language that is truly language, with chemicals
expressed in a manner to flexibly communicate semantic content, meaning that they use a chemical "alphabet" in a manner that they can manipulate to represent specific conditions of their internal and external

44. Ibid., 38.

environments. Ants do this, too. And there is the well-known honeybee waggle dance.[45]

There is, further, the chronic matter of jokes about dog butt-sniffing. A dog's nose is one million times more sensitive than yours or mine. When Fido goes outside in the morning to sit with his nose raised into the air, inhaling deeply, he is reading the morning news, and he knows all about what happened there overnight in a way that we never will. I have often seen dogs stop in the middle of an interaction to smell the butt of a dog friend as if they are seeking confirmation either that they have understood the situation correctly, or that the mood has changed. I have also noticed that dogs are not given to smelling the butts of every animal, and so I think it likely that there is some dog-to-dog communication at work. In fact, I think they are being socially intelligent good listeners, but to know for certain, we would have to design studies to measure it. And dogs famously also love to mark, leaving chemical messages for other dogs. My smallest dog, Lexi, does literal cartwheels, aiming her mark for the top of the arc. I sometimes wonder if she is trying to appear taller to other dogs, as she tends to greet them in person by wagging her tail and growling fiercely at the same time, as if to announce, "I am a dog, not a squirrel!"

On the subject of dogs, many a dog-loving scientist has been disappointed to learn that dogs are not on the list of self-aware animals that includes humans, chimps, macaque monkeys, dolphins, and elephants. Dogs have shown themselves to be experimentally non-self-aware: that is, they do not respond to the "dot-mirror-test" by trying to examine or remove an artificial dot attached to their faces and reflected to them in a mirror. Species on the "A" list can do so; their combined capacity to recognize themselves in a mirror and also to recognize that something that is not part of them appears to be part of them indicates their awareness of self and of other than self. Marc Bekoff, whose specialty is the scientific study of canines, responded to this news by devising a dog-specific study: he removed patches of urine-soaked snow made by identifiable dogs and placed these where his own dog regularly urinated. His dog, Jethro, clearly distinguished between self and other in the chemical medium of urine that is so anecdotally interesting to dogs. "Jethro infrequently urinated over or sniffed and then immediately urinated over (scent-marked) his own urine. He marked over the urine of other males more frequently

45. Ibid., 109–26.

than he marked over females' urine!"[46] Not surprisingly, this suggests that dogs experience and express self and other awareness via scent and not visually. I would not be surprised to learn that dogs have a huge chemical vocabulary for their conversations with other dogs, and that they have learned to manipulate barking, whining, and body language so as to communicate with humans.

The Human Meaning of Evolutionary Continuity

When I began this line of research, I was convinced that we have been wrong in our thinking about animals. What has changed over the course of my research and writing is how stunned I am deep within my being, in a place that those who believe in souls would certainly call my soul, by how wrong we have been, and by the tragic implications of our misguided thoughts for the world we share with other animals. But I have also been affirmed in my seeing that we love and need other animals too. It is no wonder that so many of the people who do scientific studies of animals also become activists. There are times when I almost cannot look at the tragic environmental effects and the great physical and emotional suffering caused by the combination of our erroneous beliefs and the entrenched practices that they have produced. But then I do look, and I see the equally glorious possibilities in learning not just that we were wrong, but that the whole world is demanding so much more of us than we thought ourselves capable of being and doing, and that the whole world is offering a belonging so much more beautiful than we dared trust.

One of the more touching and less anecdotal instances of this love and belonging across species boundaries occurred on March 3, 2012, the day after Lawrence Anthony died of a heart attack at his home on a private game reserve in Zululand. Anthony had worked to rescue and rehabilitate "disturbed" wild African elephants.[47] The day after he died, the elephants arrived, having walked more than twelve miles from two different directions to reach the house they had not visited in a year and a half. They processed in the manner of an elephant funeral for two days, and then departed as mysteriously as they had arrived. Except that it really is no mystery once you accept the vast, deep, and heartfelt sentience of these great animals, who like us are dependent on a social network;

46. Bekoff, "Observations of scent-marking."
47. Anthony and Spence, *The Elephant Whisperer*, 1.

who depend on that social network for proper adult development, who like us go mad with trauma and grief, who like us have a ritual way of containing the grief they feel when they lose a loved one.[48]

For some reason, the "nature red in tooth and claw" perspective has been iconic in representing the process of biological evolution, and the power of competition promulgated as the motive driving all of life harshly forward. This vision has overshadowed the fact that cooperation is the mechanism of environmental niches themselves in the way that different organisms play different roles to create the homeostasis of an environment, setting the parameters for boundaried competition at the level of species and raising the bar for creative adaptation within species. To be sure, the lion eats gazelles, especially those that are new and wobbly on their feet (or old and wobbly on their feet), but the lion who overeats the gazelles does not eat tomorrow. This choreography of the living is like a good coach, finding ways to make the gazelle a bit faster, the lion a bit more efficient in hunting, such that life itself is abundantly creative.

Having grown up and lived in an era of television "nature" programs, I was surprised, upon first visiting Africa, to learn that myriad animals on the plains hang out together from dawn till dusk, not gazing at one another from species specific enclaves, but just being out in the grass together, drinking the same water, shading under the same trees, zebras, warthogs, giraffes, gazelles and, yes, lions, among others passing through and flying over and zipping along the ground. I suppose I had imagined them all either skulking and stalking or twitching and blinking over their shoulders. How peaceful and beautiful most of the hours of most of the days are. How glorious is the African dawn for anyone who is there to experience it. It is not sentimental foolishness after all, but scientific fact, to say that all of life on earth is related, that we are quite literally family. This fact is, I think, the most important and meaningful thing we can know.

Going back to the deepest cultural roots of the Western world, the human attributes of rational thought and language have been identified as the qualities that separate humans from beasts. However, both propositions, and all their long trails of implications are wrong. The idea that humans act with careful intent, having tamed our passions in order to make rational decisions, and that animals are driven by the force of passions with no intervening intention inside of them, are incorrect when

---

48. Bradshaw et al., "Elephant Breakdown," 807.

held up to the facts for examination. In fact, animals think, and feel; they create and use language to communicate. In fact, most human cognition is unconscious, with decisions made well outside of conscious reflection and based upon emotional responses to stimuli. In fact, the feelings of internal bodily states are fundamental to the decisions of both humans and other animals. Taken together, these facts more strongly support a perspective of evolutionary continuity of mind, emotion, intention, and communication between humans and other animals. Donald Griffin's words were prophetic. Changing the way we see other animals requires that we change the way we live in the world, but it is decidedly not all bad news.

I began this book by pointing to the meme of the great divide between humans and other animals that permeates Western culture. I have now examined at least one half of the twinned equation of human distinctness and superiority, that of our supposed distinctness from other animals. We are not distinct from all other animals, but one kind amongst them, continuous with them, each species having distinctive traits. But the meme is a twinned equation and this implies that we have also been wrong about ourselves; we have not correctly understood our own distinctive traits. But, I think there is good news in that we have been wrong about ourselves, too. After all, we are not alone in the universe; we belong here with the others.

CHAPTER 3

What a Piece of Work Is Man, the Thinking Thing

What a piece of work is a man, how noble in reason, how infinite in faculties, in form and moving how express and admirable, in action how like an angel, in apprehension how like a god! The beauty of the world, the paragon of animals.

—SHAKESPEARE, *HAMLET*[1]

Out of Body Experiences

SINCE WE HAVE BEEN incorrect in our understanding of life by believing ourselves separate from all the other animals, it seems a worthy project to try to understand ourselves as animals. And so I propose to spend some time (the next two chapters, in fact), focusing in for a closer look at *Homo sapiens*, first outlining our distinctive physiology, and then delving into our true specialization, our incredibly complex psychology. Our complex psychology is what moves us away from our bodies as the primary locus of experience, and into identification with the psychological experience that we call "mind." This is extremely problematic because the body is where we live, even when we do not recognize this simple fact; there is no other location for mind to inhabit.

1. Shakespeare, *Hamlet*, Act II, Scene II.

The Favorite

"Janie, come, I want to tell you a secret, but you mustn't tell the others or it might cause hurt feelings." Janie stopped her race to the front door and turned to her grandmother, an imposing but not impossible person.

"Can you keep a secret?"

Janie paused, seeming to consider.

"It's a sign of character to do so." Well, of course Janie had sufficient character to keep a secret. It was not really a question.

"Yes, Grandmother, of course I can keep a secret. What is it?"

"Yes, then come here, right here." Grandmother gestured to a spot next to her chair. "I'll whisper it in your ear, and you are to keep it to yourself." Janie offered her ear to her grandmother.

"You . . . are my favorite."

It was the good old secret, not a new one, sealed with a piece of wrapped candy, snugged into the palm of her hand. Janie said thanks and got back to getting out the door with two sweet things tucked away, one under her tongue and one in her sense of life. She did not always like Grandmother, but she always liked knowing that she was the favorite.

When the old matriarch died, her secret came out. She had taken each granddaughter aside, and told her that she was the favorite, adding that she must not tell the others as it might cause hurt feelings. I think God must have done the same thing with all the animals.

However beautiful and smart, funny and kind, inventive and virtuous, courageous and skillful, however generally gifted we are, we are not the only best things on the earth. Not only that, we are not even the kind of thing that we have imagined ourselves to be, rational, free to choose, and independent. And I would argue that we are not spiritual in the sense of having some non-material core that can float away when the going gets rough, or even when the going quits entirely. To the extent that we have built our self-image on concepts of rationality, independence, and a presumed special place at the top of all earthly life, we have been wrong. Such core features of our collective identity may be hard to surrender, but we are not the first generation to have to modify our story, even to change it drastically, when reality intrudes upon us. Claiming poetic license, I say that understanding ourselves to be God's favorite may have helped us through some very challenging times, but it is time to grow up and grasp that we are not God's only favorite.

I am not saying, for the record, that we do not have a soul, nor that there is no possibility of life after death. But I contend that we must start our believing from what we know, and must refrain from claims to know what we do not and cannot know, claims rooted in the way that it was taught to us or that serve as a convenient platform from which to engage our self-interest. A God who would create all these exquisite beings merely to test our belief in something else is absurdly human, worthy of Shakespeare's pen but at the same time too human to be anything other than a human invention. I will return to the idea of a natural spirituality, the key theme in my thinking, in a later chapter.

Humans, Body, Mind, Soul, and Rationalizations

"I am not this body; I am a spiritual being having an experience of this body." It has become a popular expression and I hear it frequently. In a variety of similar forms, people disavow life in the body, claiming some other reality as truer or better. Such a perspective is understandable given the challenges of living in these bodies, amongst other bodies with whom we must sometimes compete and sometimes cooperate. But it is also mistaken to say, "I am not my body," because it too often leads to a denigration of life on earth, starting with one's own person and extending outward to include the only life we know with certainty to exist. This identification with something that we "believe in," outside of and beyond this physical world, has allowed us to violate the very basis of our existence, membership in a community of physical beings that is the very essence of life of earth.

Lest it be thought that I am attempting to stake a place in the so-called war between religion and science as ways of interpreting reality or experience, a war that I take to be a figment of the popular imagination fed by streams of ideology, let me insert two caveats. I am not saying that religion is "bad" because it denies us this life, subverts us from doing what we can do to improve our own lot, and makes us easy to manipulate by creating desire for an afterlife that is better than this life. I do think there is some truth in these well-worn critiques of religion, but that is apparent to anyone who looks at the wide world of religious expression. I am also not saying science is "bad" because some scientists may be deemed arrogant or because they have failed to produce a technological utopia, further observations that can be affirmed by anyone who looks at the wide world of science. What I am saying is that these two big systems of thought share valuing the "mind" and the "soul," a variously defined abstract essence, while at the same time devaluing bodies that are mere containers for the abstract essence of choice, minds in the case of science, and souls in the case of religions.

I love science because it is the best method we have for getting to some clear facts about the world we live in, and about ourselves. And I love religion because it has passed on to us both the understanding that we need to live from a spiritual perspective in order to live well and methods for cultivating a spiritual perspective. Far from dismissing a spiritual perspective, I find it profoundly meaningful right here in the shared vulnerability and contingency of life in these bodies on this earth. Valuing abstract ideas over physical bodies and pushing out of awareness the feeling of these bodies, as is required to maintain an abstract perspective, leads repeatedly to spiritual arrogance and to the greatest horrors of human behavior. The fact that we can and do identify with mental activity does not mean that it is the truest perspective, much less a good thing to do.

Consider this sixteenth-century description of a particular session of vivisection, the practice of restraining and cutting open live animals to learn the functions of anatomy and physiology. Italian anatomy professor Realdo Colombo's apparent lack of feeling with regard to the whole "procedure" as described by others stuns me. The dog is referred to as "it" and "the bitch," never as "she," much less by name. In this typical linguistic fashion, she is thoroughly "othered," and deprived of selfhood, even though she paradoxically exemplifies virtue to the clergy in attendance.

> Colombo pulled a foetus out of the dog's womb and, hurting the young in front of the bitch's eyes, he provoked the latter's furious barking. But as soon as he held the puppy to the bitch's mouth, the dog started licking it tenderly, being obviously more concerned about the pain of its offspring than about its own suffering. When something other than the puppy was held in front of its mouth, the bitch snapped at it in a rage. The clergymen expressed their pleasure in observing this striking example of motherly love even in the "brute creation."[2]

Reading this description, you might have winced, you might have felt anger, and you might have said to yourself, perhaps with resignation, that this is the path by which we have acquired the knowledge we have today

2. Maehle and Trohler, *Animal Experimentation*, 18.

of how bodies work. All of these reactions are evidence of our humanity: experiencing a lesser version of the emotional and physical pain, merely by reading about it, is an inherent part of what it means to be human. Feeling anger about the injustice and moral wrong is inherent in us, too. At a deeper level, we might feel some anxiety that such things can happen and also some relief that they cannot happen to us because we are humans. Each of these is a culturally ingrained response. Reasoning our way to something that helps us to make sense of it, and recognizing the cultural "wisdom" that animals are lower forms helps us to gain some emotional distance from the discomfort of it. Both are acquired human capacities, programmed by culture and learned by experience. But, regardless of how we respond to this description of events that took place 500 years ago, we now know with certainty that the animal who was subjected to the vivisection felt what happened to her, and what happened to her baby; we know in fact she was a self who felt pain and rage and tenderness, and emotional suffering especially because she loved and wanted to protect her baby.

There have always been those who protested the conceptual mechanization and maltreatment of animals. It is an idea that has no foundation in scientific evidence. Though it is a convenient idea for those who want to exercise their curiosity, the evidence runs contrary to it. The French philosopher Voltaire, who was strongly and explicitly opposed both to vivisection and to the underlying idea that animals are machines, expressed this vividly in his philosophical dictionary, under the heading Animal:

> What a pitiful, what a sorry thing to have said that animals are machines bereft of understanding and feeling, which perform their operations always in the same way, which learn nothing, perfect nothing. . . . You judge that I have experienced the feeling of distress and that of pleasure, that I have memory and understanding. . . . Bring the same judgment to bear on this dog which has lost its master, which has sought him on every road with sorrowful cries, which enters the house agitated, uneasy, which goes down the stairs, up the stairs, from room to room, which at last finds in his study the master it loves, and which shows him its joy by its cries of delight, by its leaps, by its caresses. Barbarians seize this dog, which in friendship surpasses man so prodigiously; they nail it on a table, and they dissect it alive in order to show the mesenteric veins. You discover in it all the same organs of feeling that are in yourself. Answer me,

machinist, has nature arranged all the means of feeling in this animal, so that it may not feel?[3]

Colombo, the apparently alexithymic vivisectionist of record, died in 1559. Voltaire wrote his protest in the 1750s, two centuries later. Between these two dates came the life and work of René Descartes.

How Out of Body Became the Norm

In 1639, somewhere in the Netherlands, René Descartes sat by the fire in his winter dressing gown wondering if he could doubt that he was sitting by the fire wearing a winter dressing gown.[4] I sometimes wonder whether Monsieur Grat, his little dog, was there with him. I am fairly certain that, had he consulted Monsieur Grat, he would have gotten direct guidance that it was more important to go for a walk than to sit by the fire obsessing over something so unresolvable as the relationship between minds and bodies. I know for a fact that Molly Brown, my little dog and constant companion, often gave such guidance to me. Over time and with some effort on my part, I learned to listen to the wisdom in it; so much, in fact, that this book flows from my exposure to that wisdom. But Descartes had convinced himself that Monsieur Grat was a robot, and so he probably did not ask Grat's opinion but only received comfort of some kind, or companionship, from his presence.

Descartes was turning his mind toward the past, to a time when, as a younger man, he discovered that he had been taught and believed things that were not true. On that day of sitting by the fire in his dressing gown, he wrote that he had always promised himself that he would come back and work from the ground up to elicit truth that was not dependent upon what he had been told. Descartes began to write his first philosophy, a metaphysics, or way of thinking about the whole of reality, that could provide a frame for his real love in life, his work in mathematics and science. It took him many years to attempt this thing he had promised himself as a youth.

Who cannot remember the general revelation if not the exact moment of discovering that something important we were taught was wrong, often by relying on that something and feeling the ground give way beneath us? We have been deceived, and now we must learn to either

3. Voltaire, *Philosophical Dictionary*, 21–22.
4. Descartes, *Meditations on First Philosophy*, 1.

ignore our own experience and join in the deception, or we can challenge it. All of us join in the communal deceptions—because we do not notice them, and also because it is so much easier, but many of us also question the givens to the extent and in the ways that we are able.

Descartes was motivated by love of science. The description of Colombo's vivisection experiment dates from a century or more before that morning when Descartes sat next to his fire. In our own time, five centuries later, Descartes has taken the brunt of the blame for generating ideas that he inherited from others, and for vivisection practices that were already in place. And he has also long been given the credit for being the "father of modern philosophy," with its humanist, rationalist, and scientific perspectives. However, as I noted in discussion of the meme of human distinctness and superiority, the sequence of ideas that leads to our disembodied perspective goes back to Aristotle, even if the disembodied perspective is not one that Aristotle took or that he would have approved. Still, Aristotle did say that only humans are rational, and in our rationality like God who logically must be timeless and abstract. Consequently, in our godlikeness we too have potentially eternal souls.

Aristotle's metaphysics was later "baptized" by Thomas Aquinas as scholasticism, the pervasive philosophy of educated Europeans at the time of Descartes. In this Catholic Aristotelianism, the human soul was deemed distinct from the body and enshrined as the enduring and real part of a human, to be rewarded or punished in an afterlife. These were the "given facts" of Descartes's time, that to be human is in essence to be a non-physical soul whose non-temporal potential would be realized in life after death, the quality of which depended on living life on earth in terms of what happens after death. And, of course, it was the church that dictated the terms that earned heaven, or hell, or even condemnation and persecution here on earth. Just six years before Descartes wrote about trying to doubt his experience of sitting in his dressing gown, the Roman church had condemned Galileo for thinking scientifically, and so removing humanity from the center of the cosmos. But, by the time of Descartes, human beings were already living a long way from their bodies, from both the traditional religious and the new scientific perspectives.

Descartes and Modern Scientific Thought

Descartes received as his inherited cultural "baggage" this cluster of related ideas: the separability of body and mind, the notion that of all creatures only human beings have minds, that we are like God in our abstract mental capacities, and that feelings are debasing in the way they come from the body, tie us to the body, and intrude upon the purity of abstract thought. It remains fair, nonetheless, to say that Descartes crystallized the implications of these ideas and put them into their modern humanist structure, and that he did so in an effort to break free of a whole set of cultural constraints into which his mind, he discovered, had been falsely trained.

This realization, that he had been taught and had believed false things, was the beginning of his philosophical journey, and the opening statement of his First Meditation: "Some years ago I was struck by how many false things I had believed, and by how doubtful was the structure of beliefs that I had based on them. I realized that if I wanted to establish anything in the sciences that was stable and likely to last, I needed—just once in my life—to demolish everything completely and start again from the foundations."[5]

Like the rest of us, Descartes was born into a set of constraints that we now call culture, though this was not a term or concept to which he had access. While seeking to break free of these constraints, he kept that part of his cultural inheritance that labeled humans as distinct and superior because of their capacity for abstract rationality, dismissing mind or soul in everything else, and especially classifying emotion and feeling in the lesser category of animal life. His unique contribution was to say that only humanity has inner experience, a marked contrast to Aristotle's notion that all living beings are aware and internally motivated by the desire to go on living, seeking what enhances their living, and fighting or avoiding things that threaten that living. Descartes freed himself and us from this soulful material world of Aristotle. And for us, Descartes's disembodied vision has become the cultural baggage that we have to unpack in our turn.

What Descartes sought was the notion of a completely mechanical universe, a place in which one thing caused another in a great chain of explicable events. He wanted to apply geometrical mathematics to describing, predicting, and ultimately controlling this great machine. In this, he exemplified early modernism with its humanist impetus that we do all we are capable of doing, free from the constraints of imagined heavens, as mediated by the very real and powerful Roman Church. Descartes and many of his contemporaries wanted the moral freedom to exercise

5. Ibid.

curiosity at any cost, and there was precedent for this in the idea that the acquisition of knowledge is a God-given mandate, flowing from our likeness to God in rationality, and connecting us directly to God while separating us from everything else.

Descartes achieved the intellectual freedom he sought by way of what is commonly thought an untenably convoluted metaphysics: his abstract and disembodied model of reality. His first great philosophical accomplishment was his "method of doubt," a method of questioning everything until something that was self-evidently certain came forward: "My reason tells me that as well as withholding assent from propositions that are obviously false, I should also withhold it from ones that are not completely certain and indubitable. So all I need, for the purpose of re-jecting all my opinions, is to find in each of them at least some reason for doubt."[6] This allowed him simply to circumvent the cultural baggage he had received and, at least theoretically, to look at the world with fresh eyes. This was no small aspiration, even if he greatly underestimated the amount and depth of his own cultural conditioning.

The first such self-evident idea was the one that he famously en-capsulated in the phrase *Cogito ergo sum* (I think, therefore I am). He reasoned, in effect, that I can doubt that I am petting my dog because I could be dreaming or imagining that I am petting my dog, but if I doubt my thinking, my doubt is actually evidence of my existence. "I am, I ex-ist—that is certain. But for how long? For as long as I am thinking."[7] With this as his foundational idea, his extended analysis led him to understand that he was essentially a thinking thing: "Well, then, what am I? A thing that thinks. What is that? A thing that doubts, understands, affirms, de-nies, wants, refuses, and also imagines and senses."[8]

Problems with the Thinking Thing

Descartes imagined that the entire universe is a great machine with no "mind" or "soul" in it, just inert matter interacting in a ceaseless chain of cause and effect. But, like Aristotle before him, Descartes's rationalism required that something must have started the great chain of cause and effect, a something that we logically call God. The idea of God as creator

6. Ibid.
7. Ibid., 5.
8. Ibid.

then became another self-evident rational fact for Descartes, one upon which he built. His articulation of God as a rational necessity was an explicit formulation that may have had some practical utility, deeply embedded as it was in scholasticism. It provided a feeling of continuity with medieval Catholicism, while simultaneously allowing science to investigate physical bodies and leaving the all-important souls to the church.

Descartes's tortuous process of doubting and of finding certainties did in fact achieve the reordering of values that was his intent, by making pure intellectual abstraction the highest of all virtues. It was God who made humans with minds, he said, as evidenced by the fact that we sense and think about the world around us. Further, proceeding from doubt to certainty step by step, he reasoned that we could see that God made us with senses and minds; and he decided that we could rely on mind and senses because "God is no deceiver."[9] I note that I have always thought that Descartes managed at this point to think himself very far away indeed from his original method of doubt; it is a quite a leap from "Doubt everything," to "There must be a God, and God is not a deceiver," and then to "Therefore we can trust our minds and senses."

Seventeenth-century Dutch philosopher Benedict de Spinoza, who greatly admired Descartes's independence of thought and the scientific project generally and to whose work I shall return, objected strenuously to Descartes's dualism and also to the "great leap" in his method of doubt, whereby everything rests on belief in God. I quote from Book V of Spinoza's *Ethics*:

> Indeed I cannot wonder enough that a philosopher of his caliber—one who had firmly decided to deduce nothing except principles known through themselves, and to affirm nothing which he did not perceive clearly and distinctly, and one who so often censured the Scholastics for wishing to explain obscure things by occult qualities—that such a philosopher should assume a hypothesis more occult than any occult quality. What I ask does he understand of the union of mind and body? . . . Instead it was necessary for him to have recourse to the cause of the whole Universe, that is, to God.[10]

Nevertheless, Descartes succeeded in describing a mechanical universe, based on belief in God who endowed humans, and only humans, with

9. Ibid., 18.
10. Spinoza, *Ethics*, 162.

minds and internal experience. In this way, he expressed central features of what became the scientific agenda, and he did so without condemnation from the Church. In the universe according to Descartes, humans by divine right inhabit an otherwise mechanical universe, made of things that knock against each other, and so change each other, while God and humans seem to watch from outside. We are, in Descartes's formulation, finally and fully outsiders in the universe we inhabit, except that our bodies and their senses (recall, that we can trust) are inside it. And therein lies the insoluble problem of Descartes, whose metaphysical model was never accepted by others as intellectually feasible. He simply could not logically explain how the immortal and godlike human mind, stripped of passions, was related to the physical body that somehow contained it. As for the animals, they became robotic at a wave of Descartes's magic philosophical wand: poor Monsieur Grat.

With his definition of humans as "thinking things," Descartes did open a kind of magical door for us, setting us free to exercise our curiosity about every physical and mechanical thing without restraint. A very important piece embedded in his puzzle is that passions, emotions, and their attendant feelings are seen as debasing us because they belong to the body and thus make us like animals. As such, they are contrasted with God and with being like God. God, who is no deceiver, made us the only beings with minds, so that when we use our minds, and especially when we use them without feeling, we are like God. In this way Descartes liberated us from debasing feelings, mere noises of the body, and he also made the exercise of curiosity a kind of divine mandate: to realize our godlikeness, we exercise reason, free of the body and its passions as God is free of body and passions. Feelings, then, are problematic as they imply both a causal interaction between mind and body, and also that pure abstract thought may not be so pure, being contaminated with feelings that drag us back towards our bodily animal nature, where they might cause us to feel with and for other beings.

Twenty-first-century scientists have amassed abundant evidence to fuel our doubt about Descartes's concept of both the universe and humanity. We need look no further than the title of Antonio Damasio's book on affective neuroscience, *Descartes' Error: Emotion, Reason, and the Human Brain,* in which he makes the strong neuroscientific case that emotions are necessary to rationality, not separable from it, and certainly not dispensable.[11] I cannot help but note the irony that mechanistic science, the endeavor Descartes loosed upon the world, has turned upon him. It is especially in the matter of affect, emotions and feelings, that contemporary neuroscience has completed the undoing of Descartes's metaphysics, for these are the living link of body and mind, the actual evidence that body and mind are one continuous thing, though we may experience them differently. However, the fact that his ideas are disproved scientifically does not keep them from being carried on and lived as a cultural artifact that has been handed down to us in a process of its own.

Scientific Progress in a Mechanistic Universe

Descartes, born the year after the microscope was invented, was himself part of a great burst of human intellectual endeavor that launched the modern scientific project. During his life, the feverish excitement of early modern science produced an explosion of new technologies: the submarine, the slide rule, blood transfusion, the steam turbine, the adding machine, the barometer, the air pump, the pendulum clock and pocket watch, the telescope, the identification of bacteria seen through a microscope, the universal mechanical joint, the pressure cooker, and the steam pump all came into being in his time. Machines of all kinds were invented to relieve the burden of hard physical work, and new technologies made possible the extension of our senses into new realms, to the very small by way of microscopes and to the very large by way of telescopes. No wonder people were able to ignore the untenable metaphysics of the scientific worldview while moving forward with realizing its technological potential. Can you imagine being one of those who first looked through a microscope or a telescope?

I was born at perhaps the very apex of that fevered forward vision of humanity's accession to power, even to our control over atoms and their energy, and I have lived my life in the growing shadow cast by what I take to be the waning light of that scientific utopian vision. As a child, I learned that antibiotics had defeated germs. Smallpox was defeated; polio and leprosy were almost completely eradicated, as was syphilis. I was taught that farming on a massive scale with pesticides and herbicides and fertilizers would feed everyone; and that clean water and basic sanitation had changed the face of human living from disease-ridden and hungry

11. Damasio, *Descartes' Error*, xi-xix.

to healthy and satiated. No more famine, no more plagues! Everything seemed possible if we simply kept applying ourselves to the work of science and its attendant technologies. Advertising had to be invented to create desire where there was no longer need.[12] And then the burst of information technology at the end of the twentieth century brought the whole world, and all the information in the world, to virtually everyone. What a piece of work is man!

Facing the Consequences of the Thinker's Actions

There were hidden price tags in all this that were perhaps really not so hidden, though we, having just won the technological lottery, were too excited to tabulate the costs. Now we know about atomic warfare, that we may control the fission of atoms but we cannot control each other or even ourselves. Now we fight new and global plagues. Now we know that super-powered strains of bacteria have developed to compete with our antibiotics, that the nitrogen in fertilizer poisons water supplies, that we can take fish out of the water faster than they can reproduce in the water, that pesticides kill honeybees upon whom we depend for pollination of crops. Now we know that the information technology that brings the world to our handheld devices also offers our private information to almost anyone who wants it. And now we know that our cumulative technologies have large systemic impacts, including the changing of earth's climate. Ours was a short reign over the universe, and the end of that reign requires us to look again at how we arrived where we are, and to consider our path from here—a task which underlies my thinking and writing at every turn.

My purpose in analyzing Descartes's influence is to explore the way that mechanistic science has framed the way we understand our humanity and other animals in relation to our humanity, and particularly to highlight the flaw in the radically mechanistic view: that the scientist who observes and measures cannot be both one of the things observed and at the same time be outside of the order of things looking objectively at it. Scientists and all the rest of us are both thinking things and, well, things, mechanical things. And when these two modes of being happen in the same place at the same time, we call it "anima," alive, as in soulful, or "selfed," or an auto-poetic system, to use more technical language for this

12. Muller, *Sabbath*, 129–30.

unitary reality of body-mind-soul. Anima is what we and they share, all animals.

Alternative Orthodoxies

I have recently learned from Richard Rohr, who is articulating what I call a "natural Christianity," the notion of alternative orthodoxies, and I gladly borrow his phrase here to signify that there are some strong historical streams of thought other than those of Descartes with which we can fruitfully converse.[13]

Benedict de Spinoza, as already referenced, proposed a very different philosophical model, distinct from the mechanical universe of Descartes, by equating God and nature, conceptualizing all of reality as one continuous living being. It is a model that is certainly friendlier to evolutionary continuity, and one to which I will return in depth. But I note again that Descartes built upon concepts that were already dominant in the cultural and political life of his times, so that, at least on the surface, he was more in tune with his own times than was Spinoza. Consequently, Descartes's model became in time the most prominent set of ideas to which we today must apply our own method of doubt.

Human culture is never so singular as to set us only one course, one way of perceiving, believing, and acting, though by definition it creates channels or constraints that mark the easiest route by which to navigate the social context. Neither the channels of traditional religious views nor those of the mechanistic scientific worldview describe humans and our relationship to our fellow animals in ways that allow for the scientifically established facts now known to us. It is therefore incumbent upon us to develop a metaphysical model that provides a framework capable of organizing what we have learned. Yet we do not have to reinvent the wheel. In addition to the insights of mainstream religious and scientific perspectives that have struggled to win the right to define, there are many, perhaps lesser known, alternative orthodoxies that we might examine to find a way forward from here.

If our collective hopes and self-perceptions about science and technology came from the skewed worldview upon which they were built, there is a certain elegance to the fact that science itself reconfigures our

13. Rohr, *Oneing: An Alternative Orthodoxy.*

wrong ideas. So I turn now from a mechanical metaphysics of disembodied mind to a scientific exploration of *Homo sapiens* in the flesh.

Meanwhile, Back in the Body

The Sapiens Factor

Archaeologists and anthropologists seem to agree upon two ideas about the evolution of modern humans: that our current anatomical form was already in place in Africa about 130,000 years ago, and that there was evidence of a shift toward intelligent social behaviors that we associate with contemporary humans—behaviors like language and painting—about 50,000 years ago. There is disagreement about whether the expression of behaviors such as the painting of caves and the use of language was the result of sudden genetic change that accelerated intelligence in *Homo sapiens*, or whether these are the consequences of continuous development of technologies and abilities, made possible by modern human anatomy and refined by culture over tens of thousands of years.[14]

By 130,000 years ago, the brain of *Homo sapiens* was three times the size of the brains of early humans, weighing almost three pounds. The modern brain that we share with African dwellers of 130,000 years ago is about 2 percent of our total mass and it uses about 20 percent of our energy. This rate of energy consumption makes our brains very expensive to own and operate, and so evolutionary reasoning tells us that these brains must represent a great advantage in getting energy or in conserving it. But the brain alone does not define modern human physiology. The anatomy for speech did not develop to its fully modern form until about 50,000 years ago. In an essay that challenges some of the common wisdom about the evolution of speech in humans, Philip Lieberman notes that "fully modern speech anatomy is not evident in the fossil record until the Upper Paleolithic, about 50,000 years ago."[15] Whether we arrived at our modern form through changes in nature's genetic architecture or by the nurture of culture, we are a young species, very young.

Homo sapiens, like all other species, has unique and niche-specific physical forms and behavioral adaptations. Our adaptation is to be the smart generalist, able to adapt ourselves by culture change to differing

---

14. Mayell, "'Modern' Behavior."
15. Lieberman, "Evolution of Human Speech," 47.

environments by first imagining the world differently than we find it, and then making it so. The set of characteristics and capacities that make this way of being possible has given us access to a radically extended range of environmental niches, from glaciers to deserts. But quickly! Before we name this trait of being ubiquitous generalists who can live anywhere the thing that makes us unique and special in all the world, consider *Pelagibacter ubique*, a bacteria that gets around quite a bit more than we do. And if we are willing to count viruses amongst the living (something on which biologists differ, in that they do not have the capacity to reproduce independently of other life forms), let us note that virus HTVC010P is the new candidate for most ubiquitous life form.[16]

While we may not be the most ubiquitous species, we do have a unique way of getting around. We are fully and uniquely bipedal. And we have big bihemispheric brains, a vocal apparatus making possible a range of utterances, hearing that is especially tuned to the wavelength of human voices, and hand and wrist anatomy, including but not limited to the presence of opposable thumbs, that permit us to manipulate the material world.

But we are born immature, unable to survive without care. The first tasks of a human infant's life involve social experiences with caregivers that create the neuroarchitecture of self and self-regulation in the right frontal cortex of the brain.[17] We have a prolonged period of development in which we acquire the knowledge, attitudes, and life skills of our cultural milieu.

We also spend many years in imaginative and imitative play and in other forms of training for adult life. Our bodies and brains are innately oriented to social relationships and we remain dependent on them throughout our lives. Our social lives are complex, requiring both competition and cooperation in constantly shifting configurations of social organization over the course of our lives. We are long-lived and share with other members of our species predictable developmental challenges throughout our lifespan. We learn and use abstract representation, including but not limited to language, both for private thought within ourselves and for communication with others. We also have the capacity to use abstract representation to imagine things that do not exist. In other words, abstract representation, combined with our other anatomical

---

16. *The Economist*, "A Newly Discovered Virus."
17. Schore, "Secure Attachment," 10.

features, allows us great creativity, burdening us with relating not only to the given world of nature but to things that we create by way of culture, whether or not they actually exist. We can communicate with others of our kind across time and space, and we can create new technologies, and we can alter given environments to suit our purposes. And we are sometimes wrong about what will better suit us because we do not sufficiently understand our context.

Most of the features I have outlined here are not unique to humans, and it may be that none of them are unique to us, though it seems the combination of our facility with abstraction and with technology, combined together in elaborate culture, has given us unique power to change the world. But other animals are surprisingly like us in many fundamental psychological and developmental factors. Like humans, baby African elephants need good mothering to internalize resilience, and they show long-term negative effects if they receive poor maternal care during the first two years of life. This is especially true for males who do not reach sexual maturity until they are twenty-five to thirty years old, and who require a second complex developmental phase in preparation for adulthood.[18] Elephants also show similar developmental, long-term, and communal effects of trauma, including loss of emotion regulation and violent acting out.[19] As elephant populations are decimated and relocated, this is an increasing feature of elephant life throughout Africa, not so different from the suffering of displaced and traumatized human refugees.

Likewise, cetacean researchers hypothesize that complex social lives account for the very large brains of whales and dolphins relative to their body size, and support this with evidence of their abilities to understand symbolic representation, use language, apply abstract rules, perform mimicry and improvise upon it, and demonstrate self-awareness by recognizing themselves in mirrors, along with a host of other cognitive capacities which they share with us.[20] In fact, whale brains are the biggest brains, by any of the standard measures, on earth. They are the absolute biggest in volume, but also the biggest in proportion to body mass, and they have the greatest gyrification index, a way of counting the surface area of the brain if it were "unfolded."[21]

18. Lee et al., "Survival and Success among African Elephants."

19. Bradshaw et al., "Elephant Breakdown," 807.

20. Marino et al., "Complex Brains," 966, 969–70.

21. Fields, "Are Whales Smarter Than We Are?"

Further, the great apes, including chimpanzees and orangutans, experience a midlife crisis similar to that of many humans and, like us too, they tend to emerge from the crisis into a greater sense of well-being.[22]

This journey of discovering how much other animals share with us makes me wonder what we would look like if we could look at ourselves from any perspective other than our own. It is impossible to know because, contrary to Descartes's proclamations about our being essentially abstract thinking things, we are in fact inside these bodies and bound to the perspective that they provide and from which they evolved. However, science has extended our senses and disciplined our fancies, and so we can use science to give us a fairly objective description of ourselves, including the evolutionary processes through which we arrived at our present form.

We walk around on two feet with our heavy heads bobbing along nicely upon the very tops of our spines, carrying a smartphone in one hand and managing a bag of stuff with the other. Yet we are not the only bipedal animals who walk and carry. Modern apes can be seen walking on two legs while carrying things in their hands, though their anatomy cannot sustain such a walk for a long distance. Other bipedal animals include birds, lizards, rodents, kangaroos, and, when running, cockroaches.[23] Concluding a comparison of bipedalism in humans and other animals, McNeill Alexander writes, "The general conclusion is that no animal walks or runs as we do. We keep the trunk erect; in walking our knees are almost straight at mid-stance, the forces our feet exert on the ground are very markedly two-peaked when we walk fast; and in walking and usually in running, we strike the ground initially with the heel alone. No animal walks or runs like that."[24] So scientists seem to have identified a unique feature, our gait.

Primate evolution began experimenting with walking on two legs about six million years ago, as can be seen in the fossil evidence of *Sahelanthropus*, among the oldest of known humans.[25] But most primates continued to climb trees and so, along with limited capacity to walk on two legs, they retained long and strong arms, a forward inclination of the spine, and a default quadrupedal gait. The first fully modern form of

22. Weiss et al., "Midlife Crisis in Great Apes," 1.

23. Alexander, "Bipedal Animals," 321.

24. Ibid., 330.

25. Smithsonian National Museum, "Walking Upright."

human bipedalism is evidenced in *Homo erectus* 1.9 million years ago, complete with the shock resistant curvature that we modern humans have in our lower spines. Being able to walk upright on two legs allowed us to go further and faster than other primates and to expand range into a greater variety of ecological niches. Soon after the evolution of the fully bipedal model of early humans, our species spread rapidly over many environments on different continents. Anthropologists hypothesize that the combination of bipedal mobility and exposure to these environments caused increases in brain size that took place between 2 million and 800,000 years ago. During that time, the human brain approximately doubled in size.

Bipedalism, in addition to allowing humans access to a greater range of environments, also freed human hands to do other things: gather food and useful objects, carry babies, tools, and supplies while walking, and make things with our hands. Both popular and scientific discussions of the evolution of the human hand often include reference to opposable thumbs and association with tool making.[26] However, it is thought that long before tool making, the human hand was anatomically adapted over a long period of primate evolution for throwing stones and swinging clubs. Each of these activities requires particular hand and wrist anatomy and both are dependent upon established bipedalism. She who would throw projectiles or wield a club effectively and routinely must begin from a standing position with arms free.

In 1956, John Napier expressed the hypothesis that human hand anatomy for a swinging and throwing grip emerged first and that this anatomy was later adapted to tool making.[27] His analysis demonstrated that a precision grip (imagine holding a baseball poised to throw) requires opposable thumbs, a fingertip grip, and refined neural sensitivity and control.[28] Anatomical evidence for the evolution of the power grip (imagine grasping a baseball bat) anatomy is also readily available. "When the fingers are partially flexed, they form an oblique line. Together with the partially flexed thumb, a corridor is formed, a cylindrical cavity lying diagonally across the palm."[29] If you pretend to hold an axe handle in your hand and you look at it, you will see this diagonal line from your

---

26. Susman, "Hand Function," 23.

27. Young, "Evolution of the Human Hand," 165.

28. Ibid., 169.

29. Ibid., 170.

fingertips across the palm of your hand, and you will feel the cavity in which the handle so "naturally" fits.

Not surprisingly, tool making emerged along with full bipedalism and a hand already evolved for precision gripping. And tool making is the context in which we typically hear about the importance of our opposable thumbs. Just for the record, though, opossums, North America's lone marsupial, have true opposable thumbs on their hind limbs. And though raccoons do not have true opposable thumbs, they are very efficient with their little five-fingered hands.[30] Touch is the primary sense in raccoons and it is very acute, especially in water. This is why I find evidence of them having washed grapes from my arbor in the dogs' water bowl, and why they can just open the hummingbird feeder and tip back its contents. Meanwhile, we humans, with our special tool making hand anatomy, have advanced from making simple stone cutting blades and hand axes to devising magnetic resonance imaging, global positioning systems, and rocket propelled stations to collect and analyze data samples on distant planets. We are far from the only animals to use technology, but we are also far and away the most technologically creative, diverse, and prolific animals on earth.

Bipedalism and specialized hand anatomy do not account for our technological proficiency, however, much less for other forms of creativity, such as music, the arts, the humanities, sports, political organization, and the rituals of daily and seasonal living. To begin to grasp the full range of our capacities and the ways in which they are rooted in our bodies, we have also to consider our voices and our brains. Though speech and language may intuitively seem to refer to the same thing, the words represent different things, a distinction that matters very much in the matter of comparing humans and other animals. In an overview of the evolution of speech, Tecumseh Fitch says that language "is a system for representing and communicating complex conceptual structures, irrespective of modality." In other words, whether by voice or gesture, chemical messages or seismic waves, language allows for information to be conveyed in a flexible and abstract way from one animal to another. By way of contrast, speech "refers to the particular auditory/vocal medium typically used by humans to convey language."[31] Human language universally uses gesture, and some human languages such as American sign

30. Smith, "Hands."
31. Fitch, "Evolution of Speech," 258.

language are entirely gestural. However, speech is the standard "signaling modality," or mechanism of human language, in all world cultures, and thus the importance of speech for human evolution is definitive.[32] We know that other animals use communication systems that are very much in keeping with the definition of language, yet they obviously do not use what we would recognize as speech.

Biolinguistics, a comparative and interdisciplinary approach to communication amongst animals, has established a clear distinction between the anatomical mechanisms of communication and the definition of language. Marc Hauser, Noam Chomsky, and Tecumseh Fitch have suggested the terms "faculty of language in a broad sense" to indicate all the various communications systems at work in animal life, and "faculty of language in the narrow sense" to represent human language.[33] Three components define language broadly, Fitch notes. The first component is the anatomical signaling and receiving system, such as speech and hearing in humans, foot stomping and wave reception in elephant feet, and the mysterious mechanism of whale sounds underwater. Grammar and syntax are difficult to distinguish from one another, but they are the linguistic terms used to describe the structural qualities that allow for a limited number of inherently meaningless sounds (for instance, the approximately forty-four basic phonemes of the English language) to produce an infinite number of distinct utterances; or, to oversimplify the concept, to make meaningful sentences out of meaningless sound bits. Sentences, as we know, can be simple or complex, from "Ouch!" to "When you interpret my intentions negatively, as you frequently do, especially when you are overworked or worried about money, as you often are, it causes me emotional distress." The term *semantics* refers to the fact that units of sound are understood to represent particular meanings.[34] These are most often words, but sometimes phrases. Whether we pronounce the word *tomato* with an English or American accent, we understand the referent to be the red fruit that goes with vegetables in salads, whereas "Oh my God!" is a unit of semantic content that is distinct from the individual words. Of these three components, grammar and syntax are the most difficult to define, though we recognize the importance of the structure of language easily enough. If I say that the structure of language recognizes

32. Fitch, "Evolution of Language," 194.
33. Hauser et al., "Language Faculty," 1569.
34. Fitch, "Evolution of Language," 194–96.

us easily enough, I have used the same semantic content, produced by the same physical structures of my body, but in a different order that causes the words to become meaningless; that is syntax.

Language has been identified over millennia as the definitive human characteristic, evidence of our capacity for abstract rational thought, and equivalent in the material domain to the word "soul" or "mind" in metaphysical philosophy. From that perspective, it is easy enough to understand that theorists have looked for the unique and special qualities of humans that give us language when no other animals seem to have it. But the search for expected unique human features has continuously demonstrated that neither language itself, nor the physical structures that we use to exercise it, are unique to humans.

It was once thought that a descended larynx in humans was the unique anatomical feature that allowed us to develop a complex system of utterances and distinguished us from all other animals.[35] But it is now understood that the mechanism for producing a pattern of information is not definitive of language. Seismic waves can do it, human vocal utterances can do it, dog scents can do it. In fact, there is a general sense that we are just beginning to understand the vast networks of communication that weave animal lives together. The finding of descended larynxes in other animals is one moment in that now long history of comparative findings that is finally chipping away at the very idea of distinguishing humans from other animals on the basis of any particular trait. With reference to the fall of the descended larynx from the pedestal of human language, Fitch says, "These new data tell a cautionary tale: we must beware of considering any human trait unique without a thorough search among animals."[36] This sentiment permeates Fitch's article, though he (more than I, and more than specialist in this area Con Slobodchikoff) still seems to want to define the specialness of human speech.

One of the most recent features of human language to have been tentatively identified as uniquely human is "recursive syntactic patterning."[37] When I want to illustrate this concept by giving an example, perhaps by referring to the way that my editor, who is more than competent in both language and thought, and who lives 2,000 miles away, hates the complexity of sentences that I often needlessly construct, especially when

35. Ibid., 198.
36. Ibid., 199.
37. Hauser et al., "Language Faculty," 1569.

several shorter sentences would communicate the concepts more clearly, the reader is likely to grasp both the concept of recursive syntax and sympathy for my editor. Syntactic recursion, a feature of complex language, is our ability to embed clauses and phrases within a series. But we now know that syntactic recursion occurs regularly in the utterances of other animals, especially songbirds.[38]

Nuances of defining language and questions about who has it aside, vocal communication has no doubt been significant in human evolution. Describing the early evolutionary advantages of spoken language, Philip Lieberman writes that it "frees a person's hands, can occur in darkness, and does not require looking at the individuals who are signaling."[39] Our capacity for language, too, evolved interactively with changing bodies and contexts. As I noted that bipedalism freed hands to do things with our hands, I now note that hands busy with objects might facilitate the emergence of non-gestural communication, for which our bodies and brains are well equipped, though we may never know which is the chicken and which the egg in this scenario. Compared to our nearest biological relative, the chimpanzee, our vocal apparatus includes a recessed face, a small mouth equipped with a tongue that goes all the way down our long necks, a larynx positioned low in our throats, a hyoid bone for structural support, muscles for fine control of the lungs, and neuroanatomy in the brain to support the development and use of spoken language. This sound system comes at the price of vastly increased risk of choking to death, and so it must represent an important evolutionary investment.

Our language abilities require not only this intricately webbed and high-risk anatomy of speech in our faces and necks but also neural structures in the brain that support the imitating of sound, the hearing of subtle distinctions in the speech of conspecifics, the providing of filtering mechanisms for sounds that are not so clearly produced, and the means of producing and interpreting speech. The established wisdom, taught in introductory psychology classes for decades, is that the speech centers are the Broca's area towards the front of the left cerebral hemisphere, where speech is produced, and the Wernicke's area towards the back of the left hemisphere where decoding or comprehension of language occurs. These two areas are named after neurologists who discovered their functions on the basis of injuries to these areas in their patients. Damage to the Broca's

38. Gentner et al., "Syntactic Pattern Learning by Songbirds," 1204.
39. Lieberman, "Evolution of Human Speech," 44.

area results in diminished or lost capacity to produce speech, and damage to Wernicke's causes loss or reduction of comprehension of speech. It has long been known that this is an accurate but oversimplified accounting for the neural processing of speech. Brain areas that process the prosody, or music, of speech are in parallel locations in the brain's right hemisphere. To illustrate how important prosody is for speech, imagine for a moment the staccato digital recording you hear on some answering machines, "*We Are Sorry but The Per Son you wish to speak to is not avail able right now.*" The Dr. Spock-like timbre and intonation is irritating, and when it is used intentionally, the message is that you do not get to know anything about the person whose phone this is.

A more recent line of study of the brain's language processes is that of investigation of the contribution of motor learning, or learning to use the body's muscles in patterned ways. This type of learning takes place in a lower and older area of the brain called the basal ganglia. Philip Lieberman notes: "Speech also requires a brain that can 'reiterate'—freely reorder a finite set of motor gestures to form a potentially infinite number of words and sentences."[40] The motor learning that is fundamental to imitating sounds in the environment takes place in the basal ganglia and is related to other kinds of motor learning, like learning to crawl, and to walk. Lieberman concludes his argument with the rather startling idea that, in terms of the evolution of human speech, "The starting points of fully human speech and language were perhaps walking and running."[41]

Brain/Mind (or Body Is Soul)

Though it may not be the thing that distinguishes us from all others, the size and complexity of our brains is surely an important part of what makes us the dominant animal that we are. (Our dominance is obvious, but our superiority another matter.) Consider for a moment that language is just one of many complex processes in the brain. Even so rudimentary a glimpse as I have provided shows that language uses both hemispheres, significant areas of neocortex and of older brain structures as well. The work of discovering the neural processes of functions like walking, making a simple tool with our hands, and having a conversation, will undoubtedly go on for decades because each seemingly unitary

40. Ibid., 39.
41. Ibid.

function, like speaking, is actually composed of billions of micro-events. In fact, one of the greatest mysteries of neuroscience is consciousness itself. The brain is body, and in the brain, the body is soul.

It takes many complex processes in our brains for us to have the most basic experience of being here. How do billons of neuronal events combine to create the unitary experience of *the feeling of what happens*, to borrow the title of another of Antonio Damasio's books on the topic?[42] In his most recent book, Damasio writes that "consciousness is often described as the result of massive integration of signals in the brain, across many regions."[43] And Gerald Edelman and Giulio Tononi, reflecting upon the fact that consciousness is not associated with any particular area of the brain but that it changes with activity patterns that occur simultaneously in several regions, suggest that "what is required is that the distributed groups of neurons must engage in strong and rapid reentrant interactions."[44] Consciousness, then, is not a "something" that we possess so much as a continuous orchestration of experience that we *do*, except that to say "I" do this continuous construction is a misstatement; it might be more correct to say that neurons in my brain create the experience I have of being me. "They" do this on their own, like the selfish genes whose product I am; they are me.

In stepping back from the enormous complexity and detail contained in the recent burst of neuroscientific data, I find an important quality of value in the perspective provided by a new biological big-picture view of humanity, a view based more in scientific fact than in the conjectures of philosophers. By describing what is elemental and common in the experience of all humans, namely the general mechanisms of experience itself, neuroscience explicates what a human is at a foundational level. The brain is always performing multiple functions, for example, most of them outside conscious awareness.[45] The implication is that we must stitch together a story of reality from the fragments of which we are aware at any moment, and we must construct a teller of the story, a self whose story we know.[46] This is a far cry from having a cohesive "self" who re-

42. Damasio, *The Feeling of What Happens*, 30.

43. Damasio, *Self Comes to Mind*, 247.

44. Edelman and Tononi, *A Universe of Consciousness*, 62.

45. For a description of nonconscious processes, see Damasio, *Self Comes to Mind*, 273–84.

46. For neural processes, see ibid., 181–210, and for the construction of the teller, 210–40.

sides somewhere inside the brain or mind, managing the controls as she clearly and firmly grasps the wheel and navigates her way through the world. The fantasy of a rational inner self who correctly senses the world and is fully responsible for her actions is a delusion, and it is a seemingly necessary delusion. Far from the noble thinking thing, we are the necessarily delusional thing with a flashlight beam of rationality to shine in the dark theater of our unconscious minds. I know that many people are distressed by this idea, but I am heartened because it makes sense of what I see and know in others, and in myself. And it makes that flashlight very precious indeed, precisely because it is a small light operating in a vast dark expanse. This view of our rational faculties is less noble and glamorous perhaps, but truer and more adventurous.

Five General Features of the Human Brain

I have identified elsewhere five general features of the way that our brains function that seem to indicate core aspects of what it is to be human.[47] First, the brain is extraordinarily complex, so complex that our experience of life is necessarily and always fragmentary. Second, it is plastic, meaning that it changes over time as a function of lived experience. Third, body and brain have a mutually modifying relationship, meaning that events in the body influence the brain, referred to as "bottom up" in the talk of neuroscientists; and also that thoughts in the brain influence the body, or "top down" as referenced by neuroscientists. Fourth, the human brain is inherently social, meaning it is "hard-wired" (a term I use with caution) for relationships with other humans. And fifth, most of the processes that occur in our brains happen outside of our awareness, implying that we are unconscious, not just occasionally or in special areas, but routinely and as a matter of course. Again, this is a truer if more humble position.

Because it is important to understand the components of "mind" as a compound biological entity and not an abstract singular thing, let me explain each of these five aspects in a little more detail. The complexity of the human brain is difficult to overstate. We are born with a surfeit of an estimated 200 billion neurons, about half of which will be structured by experience and the other half pruned away during the first two years of life. The 100 billion neurons that remain after parcellations are of at least

47. Benvenuti and Davenport, "New Archaic," 210–15.

one hundred and fifty different types, with specialized shapes and locations, communicating with one another across a trillion synaptic gaps. Also located at these spaces across which neurons communicate chemically by way of neuropeptides and neuromodulators are teams of support cells, astrocytes and oligodendrocytes, whose function is to facilitate in various ways communication between neurons. But the complexity does not stop there; the brain is also organized into large functional systems: the sensory system, the motor system, the limbic system, the instinctive affect system, and the association and executive systems of the neocortex, each system carrying out its own astoundingly complex work and communicating that work to other systems, almost all of it outside of our awareness.

The description of the brain's complexity applies to every human brain, but that complexity extends beyond the phenotypic arrangement shared by all humans. Each human brain is modified both by culture and by individual experience to create the more than six billion unique human brains that currently inhabit this earth, in a feature known by neuropsychologists as the experience-dependent plasticity of the brain.[48] Every human is born into a culture that modifies the brain of the individual by way of experience common to that culture.[49] Cultural anthropologist Liza Cerroni-Long illustrates this principle with her concept of "expressive style," one component of which is internalized sensitivity to what is defined as a loud voice, an interpretation of the physical sensation of audition that varies a great deal by culture.[50] And each individual is born with a unique genetic make-up, which then interacts with the environment to create the specific neuroarchitecture of that individual's brain. At both levels, that of cultural formation of the brain and that of individual experience-dependent formation, the brain's plasticity is predominantly, though not exclusively, expressed as synaptic communication. Neurons do not actually touch, but "speak" in chemical messages, and these chemical messages cause the formation of neural networks, so forming and maintaining synaptic connections amongst neurons is the ongoing way in which the brain's architecture is created and maintained.[51]

48. Cf. Schore, *Affect Dysregulation* and *Affect Regulation*; and Cozolino, *Neuroscience of Psychotherapy*.

49. Cf. Wexler, *Brain and Culture*.

50. Cerroni-Long, *Diversity Matters*, 20.

51. Cf. LeDoux, *The Synaptic Self*.

The mutually modifying relationship of body and brain may readily be illustrated by the ways in which body states, even something as simple as a clenched fist or "fake" smile, can evoke specific emotions that typically accompany those states, emotions of anger or pleasure respectively; and by the fact that we can use mental images to evoke body states, such as going to a "happy place" in order to release tension. Perhaps my favorite illustration of the mutual modification of body and brain is that of being presented with a visual image of a cut lemon; it evokes immediate salivation in the mouth. I have yet to meet a person who did not respond in this way to the actual visual image, but I only need the idea of a cut lemon to salivate. I suspect this is true of many people, and it speaks to the power of imagination.

There are several factors that lead to the conclusion that the human brain is inherently and necessarily social. Among these are that human hearing is especially tuned to the range of human voices, and human vision is patterned for face recognition. There are also strong hypotheses that the brain is instinctively conditioned for language acquisition, the learning of social mores, and the making of communal music.[52] It will come as no surprise that other animals share some of these features of social brain architecture. For example, many animals are visually oriented to faces and facial expressions. I still chuckle when I remember the morning on which one of my dogs, Lolo, came dashing down the hall with the enthusiasm of the very young upon waking, only to slam on her brakes at the entry way and begin barking furiously at the stranger's face sitting on a table there, that of a carved pumpkin.

We humans, like other social animals, have mirror neurons in our motor and limbic systems, facilitating the acquisition of motor skills and empathic feelings respectively. Indeed, high levels of social cooperation, to the extent of dependence upon extensive cultural formation, may be the single most significant human adaptation, though it is far from an exclusively human adaptation. John Cacioppo, Penny Visser, and Cynthia Pickett describe the complexity of human social life thus: "In short, humans have evolved a brain and biology whose functions include formation and maintenance of social recognition, attachments, alliances, and collectives; and development of communication, deception, and reasoning about the mental states of others."[53] Relationship is not optional

52. Viz., respectively, Chomsky, *Syntactic Structures*; Gazzaniga, *Ethical Brain*; Mithen, *Singing Neanderthals*.

53. Cacioppo et al., *Social Neuroscience*, xii.

for *Homo sapiens*, but is the very way by which we function adaptively as biological creatures; and this essential sociality makes it impossible to defend any strict demarcation between our biological and social lives. In other words, we are not individual bodies having a social experience, but we are inherently social bodies having a self experience.

Our essentially social natures also have important implications for how we think about what we are as humans. The strong implication is that our sense of individuality is much greater than the reality of our individuality. It would, therefore, be truer to root our sense of identity in the greater communities in which we are embedded. This, I think, is the most spiritually vital knowledge that we have or could have, and it is not a matter of belief but of knowing with certainty that to be is to belong to something bigger than the self.

The fifth significant general feature of the human brain is that we are unaware of what our own brain is doing most of the time. The fact that most of our feeling, learning, deciding, and thinking occurs outside of our awareness is a very important feature, indeed. Who is doing all this mental processing if not I?

Recently, when I suggested to a philosopher colleague that animals essentially are persons and that all the rationales for the great divide had fallen, he responded by pointing to the complexity of the human brain. He is correct in thinking the complexity of human brain to be nothing short of awe-inspiring, but this is likely true of at least some other animal brains as well. The brain is the most complex thing we know, as complex as the universe itself. Both the universe and the human brain are systems that orchestrate billions of interactions, far more than our imaginations can begin to comprehend. And access to each of them requires some grasp of their history and development, over millions of years in the case of the brain, and billions of years in the case of the universe.

Archaeology of Brain/Mind

When reading neuroscientific research, it is common to find references to older parts of the brain, sometimes called the mammalian or reptilian brain. These areas may also be called deeper structures of the brain. There has been debate amongst neuroscientists about how valuable or truly representative this kind of language is, but it is very useful and so it persists. The human brain is conceived as having three layers: the oldest

and deepest, sometimes called reptilian, is the brain stem and is associated with the basic arousal system that causes us to be awake and aware;
the limbic system, sometimes called the mammalian brain, is in the mid-
brain and is associated with sensory input, emotion, conditioned learning, and memory; and the cerebral cortex that is largely a blank slate at
birth that gets programmed by culture and life experience to become the
"thinking cap" we associate with being human. The older regions of the
mid-brain and brain stem are sometimes called the paleocortex and the
cerebral cortex is called the neocortex. All of these regions are connected
and function together, and yet each retains some of the particular qualities associated with its evolution. As I have already said, most of what
happens in our brain is unconscious, but this is especially true of process
in the older and deeper regions beneath the cerebral cortex.

Conceptualizing the brain in a three part evo-archaeological way
became very popular after the publication of MacLean's *The Triune Brain
in Evolution* in 1990.[54] But Jaak Panksepp, in his recent book *The Archaeology of Mind* (written with Lucy Biven), summarizes his own research
career in affective neuroscience with the suggestion that the brain houses
primary, secondary, and tertiary processes, building upon its evolutionary history. The primary affective states, common to all mammals, including humans, are his particular specialization. Of this Panksepp and
Biven write: "the basic biological values of all mammalian brains were
built upon the same basic plan, laid out in consciousness-creating affective circuits that are concentrated in subcortical regions, far below
the neocortical "thinking cap" that is so highly developed in humans."[55]
Further, these motivational states are fundamental building blocks of
"higher order" processes, like conditioned learning in the mid-brain, and
thinking in the cerebral cortex. Debates within psychology and neuroscience draw fine distinctions between instincts, affects, emotions, and
feelings, but Panksepp is referring to a particular set of "*primary-process
psychological experiences*" or instincts that are "evolutionary givens of
the BrainMind."[56]

The primary affective states are very basic responses to environmental stimuli and they are evolution's way of expressing and reinforcing
biological value. Panksepp has identified seven such primary affective

54. MacLean, *Triune Brain in Evolution*.
55. Panksepp and Biven, *Archaeology of Mind*, 1.
56. Ibid., 9.

states shared by all mammals: SEEKING, RAGE, FEAR, LUST, CARE, GRIEF, and PLAY.[57] (He notes that he uses upper case letters, for example SEEKING, to designate these terms as describing an identified brain circuitry and chemistry, as distinct from the internal subjective experience of animals.)[58] These instinctive evaluations are body states as well as "feelings." They are recognizable in other animals; FEAR, for example, looks horrified with wide eyes, raised eyebrows, open mouth and a contracted torso. These features represent the body's preparedness to act, but they are also felt as internal experience that is intrinsically rewarding or punishing. This is a point worth underscoring: the fact that PLAY feels good conditions the organism to want that same environmental stimulus the next time, and the fact that terror is uncomfortable as a feeling state causes the organism to want to avoid that stimulus the next time. Of this inherent conditioning, Panksepp and Biven say, "We learn to dread FEAR itself if we have already endured terrifying experiences."[59] These affective primary process states are of the greatest importance since they are the most fundamental level of behavioral motivation and of learning. In fact, these states are indications of an awakened animal, which is why Panksepp calls them "consciousness-creating." The animal is awake and energized for action, but not thinking about his or her situation in a deliberative way.

The next layer of brain is the mid-brain, or mammalian brain, often referred to as the limbic system. Panksepp and Biven refer to the functions of the midbrain as the home of "secondary processes," those built upon the first layer, including things like conditioned learning and memory. Again using FEAR, one of the most thoroughly studied fundamental affects, to illustrate, they say, "From birth, this capacity for free-floating FEAR is built into our brains; initially it can be activated only by a few unconditioned stimuli, but experience can create fearful memories that henceforth can be triggered by previously neutral events in the world."[60] This explains why people with post-traumatic stress disorder can suddenly have a flashback and experience terror out of nowhere. Some trigger in the environment, some neutral thing such as a color or an odor, has

57. Ibid., 35.
58. Ibid, 2.
59. Ibid., 175.
60. Ibid., 176.

become associated with danger and now has the power to activate a flood of FEAR responses in the body.

We share these evolutionarily old layers of brain and the internal experiences of them with all mammals, and with some other animals, too. This is not to say that we experience primary affects and conditioned learnings in exactly the same way across species lines. The neocortex of each species is distinct and the neocortex is connected to more primitive regions of brains, creating different kinds of feedback loops. Of this diversification that occurs at the level of the neocortex, Panksepp and Biven say: "The neocortex varies dramatically in size and complexity from one mammalian species to another, resulting in rather different levels and types of cognitive abilities and intelligences. As already noted, higher-order emotions are bound to diverge enormously among different mammalian species."[61] In other words, we share basic affects such as FEAR and PLAY with mice and with hippos, but we do not know if the hippo and the mouse experience shame and pride and other complex social emotions in the way that we do. Conversely, there may be complex mouse and hippo feelings that we do not have and cannot yet imagine.

Thanks to the work of scientists such as Panksepp, we know that many other animals have complex brains, similar in structure to our own, and we know some of the contents of those brain/minds because it has been demonstrated that we share with other animals some mental processes. But at the level of the neocortex, animals differ. What whales and dolphins are doing with their big complex brains is a mystery that fascinates many a cetacean researcher, as well as many a naïve human who has gazed into the eye of a whale, and who sees and feels the whale gazing back, seeming to wonder about us, too.

The human neocortex received a great deal of excited attention in the years immediately following enhanced brain-imaging technologies. Suddenly we could see on magazine covers images of the locations in the brain of our vision, our language, the feeling in our fingers and toes, the place where we decide to pay attention to something, the pleasure center that can hijack us into addictions. The "thinking cap" is the part of the brain that most people easily picture, the crinkly gray folds just under the skull, divided into two hemispheres, looking something like a big walnut. In terms of the brain, it is in the cerebral cortex that human uniqueness

61. Ibid., 19.

resides. Perhaps most telling about what it is to be human is that the cerebral cortex is essentially a blank slate when we are born.[62]

Before turning in detail in the next chapter to the programming of the human cerebral cortex and its attendant problems, this seems a good time to reiterate my two main points. First, *Homo sapiens* cannot be defined by any single trait such as rationality, intelligence, language or tool making, but by the interaction of all of these traits, and these together interacting with a variety of social and ecological environments. Second, not only is this true of humans, but it is true of all animals. The unavoidable conclusion is that being alive is inherently complex and interactive, such that any truthful description must have this fact as its foundation. And, just in case I were tempted to jump on complexity as our special trait, as I once did, I refer back to Fitch's concise point that we now know enough to refrain from such claims until a thorough investigation of the trait amongst animals has been conducted. In the matter of complexity, we are very far indeed from having completed such a thorough investigation of the animal world. To give one small example, we do not even know the mechanics of how whale sounds are made under water, much less the semantic content of those sounds or the intentions of the singer, but we know enough to think it likely that there is semantic content and that the singer does have intentions.

The fact remains that there are other animals who may be as complex, as smart, as full of heart and soul as we are, especially highly intelligent social animals, though clearly no other animal is as technologically proficient. And even as I articulate an "especially" group, the very social, amongst other animals, I feel caution arising in my psyche. I think of studies demonstrating that ants teach and learn, implying that they, too, are creatures changed by their experience and able to communicate in social relationships.[63] In fact, some researchers think that the collective "thoughts" of social insects may operate on a model very much like neurons in the brain, so that the same quality of complexity of mind that we associate with individual human brains may exist at the group level in some species of social insects. The implication is that convergent evolution has produced two similar models for making decisions related to survival.[64] Moths remember lessons learned through interacting with

62. Ibid., 10.
63. Morell, *Animal Wise*, 27–48.
64. Ibid., 47.

their environments as caterpillars, exhibiting the kind of experience dependent plasticity I mentioned as a feature of human brains.[65] Coming much closer to mammals who are, by definition, much more like us, recent studies have demonstrated social intelligence and empathy in rats.[66] And I think, too, of the newspaper story that just crossed my desk of "mighty mouse," a mouse in a Chinese zoo who was released from captivity after attempting to rescue his friend from the jaws of a poisonous snake. Both mice had been fed to the snake by zoo staff. As the snake's jaws closed over his friend, Mighty Mouse jumped up and down on the snake's head, then bit its head and repeatedly tried to pull his friend out of its mouth.[67] Perhaps God whispered to Mighty Mouse, "You are my favorite." And God may have said that to the moth and the ant as well.

65. Blackiston et al., "Retention of Memory."
66. Bartal et al., "Empathy and Prosocial Behavior in Rats."
67. Collis, "The Moment a Brave Mouse Tried."

CHAPTER 4

Lost in Thought: Human Psychology

God guard me from those thoughts men think
In the mind alone;
He that sings a lasting song
Thinks in a marrow-bone.

—W.B. YEATS, *A PRAYER FOR OLD AGE*[1]

Human Psychology

THOUGH THERE IS NO evidence for minds outside of bodies, we do have internal experience of life, including the capacity to re-experience the past through memories, and the capacity to experience the future through imagination. We likely share this feeling of "mind" with many animals. However, humans program this experience of mind from one generation to the next by way of culture, seemingly much more than other animals do. Combined with our particular anatomical arrangement, this capacity to have mental experience shared across generations, gives us tremendous creative capacity and tremendous destructive capacity, too. But the most subtle and difficult aspect of human psychology is that, due to the unconscious nature of both mind and culture, we do not know what our minds are doing, even as we establish false beliefs and hand them on, generation after generation.

---

1. Yeats, *Collected Poems*, 282.

Places in the Food Chain

Dressed for combat with military fatigues tucked into tightly laced black boots, a heavy belt adorned with a sheathed knife, and camouflage sleeves rolled up to give a peek at the tattoos underneath, Rambo stood at the counter to ask for help for his son. The school counselor had told him that it was mandatory to get help for the boy or he would not be allowed back in his fourth grade classroom. The boy stood at the counter with him, quiet, head down, shoulders rounded, eyes and ears open, like a rabbit.

The receptionist had told the man that he could not wear a knife in the facility, and he had refused to give it up. They called me, the psychologist on duty, to talk with him. In my mind I called him Rambo, and that is how I remember him. I explained to him that we did not allow weapons in the county mental health facility, that it was a safety precaution that applied to everyone and that he would have to hand over the knife, or leave. He told me that he was not dangerous but responsible, and that I should be glad to have a person like him around in this dangerous setting. He added that he was never afraid because he was always prepared.

The boy, though, was afraid, standing frozen (in fact, his anxiety problems were causing him to break down in school). Rambo loved his son enough to be in this place, trying to get help he really did not want or trust. He loved his son enough to relinquish his preparedness by handing over the sheathed knife. I recall Rambo and Rabbit vividly, because in their very being they spoke to me about the difficulty of being *Homo sapiens*.

By way of contrast, I share what I learned over the course of one surprising autumn night when I was the guardian of a severely injured fawn who had made actual contact with some headlights. I named her Rosebud after she ate every rose petal in my garden. That morning, as I had driven the mountain highway and saw her sitting there with her big mule deer ears silhouetted in the dawn light, I had thought, "That's so odd. Why is that fawn sitting at the roadside?" I pulled over, and saw that her head and body were intact but her legs were severely fractured and one of her eyes was ruptured. I knew she would have many hours of suffering before the coyotes came howling at dusk to devour her. So I spoke softly to her as I picked her up and put her on the big dog bed in the camper of my truck. I doubted she could be saved, but I did not know much about deer legs then (I know more now). Her breathing, pulse, and awareness were all strong and steady. I was thinking to ask wild animal rescue or the local vet to help, people I knew in my little mountain town. But none of them returned my calls that Sunday, and so I had the close company of a fawn for one unforgettable night.

First I made camp on the deck, but when dusk came and the dogs in the neighborhood began to howl, she frantically tried to move on her one good leg. I took her inside. She calmed down immediately and so we spent the night side by side on the floor. There were moments when Rosebud was in great pain, and moments when pain was just the backdrop. She mewed when I picked her up, and though I do not mew, I have had multiple broken bones and know well the sharp moan that movement elicits. Tears streamed down my face as I tended her. But in spite of her injuries, Rosebud's face lit up when she came to understand that the hard thing I kept putting under her head was an offering of water—she was tickled at the revelation, visibly—and then she drank the water from the bowl. Along with being in pain, she was also thirsty and sated, interested, curious, and affectionate. She was only afraid when something frightening entered her environment; and the pain only tethered her in those particular moments when it was heightened. It took me a while to understand what I was seeing, or rather what I was not seeing that I had expected to see: that she was not living in the shadow of an imagined predator. She drank water, she ate my roses and ficus leaves, she did her little fawn business on my floor, and then scooted away from it. She snuggled against me. And in the morning, as I gently cleaned the crust over her eye with a warm washcloth, trying to make her look salvageable for the vet, she ran her muzzle up and down my arm.

As I went to prepare the truck bed for her transport and to open doors we would need to pass through, I left Molly Brown in charge, telling her to be gentle. Molly was a seasoned companion by then so I was not at all surprised that she knew what I was asking or that she did what I asked in such seriousness. I stayed with the two of them long enough to see Molly gently sniff the little deer, and I was surprised by Rosebud's easy acceptance of Molly's curiosity and care. I had expected that her fear of dogs might be more general, but once again, Rosebud's response was attuned to her situation.

The first vet thought that Rosebud would live, and that she would need tending as a backyard deer. She told me I would need to take a course and get a license. But she did not possess the hardware for pinning Rosebud's leg bones. As Rosebud nuzzled my arms, Dr. Vicki told me that she was surprised to see the strong emotional bond of a wild animal with a human being; she thought it might account for Rosebud's resilience. She also told me to cancel my plans for the day because the ruptured eye needed to come out immediately and my calming presence would be required during the surgery. We called the second vet, who had the hardware, and he asked that I bring the deer to his office for evaluation. I did, and left her with him for a while, having explained how I had come to be her companion. When I called a short time later to see how she was doing, I learned that he had decided that Rosebud was in too much pain and that he had put her down. And though I had initially supposed that I would be called upon to help her to die, I now knew her, and I had already begun making arrangements for the classes I would need in order to be licensed to keep and care for her. I was overcome with wailing animal grief.

In me, though, Rosebud will always be alive because of the life-changing revelation I had in her company. She had a purity of being that I had never encountered in another creature. I finally understood that it came from this: she did not know her place in the food chain of the imagination. She did not know that she was prey. When I understood this, I simultaneously came to understand that this food chain metaphor for a way of being is relevant only to predators, whose way of being it is. She was just Rosebud, a fawn, single eyed and full of light, living moment by moment, even in her injured state, even in the very odd circumstances of sleeping on the floor with a member of a predator species in a predator's lair. She easily grasped that this particular predator was not doing predation that night. Rosebud was never anywhere other than where she was, she was not consumed by the past or fearful of the future; she was not for an instant lost in thought but gave her everything to the now.

The contrast I am drawing between Rambo and Rosebud is obvious and perhaps overstated. Yet these are two true stories that come to mind to illustrate the problem that we humans have as a result of having such a huge and highly programmable cerebral cortex on top of the smaller and more basic mammalian brain, itself a narrow gateway for the flow of information from the brain stem and body.[2] Like Descartes, I grew up being taught false things, as did my parents and teachers and their parents and teachers. I was taught false things about humans and about deer, and about mice and rabbits, sparrows, and gazelles, along with all others

2. Damasio, *Self Comes to Mind*, 249.

whom we call prey, as if that word says everything there is to say about them. And into that single word is packed a single concept, fear. I had always imagined that these animals spent their lives in constant anxiety, waiting for the attack that would kill them in a bloody mess of pain.

I am not naïve about relations between predator and prey. I have watched an eagle swoop down and carry off a bunny. I have seen an owl tearing the feathers from a living sparrow to get at its meaty chest. I have heard the coyotes of the northern woods pack-hunting white tailed deer, the sounds of their shrill syncopated yelps enough to stop a heart in its tracks. I have watched people prepare their gear for deer hunting in the fall, and I have stood in line at a fast food eatery (though not in a very long time). I have been the intended victim of a predator (hint: not a wolf) who broke into my bedroom in the wee hours of the morning. Though I fought him off and got on with my life, I would have done well with earlier lessons from Rosebud. Of course Rosebud was severely injured or the two of us would not have been keeping company that night, but this fact deepens the illustration that, even with such injuries, she assessed her situation and made the best of it; and the best she could do was very good. I know that she experienced pleasure along with her pain because we shared it.

I grew up knowing the "fact" that humans and only humans are rational. But Rambo was not rational. He lived in a constant state of fear so powerful that it dominated his life, and that of his son. He was hypervigilant, constantly scanning and vibrating with the tension of preparedness for something that was not there. His rational faculty told him that there were hidden predators watching him, and it also told him that he was fearless. On both counts it told him wrongly. He was angry with his fearful son who embarrassed him and, worse, who was the living chink in his carefully constructed armor. For all his strength and preparation, Rambo was betrayed by a child's vulnerability, something outside his control. More troubling for their shared prognosis, Rambo would have to allow his own vulnerability into his consciousness, his self-story, if his son were to be helped. It is possible for this to happen when a person is motivated (as any psychotherapist can attest) but in Rambo's case, this would entail a delicate demolition that allowed for life to go on in a functional way while at the same time shaping a more flexible self-structure.

Rambo was not someone who would be considered seriously mentally ill. He was just a little further out than all the people who stay awake at night wondering if they will be able to pay the bills, or if they will be able to avoid going to war or have war come to them, or if their kid will be safe going to school in rural Afghanistan or urban America. He was within the range of persons who are required by law to parent (that is, if they have produced offspring), who have a right to decide what their children will learn and how they will learn it. As for his son, Rabbit's every breath was already filtered through fear, and each fearful breath stoked his smoldering unconscious rage. Poor Rabbit: he might have been better off as Descartes's dog.

What I had been taught about Rosebud was wrong, but it was closer to the truth than what I was taught about Rambo. How can the godlike thinker think so badly? How can that miraculous animal *Homo sapiens*, of the unique bipedal gait, of the grasping hands, of the melodious voice, and of the huge brain, have come to this? The answer lies in a list of facts about the ways our brains are constructed. There is the complexity of the brain as a whole, and the three-layered evolutionary arrangement that we have already explored, in which our primal and instinctual motives happen with immediacy in the deepest and smallest parts of our brains, and our elaborate explanations occur neural miles away in the left cerebral hemisphere. For information from our bodies to become part of our self-story, it must pass through anatomically underequipped routes of transport. Of this, Antonio Damasio says: "One does not need to be a neuroanatomist to realize the strange mismatch between the size of the human cerebral cortex and that of the human brain stem."[3] The information that does flow to the cortex may ultimately become part of the system of elaborate explanations characteristic of the left hemisphere, explanations that continue to be edited long after the events that first caused us to create and process them.

Part of the challenge of being *Homo sapiens* is that the right and left cerebral hemispheres of our neocortex are in fact two different minds, with differing interests, differing capacities, and differing levels of access or security clearance for us, the alleged owner-operators of these brains. The difficulties of keeping such complex machines in smooth operation—machines that operate for the most part without any awareness on our part—are difficult to describe but easy to experience. So, so many working parts, and so few of them visible to us!

All this internal complexity is simple, however, compared to the fact that the person, any one of us, is not contained within his or her skin, but

3. Ibid., 250.

extends out quite literally into a social world that can take the controls of the brain at almost any time, given the right conditions. Conscious thought is only a very small part of our actual being in the world, and so it is lack of genuine self-knowledge that creates the fundamental gap through which we fall repeatedly over the course of our individual lives, and continuously in our collective life.

The "I" Is Invisible because We See through It

My earlier suggestion that our rationality is a flashlight in the vast warehouse of largely unconscious mental processes is surely less flattering than the construal of godlike rationality given us by the aforementioned philosophers. But it does have the optimistic feeling of being on an interactive adventure ride with a task to accomplish, that of finding our way around in the dark warehouse using our single flashlight beam. In reality, however, the warehouse of our minds is not unitary, not one big room with a good floor plan, but a series of rooms and corridors, some of them dead ends, most of them in darkness much too profound for meaningful illumination by our little flashlight.

Summarizing the complexity of brain structures and functions and the difficulties of correlating the biology of brain with the psychology of lived experience, John Cacioppo and Jean Decety note: "It is now widely recognized that cognitive, affective, and behavioral processes often unfold unconsciously and that this unconscious processing is adaptive and frees up limited processing resources."[4] This description of our routine unconsciousness is a far other shore from Descartes's definition of humanity as thinking things, yet it still emphasizes our cleverness over the fragmentary nature of our mental lives. The implication is that most of what we are, by definition, is something about which we are unaware. This is efficient, and it is also problematic, sometimes problematic in the extreme.

So now we have added to the fact that the three levels of brain described from the archaeo-evolutionary perspective differ significantly from one another in what they do and in how they do it, the news that the cerebral cortex (the thinking cap) is two minds that operate for different purposes and in different ways. In an address to the American Psychological Association in 2009, Allan Schore observed: "A large body

4. Cacioppo and Decety, "Brain Mechanisms," 11.

of research shows that the right hemisphere differs from the left in mac-rostructure, ultrastructure, physiology, neurochemistry, and behavior."[5] Scientists conducting brain imaging studies have shown that the right hemisphere of the cerebral cortex specializes in unconscious processing of emotional stimuli, and the left hemisphere is involved in conscious de-liberation, elaboration, and articulation.[6] We perceive first with our right hemisphere and may or may not engage further cognitive processing of that percept in the conscious mind of our left hemisphere; the decision to continue on to thinking cognitively is made outside of any conscious awareness in the brain's right hemisphere.

It is fair to say that we know and identify with our brain's left hemi-sphere. The left hemisphere is the "me" that belongs to the implicit or unconscious "I" of immediate experience. However, any information we are processing in the left hemisphere's elaboration of "me" has already been filtered by non-conscious processes. Indeed, we know ourselves as thinking things, but our thinking is but a small part of what we perceive, intend, and choose. But the fact that the left hemisphere is the place where we consciously participate in thinking does not cause the contents of our thoughts to be true. Neurologist Kevin Nelson explains: "The left generates hypotheses, interprets patterns, and makes associations (even where none exist!). It creates stories, constructs theories, seeks explana-tions, and gives us the 'why' for our experiences. Accuracy is not the primary concern of the left hemisphere; rather, its priority is weaving experience into a comprehensible or at least explainable whole. . . . In other words, the left hemisphere not only talks—it also makes things up! The left hemisphere is driven to explain behaviors arising from the right hemisphere."[7] Pause. Consider that the noble rational soul of Aristotle, the grand thinking thing of Descartes, is but a small part of the mind, and that part a spin-doctor who routinely convinces us of things that are not true.

The right hemisphere of the cerebral cortex is largely the home of our unconscious minds, specializing in speedy judgment about what is and is not good for us. It uses emotional information to process quickly decisions about whether we should move towards or away from things we encounter in the world; and about whether we should fight them or

5. Schore, "Paradigm Shift," slide 8.

6. Mlot, "Unmasking the Emotional Unconscious."

7. Nelson, *Spiritual Doorway*, 85.

court them if we do choose further encounter.[8] The right hemisphere is directly connected to the lower brain regions: especially to the limbic system, where memory for life events is stored and emotional evaluations take place, and to the brain stem where primary affects (or biological motives) are experienced. So the right hemisphere is where we have direct experience of the internal states of our own bodies on a moment-by-moment basis, but these are experiences about which our thinking mind is unaware. Though we can become more aware through practices such as meditation, most of the activity of the right hemisphere happens, by evolutionary design, without our conscious participation. In other words, this you who does not participate is by definition an illusory you because it does not include all that unconscious part of "you."

Our brains make a continuous stream of instantaneous decisions on the basis of emotional evaluations that take place deep in the oldest reptilian and mammalian parts of our brains, evaluations rooted in fear and anger, lust and care.[9] Practically speaking, this makes it possible that we turn the corner and take a different route than the one we intended in order to avoid something we never even noticed we had perceived in the first place—perhaps the flash of a color that we experienced in a painful incident somewhere in our past. Another illustration of a routine kind of unconscious decision is in the way that we make instantaneous emotional decisions about one another on the basis of our personal histories, and not on any real knowledge of the other. For example, I may have already braced my body in an aggressive stance by the time I am introduced to someone who reminded me of my abusive uncle, without ever having had a conscious thought about that uncle, perhaps while I was consciously thinking about how I might approach this person for employment. Further, the person I have just met is likely to have unconsciously registered my hostility towards him.[10] If I had been hoping to gain employment through his agency, chances are I have now blown it, with neither one of us being aware of what has transpired between us.

But who is it that wanted the job? And who is it that blew her chances? As Timothy Wilson says in his book on the adaptive unconscious properties of our minds, "Even while our conscious mind is otherwise occupied, we can interpret, evaluate and select information that suits our purposes.

8. Schutz, "Perceptual Disorder of the Right Hemisphere."
9. Ibid., slide 16.
10. Schore, "Paradigm Shift," slide 25.

That's the good news."[11] The fact that so many decisions are made by our brains unconsciously is an important feature in explaining how we can live such complex lives; we could not possibly think through every one of the encounters on an average urban commuter train, rationally weigh all the relevant evidence, and make a series of timely decisions. However, we do not need to; our unconscious processes do it on our behalf.

But Wilson goes on to describe the other side of this efficiency, namely the fact that there is in a sense nobody home, or at least not the somebody I imagine myself to be. "The bad news is that it is difficult to know ourselves because there is no direct access to the adaptive unconscious, no matter how hard we try."[12] We do not experience ourselves first hand, and this is a very difficult concept to grasp because the aware and thinking "I" believes she is in charge.

A generation ago, it was still popular to question the existence of an unconscious mind, and Freud's attribution of so much of human motivation and behavior to unconscious processes evoked smirks in scientifically minded behaviorist and cognitive psychologists. But contemporary brain scientists not only validate Freud's suggestion that the unconscious exists and that it is distinct both in what it does and in how it does it, but also demonstrate that it is likely the dominant mode of our mental processes.[13] Wilson narrates the shift from behaviorism and cognitive psychology to a reconsideration of an even greater role for unconscious motivation: "According to the modern perspective, Freud's view of the unconscious was far too limited. When he said . . . that consciousness is the tip of the mental iceberg, he was short of the mark by quite a bit—it may be more the size of a snowball on top of that iceberg."[14] The "I" of my own story is a small part of the actual animal I, the organism that makes my self-story and that interacts with other people and the world. Not only is the right hemispheric unconscious mind the greater part of mind, but other people are also literally a great part of the self, from just before birth until death.

11. Wilson, *Strangers to Ourselves*, 16.
12. Ibid.
13. Freud, "The Unconscious."
14. Wilson, *Strangers to Ourselves*, 6.

Obligatorily Gregarious

In their book *Loneliness,* John Cacioppo and William Patrick draw upon data from diverse fields of research to show the evolutionary and biological depths that make individual humans completely dependent upon skillful interactions with each other from birth to death. The foundation for a life of skilled socializing takes place during infancy in the acquisition of self-regulation of internal biological and emotional states, and the capacity to interact effectively with others by engaging and disengaging in ways that enhance our individual well-being. Cacioppo and Patrick suggest that evolution has provided us with a "carrot and stick" system of reward and punishment to support us in learning behaviors that will keep us connected to others; the carrot is the pleasure we feel in being connected and the stick is the pain of loneliness.[15] Both are biological givens for humans. They conclude: "Our brains and bodies are designed to function in aggregates, not in isolation. That is the essence of an obligatorily gregarious species."[16]

Cultural commentator David Brooks underlines their point in reflecting on the findings of the Grant study, a longitudinal health study conducted by Harvard University scientists from 1938 onwards.[17] The original plan was to follow a group of 268 male students over the course of their lives with periodic interviews and various tests and measures of well-being. In keeping with the intellectual frame of the times, the early research focused on physical factors, like robust or "masculine" body type, but also included family demographics such as birth order, intelligence, achievement, race, class, political affiliation, relationship status, and career success. Two traits emerged from the data as the most significant for well-being over the span of seven decades: the ability to be warm with people and to be organized about things. But the single factor that most accounted for flourishing was the capacity for intimacy, and this was directly related to having had a warm childhood; not necessarily cozy or easy, but with at least one emotionally warm relationship.[18] Though this would come as a surprise to those who initially conceived the study, even a rudimentary contemporary understanding of infant development

15. Cacioppo and Patrick, *Loneliness,* 120.

16. Ibid., 127.

17. Brooks, "The Heart Grows Smarter," *The New York Times,* November 5, 2012.

18. Vaillant, *Triumphs of Experience.*

explains why this factor of emotional warmth was so important over the lifespan of the men in this study.

Tabula Rasa

The first developmental task of the newborn is to create in the right hemisphere of his brain the neuroarchitecture of emotional self-regulation. This is accomplished as the infant internalizes the responses of adults to his spontaneous emotion expressions. His amygdala is one of the few brain structures fully functional at birth, and so the helpless child is born with the capacity to feel and express danger. He experiences hunger as a crisis—indeed it is a crisis, since he cannot feed himself. He screams and kicks. When someone responds by soothing and feeding him, he internalizes the soothing and learns to regulate his response to hunger, simultaneously learning to engage others to help him and to trust that others will respond to him helpfully. As oxytocin (the bonding hormone) is stimulated in him and in his caregiver, he begins to experience the pleasure of being connected to other humans and to internalize this pleasure as a stable platform for everything else he will do in life. It is important to understand that these early relational experiences are not just the stuff of deep memories but become the actual neuroarchitecture of the brain.

As an aside for any anxious parent reading this, parental attunement need not be perfect. In fact, it should not be perfect because infants must learn to tolerate some frustration and discomfort. However, they can only learn to tolerate these from a position of having generally responsive and helpful adults in their world, people who help to modulate experience to manageable levels. The wish to avoid mistakes can result in parents becoming overwhelmingly intrusive, not allowing the infant sufficient mental space in which to assimilate experience. Allan Schore expresses it this way: "The more the mother tunes her activity level to the infant during periods of social engagement, and the more she allows him to recover quietly in periods of disengagement, the more synchronized their interaction. In this way, not only the tempo of their engagement but also their disengagement are coordinated. By doing so the caregiver facilitates the infant's information processing by adjusting the mode, amount, variability and timing of stimulation to the infant's actual integrative capacities."[19] This internalized emotion regulation will reappear

19. Schore, *Affect Dysregulation*, 7–8.

later in life as the ability to ask for help, to rest when tired, to walk away from a fight.

What motivates parents and newborns in the complex development of biological and psychological self-regulation is the experience of euphoric attunement: it is the template for the feeling of being in love. New parents often express this as the ineffable joy of gurgling and gazing into their baby's eyes, overcoming exhaustion to want to do it again and again. I turn to Allan Schore for the scientific description of this state of attunement: "Dyadically resonating, mirroring gaze transactions thus induce a psychobiologically attuned, affect generating merger state in which a match occurs between the accelerating, rewarding, positively hedonic internal states in both partners."[20] This biology of joy in relationship is what evolution has provided to motivate connection and the effort that connection requires. Infants naturally want to enter such a state of engagement because "euphoric states are perhaps the most appetitively compelling experiences available to life forms as so far evolved."[21] Being positively connected feels good from birth to death, but for a human baby it is the process whereby he becomes capable—or relatively incapable—of living a human life.

In this dance of mutual interaction between adults and infants, several of the most important structures for living a human life are interactively co-created by the infant and her caregiver: her physiological stress responses are set at a healthy level so that she will respond to danger but will not be overly sensitized to discomfort or mild threats; and her sense of herself becomes one of basic security, of capacity to cope, especially by using relationships with others to guide her behavior. She internalizes the experience that sets a foundational belief or disposition towards expecting that others are fundamentally reliable and that relating to others is pleasurable.

It is a slow dance in the first six months of life, cheek to cheek, with taste and smell, touch and temperature forming the communication between baby and adult. The early life in which the infant is held often and in which she expresses basic pleasure and pain, and in which the parent responds effectively to her communications, leads to her gradually taking over such basic aspects of her existence as fluid balance regulation and temperature regulation, life-sustaining functions that become

20. Schore, "Secure Attachment Relationship," 7.
21. Schwartz, "On Narcissism," 125.

auto-regulated in the infant after first being regulated in context of relationship with a caregiver.

By six months the infant's brain is sufficiently developed that the music of speech and eye gazing (or prosody) becomes a mode of communication that no longer requires such close physical contact. The pleasurable "nonsense" mimicry and imitation that is the typical exchange between adults and infants, the cooing conversations and the funny faces, the eye gaze that creates contact as the infant acquires basic capacities to move greater distances away from her caregiver, all of these are building the mechanisms of self-regulation of body and mind in the actual brain structures of the infant. This capacity to move away from others towards increasing autonomy while also staying connected and responsive to feedback is a delicate balancing act, and it is perhaps the most essential requirement to live successfully as a human. In the words of Cacioppo and Patrick: "Reconciling this split between the self and the other—the desire for autonomy set against the desire for the calm assurance of intimate connection—remains a lifelong challenge, one that places a premium on self-regulation."[22]

During those neurally busy first eighteen months of life, the infant brain also makes from early relational experience the set of switches for self-regulation of emotional arousal, and this process in turn sets biological systems of stress response and modulation in the body. If the baby's arousal level is not regulated by a caregiver, his stress responsiveness will remain chronically over-stimulated and his body will be flooded with cortisol, the "fight or flight" hormone, resulting in long term health damage. At the same time that they are setting stress response levels, the same interactions between infant and caregiver build the neuroarchitecture for an implicit sense of self, the "I" who is distinct from the brain's archetypal "you," the other.

This "I" will increasingly evaluate, direct, and construct its "me," especially in social performance, throughout life. The implicit self of the right hemisphere is the unknowable I, the part of the self that will continue to have the most immediate experience both of the person's own internal body state and of the conditions in her environment; but this I is also one who is too busy quickly processing a cacophony of experience to be self-reflectively telling a story about that experience. However, out of the child's collected experience, accumulated as memory for life events

22. Cacioppo and Patrick, *Loneliness*, 121.

in the right hemisphere, and also out of the basic social and emotional dispositions that he has built into his right hemisphere, will come the material to create in the brain's left hemisphere the verbal account he will know as himself. This is the "me" that each of us can describe in terms of personality traits and interests, and the autobiographical narrative we create to find the patterns in our lives. Recall that the purpose of this story is not to be factually true, but to be a good enough story to provide a psychic holder, a container, for all of life's experiences.

I understand from seeing Rambo as an adult that his infant distress cries were likely met with anger or neglect, perhaps with physical abuse or actual abandonment by an overwhelmed caregiver, one who himself or herself had not mastered self-regulation of emotion. If mother cannot be soothed, she cannot soothe, and so her baby becomes one who is chronically over-stimulated, afraid of everything, and who dares not ask for help. So he is programmed for a life of social isolation that will continue to create the pattern whereby his needs are never met. His hyperarousal is all he has ever known, and so it feels normal to him. He self-regulates his extreme and now unconscious fear by being "afraid of nothing," but "prepared" for anything, and no one wants to be around him. In this way, he carries on a self-perpetuating cycle of not being able to get help.

I further make the educated guess that his stress hormones are chronically over-stimulated and that he is prone to inflammatory conditions in his physiology, the biological substrate of a plethora of physical pathologies, like heart disease and diabetes. When Allan Schore describes infant relational trauma that occurs by way of either abuse or neglect, he describes a lifelong form of suffering and social disadvantage that goes far beyond feeling sad about not having had the love one would have liked to have had. The power of interpersonal trauma during infancy is such that it can "override any genetic, constitutional, social or psychological resilience factor, and . . . have ensuing adverse effects on brain development and alterations in the biological stress system" that create a complex developmental disorder, including susceptibility to post-traumatic stress in later life.[23]

I saw in Rabbit a different pattern, another form of a recognizable lack of ability to self-regulate. He is paralyzed by anxiety. His father is so focused upon the immediate environment that he barely looks at his son, much less notices and cares for his son's feelings and needs. As for

23. Schore, *Affect Dysregulation*, 237.

Rabbit, whatever he does is under the over-sensitized eye of Rambo; and anything he does may be the something that pushes Rambo's emotional buttons and aggressive responses. There is nothing Rabbit can do that will be effective, and so Rabbit dissociates, disengaging from an external world that he cannot predict, control, or constructively relate to, in order to attend to his very demanding inner world. Again quoting Schore, "The child's dissociation in the midst of terror involves numbing, avoidance, compliance, and restricted affect."[24] And this is what I saw in Rabbit, standing compliant within his father's strong grasp, eyes wide. These symptoms are indicators of impaired self-regulation of a particular kind, a system that rapidly disorganizes under stress. When Rabbit goes to school, he does not have the self-regulation system to interact with normal demands of social life and so he simply dissociates, using the defense of "escape when there is no escape."[25] Under pressure, he breaks down, freezes, and loses contact with what is happening around him.

These two, father and son, remain a poignant and compelling portrait of intergenerational suffering. Each in his distinctive way continues to suffer from distresses of infancy throughout the course of his life, and each in his context imposes suffering on others. Before I leave them, though, I have to say that because of our lifelong neural plasticity, they can be helped, and I have also to say that their dysfunctional patterns are likely a matter of degree different from ours because the vulnerability to social factors is inherent in being as programmable as *Homo sapiens* is. Stated simply, we all have some bugs in our programs.

Culture as Internalized Behavioral Constraint

The fact that the cerebral cortex of *Homo sapiens* is an almost blank slate at birth grants us enormous flexibility as a species. Cultural neuroscientist Bruce Wexler makes the case that this neuroplasticity is definitive of humanity: "the phylogenetic emergence of human beings rests, to a significant degree, on selection for an extended period of postnatal plasticity in the fine-grained shaping of the structural and functional organization of the human brain."[26] Human infants are born equipped with about two hundred billion neurons, twice as many neurons as will

24. Ibid., 251.
25. Ibid., 248.
26. Wexler, *Brain and Culture*, 17.

be needed to construct infant neuroarchitecture; the remaining hundred billion neurons will be pruned away when the infant's construction project is complete.

At the same time that the infant is co-creating with his caregivers some of the basic templates upon which he will rely relationally for the rest of his life, it is important to understand that, whatever the interpersonal experiences he may integrate as his own self-regulation system, they come packaged in the cultural forms that his parents share with their community. His family and neighbors all were programmed by culture that they express in their every thought and gesture, and he internalizes these cultural constraints along with the smiles or frowns, closeness or distance, and food and warmth that he receives (or lacks). It is culture that sets the parameters for broad values in behavior, like how competitive or cooperative one should be, how loud or how quiet in expression, how eccentric or conforming, how emotionally constricted or expressive, how much physical space to allow or resist between bodies, how rigidly to adhere to gender norms.

Wexler makes the point that the process of intensive formation that takes place by way of the caregivers' relationship with the infant exponentially increases variation in the species, as does sexual reproduction at the biological level. Development through social interaction makes for another level of unique individuals and a great range of variation in sensitivities, interests, and capacities. Increasing the range of behavior in the species as a whole increases the chances that some members will thrive when environmental conditions change.[27] But it also makes each individual vulnerable in relation to his social context. To the extent that he is surrounded by attentive people who program him effectively, and who are also able to meet his material needs for food, clothing, and shelter, he will stand the chance of living a happy and healthy life. But to the extent that he lacks attention and care, to the extent he is taught incorrect information and given behavioral maps that do not provide adequate guidance to help him navigate a complex social life, he will suffer mentally and physically; and he will create problems for other people, before dying younger than a better cared for baby. As I have said elsewhere, the minds of humans past exert formative pressures—or bend back upon—the brains of humans present.[28] One of the great challenges of

27. Ibid., 3.
28. Benvenuti and Davenport, "New Archaic," 208.

our times is the necessity to become aware of cultural influences, within which former generations existed without noticing their presence. The cultural context when there is only one, or even predominantly one, is like breathing air or walking on earth. But cultures are no longer bound by the physical geographies out of which they grew, and they no longer exist in homogeneous settings, with perhaps some challenges at the edges of the physical and social worlds that produced them. In our time multiple cultural influences routinely contradict one another within the same environment, so that what evolved to contain our fragmentary existence now requires our containing. This is a new kind of demand, at least on the global scale we now experience, and it is an issue to which I will return in depth. We must find a way to contain the intergenerational systems that once contained us. To the extent that we succeed, we stand to gain much greater degrees of liberation from constraint and from suffering. To the extent that we do not find a way to make new containers, we will increasingly suffer the fragmentation of our natures. The stories that we tell of our collective life and of our individual lives are perhaps the most flexible containers we can make, and it helps, as noted already, if they are true.

Existence Precedes Essence: Constructing a Self

One of the major accomplishments of the human brain is the construction of a self, a project that is done in a developmental sequence roughly corresponding to the three levels of the brain: beginning in infancy, with the neuroarchitecture for basic self-regulation and relationship patterning, and continuing to the adding of layers of consciousness and complexity during young adulthood. The constructed self then becomes the perspective through which we humans are aware of our own minds. Jean-Paul Sartre, the French existentialist philosopher, articulated a basic premise, "Existence precedes essence," by which he meant that humans are born first and then construct themselves. While this might seem to point to a great deal of personal power, an "I make myself" not far in emotional tone from the swaggering self-made man, it is not so simple as that. In fact, we are in a considerably more humble position. A significant problem in being human is that, in Damasio's words, the self is one part of the mind and "a self process that we have good reason to believe cannot provide a comprehensive and reliable account of what is going on."[29]

29. Damasio, *Self Comes to Mind*, 13.

Self is a psychological construct that is easy to use; everyone knows what it means—until they try to define it. Try now to say what your self is, and after you have said it, ask who is the self and who is talking about the self? Are these the same person? It becomes immediately apparent what the problem is: the self is actually an observed entity created by, by . . . hmm. We return to that "I-Me" relationship that was first articulated in the field of psychology by William James.[30] The "I" experiences living, conducts self-evaluation, articulates desires, develops goals, and ultimately constructs a story about and description of its "Me."

Dan McAdams, whose research interest lies in the dynamics of stories and narratives, has proposed a theoretical model of the "Self," grounded in psychological research data.[31] His model articulates several important features of the self-process and arranges them in both a developmental sequence and in terms of the major challenges of "having" and being a self over the course of a life. He ascribes to the Self three roles, Actor, Agent, and Author, and describes the way in which these come into being in a developmental sequence. The Actor self emerges in early toddlerhood, and it will come as no surprise that the Actor's task is to apply and to amplify the skills of self-regulation in ever broadening social circles. The goal of such extended self-regulation is to gain acceptance and status, or to get along and to get ahead, outcomes that can easily be mutually contradictory.[32]

Humans begin to recognize themselves in mirrors at about eighteen months of age. Simultaneously, they recognize their actions as their own, using self-referential language of me and mine. As the toddler uses feedback from others to evaluate his performance, he experiences powerful social emotions like shame and pride to reinforce his self-evaluation.[33] Increased self-control is the capacity building work of the little Actor. McAdams summarizes the work of the early Actor: "Through effortful control, actors manage to inhibit impulses and summon the strength needed to perform behaviors that will win social approval."[34] The Actor aspect of the Self is the first to be developed but it continues to evolve

---

30. James, *Psychology.*
31. McAdams, "Psychological Self," 295.
32. Ibid., 274.
33. Ibid., 275.
34. Ibid., 283.

throughout the lifespan, as the self uses social feedback to correct course in the ongoing balancing act of getting ahead while getting along.

The role of Agent begins just at that time in development when the child goes out into the larger social world beyond home and family, about six to seven years of age, a period of beginning intensive acquisition of knowledge and skills. With broader exposure and a new breadth of expectations placed upon him, the child finds that he is better at some things than others, that he likes some activities and some people more than others. As he begins to articulate desires and develop goals, he applies the self-evaluation and effortful self-control he began to learn as social actor. Now, however, the evaluation comes from within and is applied to his ability to realize his own desires, to accomplish his own goals. Before this stage of life children are universally positive in their self-assessments, but with this new level of demand comes a different kind of self-evaluation, self-esteem. "Self-esteem is fundamentally about the self's relative success or failure as a motivated agent who strives to achieve goals in strongly valued domains of life—goals upon which one's very worth is at stake."[35] Now he can enjoy not only care and the pleasure of biological homeostasis and interpersonal attunement, but also feel the satisfaction of accomplishing his own desires. Now he can suffer not only from neglect or abuse, but also from shame and self-loathing. Such is the complexity and the challenge for *Homo sapiens*. Complexity, and its shadow of potentially dangerous disintegration, starts immediately, and it never stops but only grows more complex as the years pass and the episodes in memory accrue their varieties of interest.

By the time a human youngster reaches adolescence, coherence of the self (in psychological terms, self-continuity) becomes a necessity. The adolescent has had many years of living, many autobiographical memories, many different performance contexts, and has experienced himself as being both bad and good, both a success and a failure. He begins to see that he can be a very different person at home with his parents, on the street with his friends, at church with the choir, in the car with his girlfriend, and so on. He is under pressure to create a future to which he must in the present apply the lessons and experiences of his past, so he has a need for temporal continuity, as well as self-continuity across roles.

The autobiographical self includes not only the various selves of differing times and places, but also the extended self, by which I mean

35. Ibid.

everything that is "mine." William James suggested that this self is not just the body and its experiences, or even the total collection of memories, but includes "his clothes and his wife and children, his ancestors and friends, his reputation and works, his lands and horses, and yacht, and bank account."[36] I might add to this exuberant list, his debts, his enemies, and his failures, especially that of having placed his clothes before his wife and children in the lineup of self-objects.

In his book on the neural construction of the self, Damasio makes the point that aspects of the self-story include anything that evokes the feeling of self as a response to perception of that thing.[37] The "self-feeling" originates in the brain stem when objects in the world feel "selfy," and is communicated to the right hemisphere of the cerebral cortex, then passed to the left hemisphere where the feeling becomes autobiographical story. Note that this self-feeling that makes fundamental decisions about what is me and what is against me and what is neutral in the world takes place in primitive brain regions, but the story is authored in the left hemisphere of the cerebral cortex using the elaborative qualities of language.

Damasio describes this elaborative consciousness: "What your life has been, in bits and pieces, is available to you rapidly in recall, and bits and pieces of what your life may or not come to be, imagined earlier or imagined now, also come into the moment of experience. You are busily all over the place and at many epochs of your life, past and future. But you—the me in you—never drops out of sight. . . . The center holds. This is big-scope consciousness, one of the grand achievements of the human brain and one of the defining traits of humanity. This is the kind of brain process that has brought us to where we are in civilization, for better and worse."[38] I would add to his description that the center holds to the extent that it does, most often sufficiently to function in life. But the center often fails to maintain sufficient gravitational force to hold the pieces of self in a coherent dance of consciousness, as can be seen in the mental health issues of everyday life: anxiety, depression, addictions, violence.

I referred earlier to the relationship between human complexity and the need to create containers for experience that would otherwise be too fragmentary to bear. The self-story, the autobiographical narrative, or what McAdams calls the Author is such a container, and its construction

---

36. James, *Principles of Psychology*, Volume II, 536.

37. Damasio, *Self Comes to Mind*, 9.

38. Ibid., 168.

is a task accomplished by using both memory of autobiographical events (right hemisphere) and semantic memory, or knowledge of facts about myself (left hemisphere). Weaving these two kinds of self-knowledge together into an autobiography is a continuous project for holding aspects of the self in the context of the world as new experiences and lessons get added to the narrative.

The narrative self is a universal feature of humans. Using a framework of evolutionary interpretation, this suggests that making a self-story has adaptive value. Indeed the value of self-narrative has been articulated in the scientific research. Mark Landau and colleagues have found that actively maintaining self-continuity across time with a biographical story provides a sense of order and meaning and helps to protect against fear of death.[39] Another team of self-narrative researchers, led by Kate McLean, found that having an organizing theme of personal growth helps to support higher levels of ego development and provide a sense of self-continuity.[40]

There is no doubt that humans need this autobiographical self in order to function well and to feel good, but there is also no doubt that the "Me" story is problematic to the extent that it is not true. Notice, for example, that Damasio's list of what can come into consciousness as part of the autobiographical self includes what one has in the past wished or feared about one's future. Not only do wishes for the future become memories of the past under the magic wand of the left hemisphere, but we can also easily be planted with false memories, as illustrated convincingly by the research of Elizabeth Loftus.[41] The fact that the story is not true means that the person must either learn to be very flexible in the ongoing construction of his story, developing a capacity to reinterpret memories in light of new experiences, or must screen out information that would violate his self-story.

By adulthood we increasingly use those self-confirming cognitive biases to which I have already made mention to confirm us in our self-story. Imagine the tension within Rambo between his always prepared and never afraid self-narrative and the depths of fear programmed into his implicit self of the right hemisphere, the very frightened "I" that required him to produce such a warrior narrative "me." Imagine, too, the

---

39. Landau et al., "Defending a Coherent Autobiography."
40. McLean and Fournier, "Autobiographical Reasoning."
41. Loftus and Pickrell, "Formation of False Memories."

tension experienced by people who must interact with him, like the public mental health workers who are not comforted by his wearing a knife to ask for help. It is not hard to see how self and story can be quite divergent, and also to see the value of having a truer rather than less true self-story.

The trueness of one's self-story is what Timothy Wilson considers its most important feature. Of this he says: "On what basis can we say that one self-story is better than another? Self-stories should be accurate, I believe, in a simple sense: they should capture the nature of the person's non conscious goals, feelings, and temperaments."[42] The barrier to constructing such a self-story is that we are often not aware we are constructing a story at all, and we assume that our ideas, our reasons for behaving as we do precede our decisions and actions. It is a well-established fact of cognitive science that the opposite is true: decisions are made with unconscious efficiency and then reasons that are consistent with our self-story are provided after the fact. Reflecting on the way that self-stories come to be out of alignment with our actual selves as we live in the world, Wilson explains, "Because people have too much faith in their explanations, they come to believe that their feelings match the reasons they list."[43]

And one final caveat about the constructed self: she must be placed always within the set of cultural constraints that are her social milieu. McAdams hypothesizes about the role of culture in forming the psychological self: "In a nutshell, culture may (a) set norms and constraints for the behavioral expression of the actor's traits and roles; (b) provide timetables, scripts, and strong priorities for the agent's articulation of goals and values; (c) provide the psycho-literary menu off of which the author chooses the very images, metaphors, and narratives that can be used to make narrative identity."[44]

By the time that Actor, Agent, and Author have all become functions of the psychological self, the person has a great deal of time and energy invested in that constructed self, such that change becomes a serious energetic expenditure to be avoided if possible. Cultural neuroscientist Wexler concisely references the interaction of individual human development and culture:

> During the first years of life, interpersonal and other sensory experiences create internal neural structures in their own forms.

42. Wilson, *Strangers to Ourselves*, 181.

43. Ibid., 168.

44. McAdams, "Psychological Self," 286.

Once established, these internal structures alter a person's perception and experience to make them agree with the internal structures. People seek and create experiences that match their particular internal structures, and select information from the environment that most closely approximates these structures. When faced with information that does not agree with their internal structures, they deny, discredit, reinterpret, or forget that information. These maneuvers increase the sense of agreement between the internal and external worlds.[45]

It makes evolutionary sense in terms of energy conservation that we would switch to a strategy of maintenance once we have constructed a self, but it also means that discrepancies between our constructed self and "the real world" of our social and physical environments can grow undetected, as our unconscious strategies protect us from awareness of the divergence.

When the Dance Carries the Dancer Away

I have described ways in which the outer world becomes the inner world, especially in reference to human relationships and the construction of a self. But the mirror image is also true, that the self is not confined to the boundaries of skin that contain a human being. That obligatory gregariousness of *Homo sapiens* causes us to conform to social groups throughout our lives. The social context is a powerful determinant of behavior, as has been illustrated by decades of research in social psychology. In fact, experimental social psychologists have articulated a general principle to describe the way in which we typically err in our interpretations of human behavior, naming this principle "the fundamental attribution error."

The fundamental attribution error refers to the fact that we interpret human behavior as caused by individual motives and choices, even when it is clearly better accounted for by social context. An instance that is easy to accept is the fact that people are well dressed at a formal event because it is a formal event, and probably much less because they are formal people. Though there may be some selection factor in that formal people choose more formal events to attend, many more people dress formally when it is expected than would choose to do so of a Sunday afternoon. A more difficult scenario to accept is that, under various kinds of

45. Wexler, *Brain and Culture*, 180–81.

social pressure, particularly where anonymity is assured and pressure to conform is applied, good people routinely behave badly. There are many, many studies that show human behavior can be much better predicted by situational variables than by personal choice, yet we persist in thinking that personal choice motivates us.

Perhaps the two most famous lines of research to demonstrate the power of social context in predicting behavior are Stanley Milgram's obedience studies and Phillip Zimbardo's Stanford Prison Experiment. Milgram's studies, conducted at Yale in 1961, were designed to answer questions driven by images and reports of the behavior of normal people during the Holocaust. Zimbardo's prison experiment at Stanford was conducted in 1971 to investigate the impact that social context and assigned roles of prisoner and guard had in influencing behavior. Both studies led to results that still feel shocking to us in the way that they demonstrate the power of social context on our behavior, with people doing things that they would consider morally reprehensible if they observed someone else doing them.

Milgram demonstrated repeatedly the power of legitimate authority to define situations and to define "good" behavior for the situation. Sixty-five percent of his research subjects administered what they perceived to be potentially lethal levels of electric shock to people whom they thought were other research participants like themselves, but who were in fact confederates acting the part of research subjects. The research director's role involved encouraging subjects to continue to administer electric shocks and assuring the subjects that the scientist was fully responsible for the study.[46] What became apparent over the series of experiments is that obedience is a pervasive motive and that it is supported by powerful social emotions of self-doubt and fear of embarrassment. When people experience a conflict between their interpretation of a situation and that of an authority, they tend to defer to the authority because they doubt themselves and they fear humiliation.

In Zimbardo's prison experiments, even he, the lead researcher who had assigned to himself the role of prison director, came under the psychological sway of the simulation of a prison. Research subjects (students) were assigned to the role of either guard or prisoner. The simulation of a prison environment and roles proved so powerful and destructive that the study, which had been designed as a two-week experiment, was

46. Milgram, "Obedience," and Zimbardo, "Interpersonal Dynamics in a Simulated Prison."

disbanded after six days. Guards were abusing prisoners, and prisoners were suffering extreme distress. Zimbardo himself had so lost perspective that he had to be told by a research assistant that the study had become unethical and must be terminated. He attributed the changes in himself and in the behavior of student research subjects to the motive of social power, the desire to be part of the privileged in-group and not to be identified with the vulnerable out-group. Zimbardo's prison experiment demonstrated the ways in which a number of variables can communicate and support social power dynamics.

In both series of studies, the social framing of the situation set the stage upon which the participants acted out assigned parts. The context itself, including physical setting, uniforms and other props, combined with verbal explanations from one or more authorities, diminished the sense of personal responsibility and choice, and supported conforming behavior. I am reminded of an incident in my own career when a college administrator smirked and said, "Faculty are like children, you give them three choices, red, yellow, or blue and they will argue over those choices without ever thinking of purple or green." I was appalled by her Machiavellian attitude, but as a social psychologist, I see that she was essentially correct in noting that people tend to accept the frames in which information is given, especially when given by a sanctioned authority.

In her book exploring the idea of ethics without the concept of free will, Heidi Ravven notes: "not only are we likely (or inevitably, to a large extent) to be driven by social forces; we are just as likely to deny that they exist and to be convinced that we are independent creatures making personal decisions. And this blindness further intensifies the power of the social forces upon us, making us even more vulnerable to them because we are so sure that nothing of the kind could ever affect us. We overestimate our own power and underestimate that of situations."[47] The persistent belief in ourselves as morally free choosers and actors is yet another aspect of our problematically incorrect self-story.

My description of the postnatal development process of human beings is intended to demonstrate that we have been incorrect in understanding what an individual human being is, beginning with the fact that there is no such thing as an individual human being. As psychologist Hans Kohut notes, "Values of independence are phony, really. There is no such thing. There can be no pride in living without oxygen. We're not

47. Ravven, *Self Beyond Itself*, 109.

made that way. It is nonsense to try and give up symbiosis and become an independent self."[48] I would add to this that it is nonsense to ignore the futility of pretending to be independent, rational, and free, while the social world within and around us crumbles under the combined weight of our extreme bio-psycho-social complexity with its tendency towards disintegrations and self-deceptions at so many levels.

If a truer story is a better story, I am compelled to ask, "How can we create a truer story?" The answer feels a bit like a cleansing confession, and perhaps that is the best place to start: we might do well to confess the many kinds of breakdown or fragmentation inherent in our complexity instead of looking the other way. To get to a truer story, we need to accept the fact that doing so will be energetically demanding and emotionally threatening to the value of self-maintenance. Yet, in a manner reminiscent of twelve-step recovery programs, the first step is recognizing the necessity of admitting to our problems. Hello, my name is *Homo sapiens*, and I cannot manage my own complexity. A good start, but this is only the starting point for real change.

From birth, our brains have been programmed by our experiences and later by our own individual and collective narratives, all in the context of culturally defined behaviors and symbols. As we invest in our constructed self, we begin to filter and select experiences that reinforce what we think and to avoid or punish experiences that do not support our constructions of self and world. Throughout this developmental process, we create a cluster of problems that may be unique to human beings. By several mechanisms originating in the evolution of our brains, we get lost in thought. We mistake cultural givens (memes) for facts, like the "fact" that our minds, bodies, and souls are distinct and separable, or the "fact" that other animals are really machines. Because of the distracting noise made by our story generator, we are unable to hear the direct messages sent by our bodies, and so we join James Joyce's Mr. Duffy in living at least a short distance from our bodies.[49] Problematically, and like the archetypal Mr. Duffy, we tend to evaluate this as a good thing, a sign of our having overcome the weakness of the flesh. But the fact that our elaborative autobiographies override necessary instinctive advice renders us vulnerable to all that we do not know about our own motivations. We have the terrible capacity to say we are not these bodies, and to believe it,

48. Kohut, *Self Psychology and the Humanities*, 262.
49. Joyce, "A Painful Case."

and to act as if it were true. We have the equally terrible capacity to say that other animals are just machines and to ignore the information from our own bodies that, in their suffering and their joy, they are as we are.

Being easily overwhelmed by our own psychological and social complexity, our centers do not always hold and we become unable to regulate our inherent tendencies to fragmentation. Being substantially and inherently unconscious in our decision-making, we have a hard time becoming aware of where we have gone wrong. Add to this that our self-stories are not just about "me" but about "mine," that they extend to us and ours. So when I encounter self-objects in the extended left hemisphere of media, I am soothed and I use them to support my fragile story. Conversely, when I see objects that threaten the veracity of my story, I am upset and I want to be rid of them. Needless to say, such events are increasingly the stuff of human life, and they take us further from the homes that our bodies are. Practically speaking, this I think may be our greatest human distinction, that we are utterly lost in thought.

Looking at *Homo sapiens* from different perspectives as we have done over these last two chapters, we see that biologically and fundamentally we are inescapably animal, and that our brain stem knows this. However, we are animals of a heavily programmed kind, with suscepti-bilities related more to our program bugs than to any other feature. It is easy to see that being so programmable might work in the right setting, a setting of face to face interactions with a small group of people and sufficient time to assimilate messages from the social world, and from one's own body. It is also clear to see how our capacities—and particularly that necessary link between motivational feelings in the brain stem and stories in the cerebral cortex—can be overwhelmed by too much information at the level of cortex and too little awareness of messages from the body.

Physically, it seems that our gait is our greatest claim to fame: it would be fun to say it is our feet, such a grounded metaphor! But, while our gait is located in our leg bones and spine and hips as well as in our feet, our problems are clearly most pronounced in our heads, and particularly in the communications between brain stem and cortex. Our suffering is not quite all in our heads but, as the Buddha noted, most of it is. Speculating on the interaction between increased pressures on cognition brought about by the digital revolution, Damasio put it this way: "Increased cognitive demands have made the interplay between the cortex and brain stem a bit rough and brutal, or to put it in kinder words, they have made the access to the wellspring of feeling more difficult. Something may yet have to give."[50]

Wherefore I know not, lost all my mirth

Something is giving. In fact, two things are giving, our shared natural environment and our collective center. Suffice it for now to say that a further area of disintegration that must necessarily be added to the list of neural, psychological, and social dysregulations to which we are susceptible is that of ecological disintegration. Virtually all urban people, and increasing numbers of rural people too, do not experience their actual deep rootedness in nature, as information from inside our bodies about the world is overridden in our consciousness by media and technology. We are out of touch with the physical world and we mistakenly think this is both natural and good. Our positive evaluation of being mental to the exclusion of physical is that it makes it even harder for us to notice and recognize the feelings in our brain stems that are motivating our actual behavior. Identifying with the mental reinforces the problem without us ever having had an experience that there is a problem. But being cut off from our own bodily information, much less the rest of physical reality, is problematic.

Our individual quality of life and our communal life are dependent upon our internalizing self-regulation from others who have it, and passing it on in the ongoing dance of emotion regulation that is as necessary to our species as is food, air, and water. Again, it is easy to see that this system would have worked better in times when social living happened on a smaller scale, like village or tribe. Human life on a larger scale means that this aspect of face-to-face and body-to-body emotion regulation simply falls through the cracks. And, of course, there is a gendered cycle of victim and perpetrator that assures an unending cycle of depression when males act out, females are victimized, and babies are neglected or abused (and nature violated).[51]

Much to the point are global statistics on depression: the World Health Organization lists depression as the third most common non-communicable disease in the world, set to become the most common by 2030. Depression is already ranked first for women, and male depression,

50. Damasio, *Self Comes to Mind*, 251.
51. Benvenuti, *Gendered Forms of Depression*.

symptomatically characterized by substance abuse and violent behavior, is just beginning to be named and counted. The most recent global epidemiological study ranks depression as the second cause of all disability, with back pain being first ranked.[52]

In spite of its prevalence, there is broad confusion about what depression actually is. Symptom checklists in documents ranging from the *Diagnostic and Statistical Manual* to advertisements for pharmaceutical antidepressants typically list two differing kinds of symptoms: symptoms of active suffering, like sadness, loneliness, despair, hopelessness, crying, and symptoms of lack of motivation, like loss of appetite, loss of interest in sex and friendship, and socially isolating behavior, lack of interest and energy in things that once were engaging. The media-educated public often sounds confused about depression, thinking it to be "biological" and thus both not one's own fault and treatable by medication, and at the same time confusing all kinds of feeling bad with depression.

Feeling bad is most often a normal part of life that cues us to change our behavior or circumstances. Taking medication for feeling bad is likely to cause depression by inhibiting the effort to make positive changes that feeling bad cues us to make. When we are unable to do this, to get away from what is causing pain and distress or to find a way to what will bring comfort, joy, and laughter, this combination of feeling bad and being unable to call up the energy to improve our feelings is depression. What characterizes depression and makes it distinct from other dysphoric conditions is lack of motivation, and not the depth or intensity of bad feeling per se.

Commenting on the combined prevalence of depression and lack of understanding about what causes and characterizes it, affective neuroscientist Jaak Panksepp says: "Our failure to understand depression may arise, in part, from the fact that neuroscience has not yet studied the most relevant ancient affective circuits of the mammalian MindBrain closely enough." Of the seven foundational affective circuits that he has described in all mammals, he suggests that two are especially relevant in causing depression: GRIEF and SEEKING. The GRIEF system is the brain circuitry responsible for the "psychic pain that arises from sustained separation distress."[53] As the process whereby infants internalize the capacity to regulate their emotions would suggest, healthy social

52. Ferrari et al., "Burden of Depressive Disorders."
53. Panksepp and Biven, *Archaeology of Mind*, 459.

bonding is necessary for *Homo sapiens*. The distress that results from lack of social bonding or disruption of social bonds—death of a loved one, divorce, social shunning or public shaming—is one of the most painful and difficult experiences of life.

Panksepp hypothesizes that depression reflects "diminished activity of the natural brain chemicals that make us feel good when we are safely and securely attached to others," and goes so far as to say that "loving social attachment bonds are a primal form of addiction."[54] Put differently, we are addicted to each other naturally by evolution and, when we cannot get our bonding "fix," we must necessarily look for it in other places, or break down trying.

GRIEF alone is not sufficient to describe depression because depression is characterized by motivational impairment. It is feeling bad, plus being unable to even anticipate doing something to feel better. The death of a loved one or a divorce can cause enormous psychic pain, but even a very intense level of emotional pain does not imply the presence or necessity of depression. I met a woman who was compelled to go out for a 2,000-mile walk in response to the death of her mother. This represents an admittedly big grief response, but it is a highly motivated response and so it is very far from depression. When a person is suffering psychic pain *and also* lacks energy, interest, and pleasure, this is a characteristic description of depression. It implies that what Panksepp calls the brain's SEEKING system is pathologically unresponsive. The SEEKING system is brain circuitry that causes an energized state of anticipation; it feels like a wanting to do something, whether the something is buying an especially pleasing gift, achieving an especially satisfying revenge, or simply eating a good meal. "When the SEEKING system is aroused, animals exhibit an intense, enthused curiosity about the world . . . [W]hen the SEEKING system is chronically underactive, we experience a hopeless form of depression, characterized by lethargy and an absence of get-up-and-go." SEEKING activation can be caused by a bad feeling like hunger or loneliness, or by a good feeling, like love or curiosity, but "the encouraging sense of purpose that emanates from SEEKING arousal still makes the animal curious about its environment and sufficiently optimistic to engage."[55]

54. Ibid., 459–60.
55. Ibid., 98–99.

Let me now draw the obvious conclusion: at the rate we are going, the most debilitating of all human health concerns in another fifteen years will be depression, caused by disruption of social bonds of sufficient depth and severity to cause a continued lack of energy and motivation to try to help ourselves. I am attributing this to a great extent to the fact that we have insufficient connection with each other in ways that our bodies can recognize and incorporate to create a sense of well-being. I am saying too that, whatever the blessings and curses of social media, we are evolved to make contact with expressive faces and rhythmic bodies, not emoticons and bells. We have lost connection with our own bodies as well; while they continue to tell us what we need, we do not hear it because we are lost in thought, elaborating our stories, even though they are not often true or helpful stories.

In place of connection with each other and with our own animal natures, we have individual and collective stories that are not true and not working for our well-being; yet we fight to the death in defense of them. It stands to reason, therefore, that we need face-to-face connection with other humans, an open channel to the real motivational system that operates in our ancient brains outside our awareness, and we need a truer story. Just as lack of these is creating for us a negative synergy, enhancing them is likely to create a positive and healing synergy.

I have already referenced two items that represent a shift towards a truer story: Allan Schore's 2008 address to the American Psychological Association, "The Paradigm Shift: The Right Brain and the Relational Unconscious," and David Brooks' *New York Times* piece, "The Heart Grows Smarter." Both of these point to a truer collective story that includes the vital importance of warm social connections, and inclusion in our awareness of our own embodied intelligence that is older, deeper, and truer than our explanatory stories. Both reference scientific studies. Schore references many studies, and Brooks reflects on one significant longitudinal study, together showing where we have been wrong about ourselves and how to get right with and about ourselves. Ultimately this is the value of science, not primarily in the technologies that get us into trouble as much as they support us, but in the clarity of knowing what is true from what is false.

Descartes gave us a false story: we are not thinking things that can be unplugged from our bodies, or from each other's bodies, or from the body that is earth, mother of *Homo sapiens* and all the animals. The unplugged story is both false and massively depressing. Schore made reference not just to new knowledge about brains and behavior, but also to a paradigm shift, meaning that the basic model or framework within which questions are articulated and answers sought changes because of the inherent limitations or "anomalies" within the "normal science" or old paradigm.[56]

While Brooks does not make explicit reference to the paradigm in which the questions and their answers occur, his article is all about the frame, as he concludes: "Perhaps we could invent something called the Grant Effect, on the improvement of mass emotional intelligence over the decades. This gradual change might be one of the greatest contributors to progress and well-being that we've experienced in our lifetimes." In his address specifically directed to the changing structure of understanding the world and ourselves, Schore stated, "The field must create models that overcome Descartes' error. The fundamental unit is not mental but psychobiological, not the mind but the human organism, mind/body."[57] Rather than seeking to understand humans as things thinking about a mechanical universe, Schore's new paradigm turns our small beam of rationality back upon the knower and "into the problems of emotion, development, and communication, as well as the relationship of the mind to the body, individuals in particular circumstances, and to the social context."

There is no separate mind somehow driving a body through a mechanical universe, comparable to the way that a person drives a car on the freeway. Instead we are more like fish in a stream, inseparable from the world of other bodies, including that of the flowing water. In fact, this metaphor reminds me of a vivid memory of a thought, an impression I had many years ago after returning from some weeks on the Amazon River. I was on California's Interstate 5, a great, wide section of it known as the Grapevine, in a mountain pass that separates southern and central California. In its length and breadth spreading across the landscape, it reminded me of the Amazon. But as I looked into the cars on either side of me, the people who inhabited those cars greeted my gaze with pointed "look-aways," much as Lana had refused my air kisses at the San Diego Zoo. By way of contrast, on the Amazon, people who are a mile away in a dugout canoe routinely holler and wave; their set of assumptions is very

56. Kuhn, *Structure of Scientific Revolutions*, 5.
57. Schore, "Paradigm Shift," slide 68.

different, that we are connected by and in these bodies and the world that holds and carries them.

Our task, it seems to me, is to let the combined message of our own sickness, with its particular qualities of depression, and the factual messages of science guide us in making a new and truer story to consciously replace those that no longer can contain us, the memes and myths of smaller and more local cultures, of earlier times. But the challenge is to bring into consciousness what has been by evolutionary design left out of our awareness till now. How can we connect with those deep layers of our own body-minds, and how can we possibly cut through layers and layers of stories and storied lives to connect with each other? Dare we trust a new story to be truer or better, as Descartes so hoped his metaphysical story would be?

How We Are Always Beside Ourselves

I think of Karen Joy Fowler's novel *We Are All Completely Beside Ourselves*. Rosemary, the first person narrator and protagonist in this family drama, was raised as a twin to a chimpanzee sister, in one of those home-based psychology experiments of the 1960s and 70s. Rosemary is a human child who cannot quit talking, as of course, her chimpanzee sister Fern can never begin to talk. Rosemary's talking is what makes her special. Describing her own loquaciousness, she says: "I remember being told to be quiet, but I seldom remember what I was saying at the time. As I recount things this Lacuna may give you the erroneous impression that I already wasn't talking much. Please assume that I am talking continuously in all the scenes that follow until I tell you that I'm not."[58] My point is not to spoil the novel for you, but to say concisely that Rosemary had a talking problem from which she had to recover, and she could not find the sickness in it, nor a healing path for herself until she learned to be quiet. After a long and manic talking comes a long and sobering quiet, and then the healing begins.

We will have to go deeper than our stories, and so we must have a time and a place to un-story, to shut up in order to awaken. I know this well. When I was a little girl, my mother paid me a penny a minute to be quiet. Those were pennies my mother spent on herself, as you might well imagine, but they were likely the most precious of the many gifts she has

58. Fowler, *We Are All Completely Beside Ourselves*, 57.

given me. The parallel in this to core Buddhist teaching is pronounced: first we learn the nature of mind, and then we awaken to the no-self nature of reality, and then we speak and act from the place of liberation.

As human and animal neuroscientists have both learned, the stunning light of sentience does not belong to the cerebral cortex, much less to the story-spinning specialty of the left hemisphere, but to the humble brain stem shared by all animals. We have long thought we had left all that behind in our godlike rationality, risen above it existentially, never to be pulled back to the dirt. But our bipedal feet never left the ground, though our primal sentience was left out of our stories, causing them to be gapingly inadequate.

Let me quote from *The Cambridge Declaration on Consciousness*, the statement written by Phillip Low and edited by Jaak Panksepp and others for a conference on Consciousness in Human and Non-human Animals, at Cambridge University in 2012:

> The absence of a neocortex does not appear to preclude an organism from experiencing affective states. Convergent evidence indicates that non-human animals have the neuroanatomical, neurochemical, neurophysiological substrates of conscious states along with the capacity to exhibit intentional behaviors. Consequently the weight of evidence indicates that humans are not unique in possessing the neurological substrates that generate consciousness. Non-human animals, including all mammals and birds, and many other creatures, including octopuses, also possess these neurological substrates.[59]

Humans are, by definition, members of cultural collectives. Our ecological niche, for better and for worse, is our imagination, our ability to change the world and ourselves by creating an internal representation that is different from given realities and then living into and realizing that vision in the world. This is culture, which both creates us and is created by us. Culture gives to us as individuals a kind of collective substance in the neural structuring of our brains, and culture receives from us and is changed by us as we participate creatively in the forms of science and technologies, the arts, athletics, the rituals of political and civil life, and in religious and spiritual structures, stories, and rituals. Culture is how we got to this place of massive experimentation with the life of the entire planet by way of global warming and broad scale ecosystemic alterations.

---

59. Low, *Cambridge Declaration on Consciousness*.

Culture is how we got to this place of human overpopulation and wide scale depression, and epidemic violence. And culture is how we might find our way into a renewed and even sustainable future. But we will need to develop perspectives that allow us to see culture, as difficult to do as to observe the air we walk through, but not impossible.

This I think is where other animals can help us. They are enough like us and different enough from us that we can imagine their perspectives and their ways of being. Through such an effort we can become reacquainted with our disowned bodies, and with the material life of the planet we share. We can never escape story and invention because it is what we are, but we can make a truer story and so perhaps invent a better life for all beings than that which we are currently making. It will begin something like this: "I am not this egoic self-story but a spirited animal having an egoic experience that keeps me from understanding myself as a living member of a living world." This is both a true story and an inherently spiritual story in that it gives us a position within the totality of being, and a way to understand the basic meaningfulness of the facts.

If Rosebud had a self-story, I will never know it. That she had sentience and wisdom better than most stories, I do know. The knowledge that I have of her wisdom and of her self comes from having caused her pain by moving her broken bones, from having offered her water and seen her pleasure in discovering and tasting it, from having brought her rose petals, and more rose petals until all my rose petals were in her little deer belly, from having felt her pain in the memory of my own broken bones, from allowing myself such intensity of tears and grief, from her affirmation of the worth of all this as she ran her muzzle along my arm in primal loving connection. In knowing Rosebud I learned too about myself and about my potential to allow the moment to be specific and as it is, and not just an accoutrement to my self-story. Rosebud had the wisdom, presumably not elaborated rationally and linguistically, to let comfort come to her in unexpected ways, to assess and respond to real threats, to allow joy to delight her even in the midst of great pain. Rosebud knew to let her senses guide her, all the way to the end of her life.

CHAPTER 5

The Tune Without the Words

"Hope" is the thing with feathers—
That perches in the soul—
And sings the tune without the words—
And never stops—at all—"

—EMILY DICKINSON[1]

JUST YESTERDAY I HEARD a disabled husband say in a tone of entitlement that he wished his wife loved him as much as she loves the dog. Who can blame him for this wish? Life must be hard enough for him without witnessing someone else getting daily what he so craves, but I would also hold him accountable for the expectation that underlies his hurt, that no matter the context, he is more worthy of love than the dog. There is the simple fact that the dog gives loyalty, attention, and affection generously, and the overburdened wife needs these probably more than she ever has. Though the man's disabled status lends a particular pathos to this situation, I mention it because neither the complaint nor the source of it is unusual. People often love their pets more than their family members, and I suggest, with good reason—the pets are either more loving than the family members, or they offer their love in a manner beneath the tiresome and demanding terrain of verbal communication. So my advice to the disabled husband would be to watch the dog and seek to imitate him

---

1. Dickinson, *Complete Poems*, 116.

because there is something the dog is doing that his wife needs. I might also suggest that he get a dog himself.

The central point of this book is that there is something in the way many of the other animals live that we need but do not know how to do, and also that we have dismissed them and lost ourselves in the process, so we should turn and look at them, and learn to live in our bodies, and to love in ways not so convoluted by words. This may sound so simple as to be laughable. It is simple, and laughable in the very best sense of the word. It is an invitation to learn how to be simple in healthy ways, and how to play. Then we might indeed laugh that particular laughter that has a self-mocking and joyously relieved melody to it. "I was an idiot! But now I am a much happier idiot!"

Their Beauty, Their Reply

I have no idea how long ago it was that I saw footage of Jacques Cousteau in full diving suit, floating in front of the eye of a whale, and then the interview in which he spoke of looking into the eye of the whale, seeing and being seen, how it changed him forever. But from that day, I knew that one day I would look into the eye of a whale. I had heard that in the Baja lagoons, I would certainly see whales, and perhaps even touch one. But my secret highest hope as I packed for my Baja expedition, many years later, was that I might look into the eye of a whale, that I might experience that seeing and being seen. As far back as I can remember, I had never accepted the given wisdom that animals and humans are different by degrees of separation from God. But now, equipped with knowledge of evolutionary biology and neuroscience, I had reason to think such seeing and being seen might be what I would call soul to soul.

On our first launch into Magdalena Bay, the panga (fishing boat) captain told us to put our hands into the water and splash vigorously as this would attract whales. Monica, the former dolphin trainer, whistled her particular whale-whistle. We had been out for almost two hours and were approaching the end of our time allotment when finally, to our great excitement, a whale approached. I was at the prow, that part of the boat with the greatest distance to water, when the whale swam up and under. I dove for the side of the boat and was almost hanging by my ankles with much of my body high in the air when I got my first feel, my first kinesthetic and proprioceptive sense of a whale. A gray whale is big, and that is what I felt first. I admit that I was scared, but I reached out of the boat with all my strength: what a way to die!

Let me pause here to consider matters of scale. An adult female Pacific gray whale is roughly eight times my length and three hundred times my weight; that is, she is larger than me on a grand scale, akin to me standing next to a squirrel. Her commute is on a grand scale, too, roughly 6,500 miles one way. And the time scale of her life is vastly greater too, not in number of years but in quality of time. She never sleeps because she has to think about breathing constantly, so she is awake from birth to death, experiencing up to seventy years of continuous awareness. She eats during the summer only and not while making her long commutes, nor while birthing and nursing, so the period of time between dinner and breakfast is extraordinarily long by my standards. Her nursing allows her baby, born headfirst at about 1,500 pounds, to gain 200 pounds a day for the period of its infancy in the Baja lagoons.

There is some mystery surrounding gray whale vocalization. It is known that mothers make a sound to which baby whales respond immediately. Other than this, there are no recordings of gray whale vocalizations, but there is an assumption that this animal who is anatomically all about sound probably uses sound for communication, as do other whales. So, though her vocabulary has not been deciphered, bioacoustics studies suggest that she likely speaks in low frequency ranges that carry over many miles, maybe even hundreds of miles in the water. In almost every imaginable way, this whale and I live in almost unimaginably different magnitudes.

Roger Payne, biologist and career whale researcher, makes the observation that whales are the most confident and relaxed of animals because they are so very large. He reflects on the meaning of their size: "As the largest animal, including the biggest dinosaur, that has ever lived on earth you could afford to be gentle, to view life without fear, to play in the dark . . . and to greet the world in peace—even to view with bemused curiosity something as weird as a human scuba diver as it bubbles away, encased in all that bizarre gear. It is this sense of tranquility—of life without urgency, power without aggression—that has won my heart to whales."[2] This is seemingly so obvious, but it is utterly amazing in the way it is palpable upon meeting a whale. I have now been a whale's stuffed toy

2. Payne, *Among Whales*, 21.

and I, formidable human, will never forget the graciousness with which I was tossed about.

What I first touched, hanging from the side of the boat, was the whale's fluke as he swam under the boat. Powerful and not at all soft, he brushed my hand. I felt the thrill of contact—and it was thrilling—but I wanted more. I decided to ditch my camera and to give my everything to the experience, to let the story be recorded in my cells, in my heart's memory. That night, under black velvet sky, I could hear the whales breathing as they swam the lagoon, swimming all night and all day without sleeping, breathing in the quiet dark. I know that they rest by using one brain hemisphere at a time but I have no idea what that might feel like. Could they be dreaming and thinking at the same time? On the basis of Kevin Nelson's studies of the neuroscience of spirituality, specifically with reference to the switch in the brain that controls rapid eye movement sleep, it might well be so. If so, then whales are living in a state that is almost by definition spiritual for humans. And, speaking of conditions that are considered spiritual states for humans, the whale does not need a meditation cushion to develop the practice of conscious breathing. One thing I grasped in my depths is that whales' lives depend upon their making good decisions about breathing. Thus their breathing is necessarily conscious. And from my point of view, it was sheer delicious wonder to listen to them breathing above the quiet surf in the still of the night. That roundest of sounds comes over the water, over the dunes, riding the night breeze: "bPuwwwhhhh;wHa!" Can it be? Am I listening to whales breathing by starlight?

The next day, there were high winds and waves and many whales, accompanied by a great many dolphins, who are partial to the breast milk of the gray whale and who understandably like to be there when that milk is released into the water. The day was cold and wet and wonderful; bouncing on the tops of waves, I got my first face full of musty blow. Soon I began to whistle what became my own distinctive whale whistle, and one toddler whale appeared to like it very much. She came to the boat and I leaned over and touched the whole length of her as she positioned her swimming to make just the contact that she wanted. It is part of the wake-up to wonder to realize that, in order to have a whale encounter, the whale has to want you too.

There were eight of us adult humans going crazy with childlike delight, petting this playful baby whale, whose huge mother was calmly directing the show. By the next day, the little one came whenever I whistled. When she first arrived, she gently turned the boat around in a circle, seeming very pleased with herself. There, I was a whale's toy, but never a thing tossed about, always a being whose needs were taken into account. The whale recognized that I was an animal who was interested in her, as she was interested in me. I might mention that this is a good enough description of a soul-encounter for my purposes. When was the last time someone recognized your interest in her and returned that by being interested in you?

Over my few days in the Baja lagoons, I experienced everything I had remotely dreamed of knowing, including an encounter with a "boat-hugger," one of the whales who swims quietly up under the boat and lifts it out of the water. I had so wanted to feel that. But not everyone in the boat enjoyed it. In fact, the panga captain pulled his eyebrows down from the top of his head and tore out of there as soon as the whale set us down. Was that what the whale wanted? Was the whale sick of intrusion, wanting to feel his power, just having some playful fun? Certainly, he could easily have killed us, but his lift did not even jostle our equipment. In fact, he was the essence of gentleness, inviting us to relax, if we could relax with someone 300 times our size.

The main event for me, though, was courting the little whale, and seeing her court me in her turn. A mutual courtship is such a sweet and satisfying thing. I'd whistle and time after time, she'd come, not just to the boat, but to me. My fellow travelers gave me the name *Holds Hands with Whales* when this baby turned and seemed to offer her fin to my hand. I was so overjoyed that it took me a minute to register that she was putting her eye up top; she was looking at me! I whisked my sunglasses off my face, and looked into the eye of the whale. I did it again and again, same whale, every day. In this magical eros of one face to another, she wanted to see my essence, my soul, and had to position herself just so in order to look into my eyes, and so did I. This is what I cannot forget, and it is whale lore too. Those who have looked into the eye of the whale say that it changes you. It does. You have been pulled out of yourself, out of your story, by another self, another soul who is every bit as aware and as curious as you are, who is huge and who allows you the safety of her own size.

I put my hand into Barbilla's mouth, giving her stiff baleen screen a good rubbing, even though it meant a quick getting over my fear of her powerful jaw and huge muscular tongue. I felt a gestalt sense for her way of living, with her long jaw and her whiskers, her double blowholes, her flippers and her spinal knobs, her white chin and her mighty fluke, her ever-present need to breathe consciously, her bright and curious eyes. I began to feel how one might live in such a body, live in such a house of water and air, dolphins and stars, red dawns and black nights, and toy boats full of noisy little animals to play with.

I saw her from the shore every morning and I imagined that she was waiting for me—though this part could be my imagination, the projection of my own awakened liveliness and attachment.

On my last trip in the panga, I whistled and she came, this little whale whom people were calling Ballerina because she loved to pirouette in the water, a move that goes with nursing as mother and baby turn to make mouth-to-milk contact. Jennifer, our marine biologist, and I called her Barbilla Blanca, little White Chin, for her very distinctive chin splotch. Jennifer had told us as we climbed into the boat that morning that she had dreamed during the night of kissing whales, something she had never done. As she whistled, Barbilla went right to her and came out of the water for a kiss. Then she came to me and came out of the water again for my kiss, a full face-plant kiss, and this after days of gazing into one another's eyes.

For months after that whale kiss, I thought of Barbilla every day, holding imagined conversations with her. I remembered my own time of going out into the world on the cusp of being a toddler: how amazing it is, how engaging, how much you learn—in my day, how to tie your shoes, and tell time, and take a bus, how to memorize your phone number and address, and how to call home, and how to make friends, how to write your name, then someone else's name, how to gather seeds from flowers, and then to plant them, how not to knock the dust from a butterfly's wings, and not to take candy from strangers. My God, it's a busy time of life.

And I knew she was learning her whaley version of life intensely and in a similar developmental burst of demand as she swam onward with her mother, not in the peaceful warm lagoon of her infancy but in the Pacific Ocean for about 6,000 miles to the place where she would eat her first solid food. I wonder what the contemporary whale toddler needs to learn: a particular route? Directions? Heuristic rules for navigating the Pacific Ocean, closely paralleling the shore for thousands of miles? Problem solving? Orca escape techniques? Getting along with others? Depth gauging? Storytelling?

I knew that one day she would have to swim past Monterey, where the orcas wait with their playbook of strategies to separate mother and toddler so that they can eat the little one. And Barbilla's mother was hungry by then, not having eaten in months; she might have felt the need to take short cuts. Yes, I worried. That is the price of love, and I loved Barbilla and love her still. I cheer for her; I try to imagine her life, her joys, her challenges, her fears. Every day I pray for her, every day I encourage her, every day I am made so much larger for knowing her. On the scale of the heart, we are equals.

On my pilgrimage to encounter an animal other, soul to soul, I was again confirmed in knowing that others are souls too, just as we are souls, not floating around within our bodies, but holding ourselves together and holding the world in the knowledge of each other: every living being a piece of the whole living thing. That we all together are God's body is, I think, a true story, and a necessarily shared story, and because this is a big enough story to hold everything inside it, it is a spiritual story. But this is not to say that Barbilla and her people are just mirrors in which I might see myself better. No, it is to understand that there are many ways to be a soul, many ways to meet God, or the divine. This is an essential aspect of the true enough and good enough story: the multitude of others pull the multitude of selves into relational living. The soulfulness of being conscious of the relational nature of living at all is reflected in the poem by Homero Aridjis that speaks of the Baja whales plowing through the sea and God being seen through the eye of a whale.[3] Why would God not be seen through the eye of a whale, and through the eye of a grasshopper or the eye of a lamb?

No poetic license is needed to say that whale souls are old, older than ours by many days of creation. They are 60 million years old; we are about 150,000 years old, so we have been carrying our three-pound brains on our bipedal stems for approximately 2 percent of the time they have been swimming the oceans. Having spent a few days amongst them, it is hard to imagine that they would not be held together by the same qualities that indicate the quality called "soul" in humans.

My Questions Were My Attentive Spirit

"Mom, is Sherry going to heaven?"

3. Aridjis, *Eye of the Whale.*

Like a good little mammal, I had sidled up to my mother, who was at the sink, up to her elbows in soapsuds. I craned my neck sideways and tilted my face up to see her.

"No, Sherry can't go to heaven; when she dies she will be dead and we will bury her in the backyard."

"But, Mom, I think Sherry has a soul, I really do."

"Yes, Sherry does have a soul, but she has an animal soul; only humans have immortal souls. When Sherry dies, her soul will die too, but when we die, our souls will go to heaven."

"Why, Mom, why? What's the difference?" She rinsed dishes and put them in the drainer, and turned to look at me.

"We have rational souls, we can think, and animals can't."

My mother's answer to my question came directly from the scholastic theology of Thomas Aquinas. Have I mentioned that not only was Descartes taught false things, but we all have been taught false things, because throughout our lineage we have had to fill in the gaps of our knowledge by telling stories that seem to fit the gaps? That is what our left cerebral cortex does, make things up, and then we use language to pass those made up explanations as culture. It is not just me, nor even my mother, but her mother and René Descartes and his lineage, all of us all the way back, in this case to Thomas Aquinas.

Growing up Catholic, I knew how to apply scholastic theology before I could spell the words, and, to be honest, much of it served me well in giving me a sense of just how big was the project to which I belonged, and what my place in it was. I long ago parted ways with Roman Catholicism, even as I have abandoned a great many philosophical explanations, including the scientific reductionist one that says the unfeeling mechanical nature of the world can have no meaning but that created by the naïve to comfort themselves. While I outgrew much that I loved in the Church, I had never accepted the particular application of scholastic theology, that humans alone are dear to God because they think. This thought construction itself contained no meaningful explanation and it seemed to me, even at seven years old, to be a strikingly self-serving interpretation. Not only that, but I had spent a good deal of time with dogs, and, if any species qualifies for sainthood, I knew it was more likely dogs than humans. Even by dog standards, Sherry was good to the bone. She had another name, Lady Bright III, and was what my father called our "breeding bitch." We raised beagle puppies, and Sherry accepted me into the litters of her puppies and raised me with the kindness that was her signature trait. That is why I thought she would go to heaven, her kindness. Right now, I have to protest the notion that Thomas Aquinas is in a heaven from which Sherry, not to mention Molly Brown, is barred. Aquinas should be in heaven because he had a left-brain fabricator that these dogs lacked? I think not. (Note to Descartes: Did you hear that? I think not!) Given what we twenty-first-century beings know about animals and about humans, I think that Aquinas would come over to my side, that perhaps he would assure me that Sherry is in heaven, along with Molly Brown and his own good self. Or, I suspect, he would lead me to understand that none of them are in quite the heaven he imagined during his life. To his credit, and to the credit of Aristotle before him, Aquinas understood that listening to and interpreting natural law is a human rational activity that can go wrong. Further, mistakes in our thinking about nature need to be corrected if we are to understand God correctly. Of this he said explicitly:

> Errors made about creation will result in errors about God as well. The opinion is false of those who assert that it makes no difference to the truth of the faith what anyone holds about creatures, so long as one thinks rightly about God. For error about creatures spills over into false opinion about God and takes people's minds away from God, to whom faith seeks to lead them. For this reason scripture threatens punishment to those who err about creatures: (Psalm 28:5) "Because they have not understood the works of the Lord and the work of God's hands, you will destroy them, and not build them up." There can be no question that to study creatures is to build up one's Christian faith.[4]

Aquinas also understood that humans and animals share "instructions" under natural law, and he defined natural law as "nothing else than the rational creature's participation in the eternal law." The rational creature sees that this is the first precept of law,

> that good is to be done and gone after, and evil is to be avoided. . . . Secondly, there is in man an inclination to things more specially belonging to him, in virtue of the nature which he shares with other *animals*. In this respect those things are said to be of the natural law, which nature has taught to all animals, as the intercourse of the sexes, the education of offspring, and the like. In a third way there is in man an inclination to good according to

4. Aquinas, *Summa contra Gentiles*, ch.2, n.3.

the *rational* nature which is proper to him; as man has a natural
inclination to know the truth about God, and to live in society.[5]

Aquinas thought we could and should learn from animals in those things
that we share with them, and that we should follow our impulse towards
truth and goodness, as they do in their natures. He also understood that
we have the additional work of correcting errors in our distinctly human
rational grasp of nature, that we might more accurately perceive God
from our distinctly human perspective.

So if I had Aquinas in the room with me now, his job would be to
show me what it is about humans that causes them to be immortal and,
further, how this contrasts with the supposed mortality of other animals.
I believe he would accept the challenge to rethink his position on the
basis of today's scientific advances, but especially he would have to reconsider his whole project because of the realization that our rationality is
mostly irrational and unconscious. I would invite him to Kevin Nelson's
work in explicating the mechanisms of spiritual experience in the brain,
and especially to the way our left cerebral cortex is largely a spin doctor,
whose job is to make what verbal sense it can of fragmentary experience. Of that formerly elevated human rationality, Nelson writes: "We
need to be wary of our left hemisphere, the explainer and confabulator
in our brains. It has led us astray so many times in the past, giving us a
plethora of gods, including a mathematical god, to explain the natural
world around us. The left hemisphere has given others the reasons to explain away our spiritual essence, often with hubris. . . . It is all too willing
to look for natural and supernatural explanations."[6]

I suspect that Thomas Aquinas would both receive the truths revealed through the brain science and also argue the point that the use
of language is required of our human nature, and that we must humbly
recognize the limits of reason, seek divine guidance, and reform our
opinions accordingly. I would like to say to him that our souls are not
very rational at all, and that they are in a sense not within us but amongst
us, that we can only be soul by meeting another soul, be it the soul of a
honeybee or the soul of a whale or the soul of a theologian. I would say
to Aquinas that, when we meet soul in the world, we meet the divine, and
that, when we meet the divine, we meet something real and vast about
ourselves.

5. Aquinas, *Summa Theologiae*, 94.
6. Nelson, *Spiritual Doorway*, 85.

With regard to anything that may make human souls distinctive in comparison with other animals, the scientific news is not good for those who would hold *Homo sapiens* to be spiritually elevated above the others. But for those who would seek to find a spiritual home for humans in this world, a meaning that is profoundly spiritual in the here and now, and for those who would like to include the whole of creation in any reward system, the news is good. We are bodies amongst bodies, souls amongst souls. The evidence for this view is strong: it is essentially the same body of evidence that drove the conclusions of the Cambridge Statement on Consciousness, that we share the basic platform for consciousness with most and perhaps all other animals. However, the left hemisphere of our brains is essentially our definitive characteristic, as problematic as it is fantastic. To give our specialized brains their due, the story-making machinery of our left hemisphere gives us more than the capacity to be delusional. It gives us also the capacity to acknowledge delusion and to know that we have a tendency toward delusion, and so it gives us the capacity to awaken from delusions. This is our distinctly human existential challenge, and it makes me wonder what is the existential challenge of the elk, the moose, the wild turkey, and the bonobo?

Because of our left hemispheric verbal capacity to explore and describe the world as it is, to imagine it differently than it is (even unintentionally), and to transfer our understanding across generations and across locations, we have, for better and for worse, transformed the face of the earth. Our capacities for elaboration and imagination, combined with our technological proficiency, seem to describe what is distinct about us. Over the course of a few thousand short years, we humans have elaborated aspects of animal life into the many sciences, arts, technologies, philosophies, and religions that exist side by side, harmoniously or otherwise, on what Teilhard de Chardin used to describe as our humanized planet.[7] We have made symphonies of birdsong and, more ominously, an ethos of war from the dynamics of predator and prey.

Yet we have not come to any certain understanding of our essential nature as a species, much less of our behavioral motivations. We remain persistently stunned by our failures, to such an extent that it would be comic if it were not so tragic, the way that every technological fix seems to seed the next problem. We tend toward fragmentation within ourselves

7. Chardin, *Phenomenon of Man*, 246.

and in our networks of relationships.[8] In fact, it is correct to say that our very consciousness, which we experience as having continuity, is a weaving of fragments of experience.[9]

The realization of our ancient desire to overcome suffering and death remains elusive, despite our triumphal visions of various humanly engineered futures.[10] And in our current technological context, we are stalked by our old fear that we are likely to unleash harm with the unwitting side effects of our creativity. This is our humanity. *Homo sapiens* is still searching for the elusive *sapiens* factor by which we have imagined ourselves especially blessed. We are marvelous in creative capacity, terrible in destructive possibility. Having evolved to be creative technological generalists, we override systems of constraints within which other life forms exist; and so, rather quickly in evolutionary time, may have brought other species and ourselves to the brink of extinction.

The foundation of our being as humans is the animal life in us that is the sine qua non of our specifically human capacities, the animal life that will likely evolve on and on, with or without the human form. Our own lives as animals are the platform upon which all the wonders of culture depend: without bodies, no sentience; without limbic systems, no emotional responsiveness; without a cerebral cortex and a world of others to bring in to it, no creativity or culture. In our thinking, we have lost the connection to our own vast animal soulfulness, and we need to find a way back to it.

Kevin Nelson notes our tendency to lie to ourselves about what and who it is that we are: "In fabricating a running narrative of our emotions, thoughts, memories, and dreams, the speaking left hemisphere may be critical for creating the illusion that we are a whole self."[11] And I suggest that, illusory though our internal selves may be, we may yet do better than to indulge self-aggrandizing delusions by waking up to what we share with other animals, fundamental wakefulness or awareness of the world around us, biological connectedness by way of our social intelligence, and deep feeling that is the basis of our values.

To wake up to these realities, these facts of life, is to find that I am "we," and that others who share in this "we" know themselves and the

8. Newberg, *Principles*, 214; Benvenuti and Davenport, "New Archaic," 215–17.

9. Cf. Damasio, *Self Comes to Mind*, 180–209.

10. Cf. de Grey, *Ending Aging*.

11. Nelson, *Spiritual Doorway*, 86.

world, too, each according to their kind. I think it both likely to be true and truly liberating that we share a fundamental grasp that we are all here together and that the being here together is something bigger than the solitary "I" can grasp alone; and I say this on the basis of all that I learn in the biological and psychological sciences and also by way of my subjective experience of Barbilla, Molly Brown, and a host of other animal friends. In fact, the "alone," the belief that I am my own property to dispose of, is the core of a painful illusion.

The enlightenment philosopher David Hume was likely right when he suggested that our rationality must always be in service of our passions because emotion is the biological expression of value.[12] When Hume reflected upon this relationship between rationality and the passions, he was reversing the order of value given by early modern rationalist philosophers, like Descartes and Spinoza. Hume was suggesting that our passions communicate our values and that abstract reason should serve those values. However, his understanding of the passions was both broader and more fundamental than the images of lust and rage we tend to associate with that word. He referred to the impulse to take action in response to something; and today his understanding of the passions and their relationship to reason finds a noticeable parallel in the neural circuitry of primal affect described by Jaak Panksepp in his articulation of the fundamental affective circuits shared by all mammals.

These circuits include RAGE and LUST (words which Panksepp uses in upper case, in order to distinguish them as physical neuroarchitecture with chemical communication systems, locatable in animal brains, and not only as subjective feeling states), but the most fundamental affective circuit described by Panksepp is SEEKING, or the impulse to intentionally direct wakeful awareness to some interaction with the world. Panksepp and Biven emphasize that the SEEKING system is "the biggest and most pervasive emotional system of them all . . . the SEEKING system may have served as the platform (the preadaptation) for the evolutionary emergence of the other social-emotional systems. . . . It is also the system that has the most evidence for mediating a very special kind of positive affect—not the pleasure of sensation, but the positive invigoration, euphoric excitement, of engaging productively with the world."[13] Indeed,

12. Hume, *Treatise on Human Nature*, 2.3.3.4.
13. Panksepp and Biven, *Archaeology of Mind*, 399–400.

it is this big and pervasive affective seeking system in the brain that is disabled in depression.

The other four affective circuits found in the primitive (that is, shared with other animals) brain stem and limbic structures, in Panksepp and Biven's telling, are SADNESS/GRIEF, CARE, PLAY, and FEAR. These are fundamental affective motivations for responding to the world, each having distinctive circuitry and chemistry, and they provide implicit punishment and reward in the subjective experience that their chemistry creates in the conscious animal. FEAR, for example, is terribly uncomfortable and creates the desire to flee, and so it punishes contact with the object of fear. By way of contrast, PLAY offers delight, and creates the desire to engage the objects of play repeatedly. LUST is almost absolutely compelling and the intrinsic rewards of sexual pleasure encourage repeat performance, and so also the coming of future generations. These passions stand in notable contrast to Descartes's high valuation of pure bloodless abstraction, yet are seemingly the source of earthly soul.

Panksepp's career of discovering the shared motivational life of animals points toward a foundation for understanding the nature of soul, that ephemeral quality that causes animals to engage intentionally with each other and with the world around them. It is one of the lines of investigation that leads me to conjecture about a description of soul for the twenty-first century. In their chapter "Toward a Neurobiology of the Soul," Panksepp and Biven suggest that the term *self* (which they characterize as Simple Ego-type Life Form) as a universal brain/mind function might be, in effect, our animalian soul.[14] The word *soul* described in this sense can be applied equally to humans and to other animals: a self that is neurally orchestrated from a combination of motor predispositions to act, primal affective states, sensory awareness of the world, and internal map of one's own body.[15] Indeed, that is Panksepp's intention in referring to this SELF as nomothetic and as neurobiologically based.

While recognizing the broadly described self, or animalian soul, as universal in animal life, Panksepp and Northoff recognize that there is also an ideographic self that is unique in each instance. The ideographic self "emerges during each life span through the unique experiential landscape of each person and each animal."[16] It necessarily varies both

14. Ibid., 390.

15. Ibid., 393.

16. Panksepp and Northoff, "The trans-species core SELF," 193.

by species and by individual because it is created and maintained in the specific adaptations of each species as these adaptations are reflected in neocortical specializations of the species as a whole, and formed by the particular life experience of each individual animal.

To illustrate this abstract notion, consider again that whales do not sleep as we humans do, but by alternating the wakefulness of their brain hemispheres. We, whose left and right hemispheres make up different minds while awake, turn both of our waking minds into another kind of mind when we switch over to rapid eye movement (REM) consciousness during sleep. We are physically paralyzed while in REM, vulnerable as we lie unaware, and our dreaming consciousness has seemingly little to do with the world of our waking consciousness. These differences mean that we simply have no idea how the whales' alternate hemispheric rest behavior translates in terms of the subjective experience of wakefulness, dreaming, and resting. The beauty is that we can wonder, that we can be pulled out of the confines of our individual and collective self-story by the other, who is very other. If we could objectively measure and "grasp" the reality of the other, that other would not have the power to awaken us that he or she does have. As the continental philosophers have long noted, to awaken at all is to awaken *to* something, to the other.

David Goodman and Mark Freeman note, in a volume on "Psychology and the Other," that: "Others 'call us out' of ourselves, and in so doing they frequently bring us back to what is most fundamental in our relation to the world, our sense of responsiveness and responsibility. In this respect, we find the idea of the Other a vitally important vehicle for thinking anew about the human condition."[17] Pointing to the necessity of the other in lived human lives, as contrasted with psychological theories that are focused on self and self processes, Freeman describes the suffering that leads people to seek psychotherapy not so much as breakdown in the self as disconnections with the world. He says in a related essay: "the self is exactly that which they cannot get out of, and as a result they can derive no sustenance from the world, no nourishment. . . . The restoration of the self, I suggest, is ultimately a function of the restoration of the world."[18]

The reconnecting with the world that seems to be called for (and that certainly resonates with the idea of an impaired SEEKING system) is especially challenging for us humans because of our self-referential

17. Goodman and Freeman, "Psychology and the Other," 193.
18. Freeman, "Thinking and Being Otherwise," 199.

symbol systems, those words and stories and images of me and mine that occupy our mental space, keeping us from noticing the world beyond our imaginal constructs. "This challenge, one might add, has been made that much more acute in our time: put together the culture of narcissism with the age of technologically driven distraction, inattention, and you have a near-unbeatable combination."[19] It is because of this particular cast to the problem of being trapped in ourselves and disconnected from the world that I believe that other animals can and do help us. There is a natural eros of attraction and attachment that is body to body and face to face, beneath the words and symbolic images, and rather than fear the "lustful" suggestions in the word *eros*, we should engage being drawn out of our heads and into the heart of our bodies, towards the other. If we do not, we starve our own moral sensibilities that are by evolutionary design composed in part of a variety of attractions.

Whatever the differences amongst animals at the level of neocortex and subjective experience of life, animals likely share a sense of agency and ownership in relation to their lives. Panksepp and Biven describe this sense of ownership as one that "might allow people and animals to feel that they somehow belong to their world—that they are affectively embedded in the context of their lives."[20] It is a short inferential hop to claim that we are affectively embedded in each other's lives, and in life writ large. What more could we ask of a natural description of animal soul?

The feeling of belonging, of being responsive and responsible is important to living; it is not a mere illusion produced by mechanical gears but an interpenetrating organismic event. This is to say that from a scientific and objective point of view, life on earth is a genuinely shared experience and outside of that, it is nothing. I am inclined to think of soul as the experience of awakened awareness that knows that "I belong to life itself, as do these others." This is the essence of a spiritual life, and it is the "within which" that we humans so need to grasp in order to understand ourselves, in order to want to live. For us, this knowledge is expressed in words, but we can know it without words, too, as do the other animals: a knowing expressed in Sherri Rose-Walker's poem "Wild Healing."

> The wolf is at the door.
> Her wild breathing seeps through the cracks,
> ruffling my hair, her claws catch my skirt.

19. Ibid., 203.
20. Panksepp and Biven, *Archaeology of Mind*, 419.

Like moonlight her golden eyes search my face,
dissolving through my skin to my racing heart.
I open the door.
Her fur rises at the sight of me; she softly growls.
My slight fur rises also, but my jaws unclench
as I reach out timidly to touch her.
Howling, she springs away into distance.
My body, as if seeing her true mother at last,
runs after, dragging me with her.
Ears pricked, the wolf stops in a clearing;
she is waiting.
She growls; suddenly, I growl too; she howls;
suddenly, I too am howling:
anguish, loneliness, rage, then
pure, clean fire of wildness.
Following the light of her golden eyes,
I lope into the night forest.[21]

A Whole Perspective for Living in a Whole World

Scientific knowledge about the world, what it is and how it operates, is a fantastic realization of human cognitive potential. It has the particular beauty and honor of being self-correcting by design. As our brief visit to the human cerebral cortex left hemisphere has shown, we need systems for self-correction in our thinking. But knowing about the world, even about the human body and mind as part of the world, is insufficient for living because we do not exist somewhere outside of the rest of reality, somehow looking down or into it, but we are in the very middle of it. We need to know our place and we need to how to navigate within the space and time and relational context of life. This is the essence of spirituality.

I repeat for emphasis: a spiritual orientation is necessary for human living because we need to know not just *about* life, but about how to live. And I am convinced that the best place to look for the spirituality we need for living is right here, now, among the living. We do not need to search outside this material universe to find God or meaning or morality: in fact, these things cannot be found anywhere else but where we

21. Rose-Walker, "Wild Healing."

are, in the middle of it all. The idea that we know anything with some hypothetical God's-eye view is not only incorrect but terribly and painfully misleading.

Can you call to mind the image of the Milky Way with the arrow that says, "You are here"? It is beautiful and inspiring in one sense; it might make our problems seem small, but it is overwhelming and incomprehensible too, and it makes us seem infinitesimally small. It does not know our faces, and we mammals are made for knowing faces. This "somewhere outside of life" point of view makes it hard to engage our animal SEEKING gears, the something within us that energizes us to live each day.

Now picture yourself in that "here" spot on the galactic image, where you are, and ask "But what do I do?" Here in our bodies, we find knowledge of others, body to body and face to face, and together we must learn what to do as our SEEKING systems energize us. This is coming home to our bodies, to our families, to the face of the earth in proportions our bodies know. It is admitting the obvious to say that Monsieur Grat is a dog-person as Monsieur Descartes is a human-person. It is living from the middle of the mess and not from some imagined purity of perspective.

Biological life has two gears for motivating behavior, a selfing gear, and an othering gear. Morality follows from fundamental animal capacity for knowing that we are living members of a living world. It is to be found in the tension between preserving our own lives while cooperating with others, and somehow knowing too the life of the whole within which both they and we have our existence. Of course, this sets the stage for conflict; else there would be no need for morality.

The selfish side of biological life has been well understood, from Aristotle's formulation of natural law, with self-interest at its motivational heart, to Dawkins's selfish genes driving every living thing to do what they want (even though there is no "they" and no intention at that level). But there is another side of biological life, as real as the self and its interests in staying alive, and this other side may be called the Other. Animals, including *Homo sapiens*, are "wired" to know the other and to care about the other, as surely as we are wired to feel ourselves and be motivated by self interest (I am not using the tired expression "hard-wired," because the world, and especially the living members of it, are so much less mechanical than the reductionists expected them to be).

The other is the one who calls us out of our limited perceptions and self-interests into a bigger world; the other is our feast, as we are feast for the other; the other is also our competitor in getting to the feast and our companion at the feast; and yes, the other can also be our self-object, as we incorporate our sense of its otherness into our sense of our own self-ness. Abstract as this sounds, it translates readily enough into practical form: from birth I am dependent on others not just to meet my needs but also to create my very self, and so I am not merely invited but compelled to incorporate the other into my self. As I grow, I need energy to live, fundamentally the energy of food. Sometimes this is meat, and when meat is my food, I am eating the other directly, knowing too that the other could eat me directly. But we also give and take energy from other lives in myriad ways, as time and money, as physical energy and attention.

Sometimes we have to compete with others around us to get enough energy to keep going, or to harness more energy to hoard for an imagined future, or even to give away, to redistribute. Sometimes we cooperate, joining ourselves with others to get a group portion of energy to share amongst ourselves. And sometimes we give of what we have to energize another life or another group of lives. Our giving is often with the expectation of some direct or indirect return on our investment, but not always. And, even when the gift has strings attached, it supports mutuality of being and reflects the relational nature of life. Giving, receiving, competing, cooperating, these are the activities of membership in life. A spiritual perspective gives us the best motivational stance, a good attitude, and perhaps some skill in knowing when to engage which of these activities.

All mammals and most vertebrates seek interaction with others. There are multiple systems in mammalian bodies for experiencing the other, and few of them require thinking in any abstract way. Rather, knowledge of the other is direct and physical whether by way of mirror neurons, subtle muscle mimicry, or hormones stimulated by one body in another. What is communicated in these direct biological ways is much more certain than the term *theory of mind* would suggest. An animal does not need to be able to consider in the abstract what the other is thinking or planning when he can know directly what an animal other is feeling in the very moment. If animals were running the experiments on humans, they might well ask the questions, "are they aware?" and, "do they notice?"

In her book *Braintrust*, Patricia Churchland explores the biological basis of morality, giving particular attention to the many biological mechanisms that support and direct our social intelligence. It is now understood that the biological mechanisms for knowing the other are many and they are not composed of abstract reflections upon sensory information about the other, as Descartes and many others would have it, but are biological systems, formed in each individual by life experience. Among these are the attachment system of the bonding of parent and child, thought to be the foundation for all social intelligence, but also the already noted neural processes of mirror neurons and subtle muscle mimicry which causes the subjective experience of empathy, which Churchland encapsulates as "simulating, in my brain, your sad facial expression."[22] The notion that I have to form my face in a likeness of yours in order to understand your feeling state may seem odd and excessive, yet it is one of the many biological processes of social intelligence about which we are mostly unconscious.

Churchland summarizes information on mimicry as part of the moral intelligence system: "Psychological studies on unconscious mimicry in humans show that posture, mannerisms, voice contours, and words of one subject are unknowingly mimicked by the other. Such mimicry most people do regularly as part of normal social interactions."[23] Indeed, it is now widely accepted that intelligence in social species is largely a matter of social intelligence. The skill of negotiating, in shifting circumstances, how to get along with others while successfully competing at the same time—knowing not just what to eat and where to find it, but whom to trust and whom to avoid, who will make a good collaborator and who will run off with the reward—has likely driven the evolution of mammalian intelligence. Because this is an accepted principle, a biologist may legitimately infer from the presence of a big brain that it is embedded in a big social world. Those who study the evolution of cetacean brains illustrate this in saying that the large brains of cetaceans are "examples of convergent evolution of function largely in response, it appears, to similar social demands."[24] In other words, even when environments make radically different kinds of demands and require radically different sensory systems, it is complex social life that drives the evolution of intelligence.

22. Churchland, *Braintrust*, 148.
23. Ibid., 156.
24. Marino et al., "Complex Brains," 971.

The attachment system works largely via the effects of the hormone oxytocin in all mammals, not just humans, giving to the little one a sense of self and other and a trust in belonging with its kind, and to the parent it provides pleasure enough to continue caring for little ones; and we recall the importance of human infant attachment, and of the same for elephants. It is easy to imagine that because they are large bodied and big-brained and highly social, they are like us. And of course they are, but so are rats.

Maternal care in rats has been shown to alter expression of genes that regulate behavior and hormonal responses to stress, as well as to have effects on brain development. Maternal care in rats also appears specifically to alter the expression of the gene for oxytocin receptors and so demonstrates that even in rats social experience creates intergenerational effects.[25] Not surprisingly, when stressors are imposed on mother rats, the lower quality of maternal care increases stress reactivity in the next generation. As with rats and elephants, so with the six billion humans, a great percentage of whom are depressed. Depressed mothers cannot give optimal care to infants, and the negative effects roll out for generations.

Knowing that all mammals share the bond between infant and mother, biologically driven by the hormone oxytocin, we understand this chemical link to be the basis for the primary affect of care.[26] Because care is most fundamentally care for one's own offspring, extended to kin, and then out in ever widening circles, it is understood to be an evolutionary development that supports the passing on of genes in the selfish gene mechanism as articulated by Richard Dawkins. At the level of offspring this is obvious: I care for my child because he carries my genes forward. At the level of kin, it still makes simple mechanical and mathematical gene-sense: they share some of my genetic endowment, so if I support them, I advance the cause of my own genes.

However, it is quite a stretch to infer that this simple genetic mechanism fully accounts for the complexity of social intelligence and moral responsiveness known to exist in the animal world. My intention here is not to challenge the selfish gene principle that drives biological evolution, but to make the case that the many levels and permutations of subjective experience arising from it cannot be reduced to it. As I have already noted, even Dawkins recognized, discussing his concept of memes as

25. Meaney, "Stress Reactivity Across Generations."
26. Churchland, *Braintrust*, 31.

cultural replicators, that once psychological experience comes into being, it brings with it specifically psychological kinds of motivation.[27] While recognizing the power of psychological experience, he sees it as mechanically parallel to genetic behavior: "Just as we have found it convenient to think of genes as active agents, working purposefully for their own survival, perhaps it might be convenient to think of memes in the same way. In neither case must we get mystical about it."[28]

It is at this last sentence that I part ways with Dawkins. The world does indeed seem to work on a few mechanical principles, but the human work of knowledge is not complete until it describes for us both something about reality and also something about our place in that reality.[29] This finding our place within reality is the essence of mystical knowing, and it is essential to the survival of animals, who have evolved complex self-other systems in their very bodies. If "getting mystical" means looking for special supernatural interventions in natural processes, then indeed we must not get mystical. But if the feeling of belonging within the world, of being responsive to it and even responsible for it, is experienced as meaningful, then let mysticism unfurl its glory and abstract thinking take a place in the back seat as we do the urgent work of reconnecting our thinking thing selves to a feeling world.

Because we are humans, we need both clear thinking and deep feeling, but the world turns, it seems, on feeling more than on thinking, and we have lost our way at this very juncture, being so mesmerized by our left brain spin doctor that we cannot hear the right brain's affective messages, so necessary for survival. The need to take social intelligence and all that it implies into account has driven a revolution towards reconsideration of the importance of affect, as evidenced in the work of so many affective and social neuroscientists. This taking into account of affect and social bonds has had such impact on the biological and psychological sciences that Allan Schore refers to it as a paradigm shift, moving "from explicit, analytical, conscious, verbal, rational left hemisphere to implicit, synthetic, integrative, unconscious, nonverbal, bodily-based emotional right hemisphere."[30] Another way to describe it would be to say that, in order to understand ourselves as humans, we need to take into account

27. Dawkins, *Selfish Gene*, 193.
28. Ibid., 196.
29. Benvenuti and Davenport, "New Archaic," 219–24.
30. Schore, "Paradigm Shift," slide 4.

the greater part of ourselves, the part we share with all mammals: the very parts cast off by Descartes. As Thomas Kuhn would say of a paradigm shift, we were running into walls because the concepts and constructs we were using as a framework to understand human behavior were not adequate to the task. The study of the biology and neuroscience of social connections and affects has revolutionized the fields of psychology and biology by making them inseparable, as they actually are in the living world.

Not only are mammals wired for connection to each other, but biological scientists recognize among both animals and humans a compassionate instinct.[31] Some of the studies are old, and the fact that there are few from the intervening decades points to the paradigm in which scientists were working, a mechanistic paradigm in which emotions were considered unmeasurable and therefore unsuitable to study. In a 1964 study of rhesus monkeys, for example, monkeys were found to refuse food if they knew that their use of the lever by which food was gotten would also lead to electric shock to another monkey. One monkey in the study went without food for twelve days, starving itself rather than cause electric shock to another monkey.[32]

More recently, a series of experiments by neuroscientists at the University of Chicago demonstrated empathy and prosocial behavior in rats. Rats were paired, with one in a free condition and one held in a restrainer. The free rats quickly learned how to open the restrainers and soon routinely and consistently freed restrained rats, even when given the alternative choice of a chocolate treat. "When liberating a cagemate was pitted against chocolate contained within a second restrainer, rats opened both restrainers and typically shared the chocolate."[33] A host of studies reveal that mammals, from infant humans to chimpanzees to rats, routinely engage in prosocial behavior, even at a cost to themselves, such as having to overcome an obstacle or go without food, and that they seem to do so because it is pleasurable.[34]

The fact that prosocial behavior feels good is an indicator that it is part of that internal neurally regulated punishment and reward system to which I have referred, and this is an indicator that prosocial behavior has evolved because it works to promote survival. The fact that prosocial

31. Seppala, "The Compassionate Mind," citing a phrase used by Dacher Keltner.
32. Wechkin et al., "Shock to a Conspecific."
33. Bartal et al., "Empathy and Prosocial Behavior in Rats," 1427.
34. Seppala, "The Compassionate Mind."

behavior has evolved broadly in mammals leads once again to the notion of evolutionary continuity. Marc Bekoff and Jessica Pierce, in their book *Wild Justice,* refer to both the principle of evolutionary continuity and numerous studies to make the case that animals are moral beings: "We argue that animals feel empathy for each other, treat one another fairly, cooperate towards common goals, and help each other out of trouble. We argue, in short, that animals have morality."[35]

Also addressing directly the question of animal morality, Patricia Churchland says "because there are common underlying motifs and mechanisms in the behavior of social mammals in general, the question of whether nonhumans have moral values is anything but straightforward."[36] She further suggests that "it may be most useful to shelve the assumption that there are exactly two kinds of morality: human and animal. The problem with the assumption is that each social species appears to be unique in various respects, even while having features in common."[37] Finally responding to the classic argument that morality requires rationality and that only humans are truly rational, Churchland states, "Because many species of mammals and birds display good examples of problem solving and planning, this claim about rationality looks narrow and under-informed." Conceding that only humans are likely to have *human* morality, she concludes, "One might as well note that only marmosets have *marmoset* morality, and so on down the line."[38]

While the research on empathy, compassion, attachment, and social intelligence has bearing on questions of morality, and puts moral concern into a solid biological framework, questions of spiritual experience are distinctly different because they are questions about the subjective experience of that which we call spiritual. Kevin Nelson addresses matters of human spiritual experience from a multidisciplinary perspective and concludes: "Odd as it may seem, we have shown that primal brainstem reactions seem to be at the root of the experiences that we think of as spiritual and that make us most human. . . . Given that we share many of the structures and systems in our brains with other creatures, we may not be the only primate with spiritual feelings. . . . In fact, I strongly suspect

35. Bekoff and Pierce, *Wild Justice*, 1.
36. Churchland, *Braintrust*, 23.
37. Ibid., 24.
38. Ibid., 26.

that mystical feelings could exist in the many other mammals that are endowed with a limbic system that is very much like our own."[39]

Jane Goodall has long suggested that the chimpanzee waterfall dance likely reflects spiritual experience. She describes the ritualized behavior of a chimp approaching a waterfall: "As he gets closer, and the roar of the falling water gets louder, his pace quickens, his hair becomes fully erect, and upon reaching the stream he may perform a magnificent display close to the foot of the falls. Standing upright, he sways rhythmically from foot to foot, stamping in the shallow, rushing water, picking up and hurling great rocks. Sometimes he climbs up the slender vines that hang down from the trees high above and swings out into the spray of the falling water. This 'waterfall dance' may last ten or fifteen minutes."[40] It is reported that chimpanzees may sit in a trance, gazing at the water, at the completion of the dance. This behavior seems to me not so far from some human spiritual practices, such as the animal dances of Native American powwows, and Sufi whirling dervishes. An even more ancient human use of dance as spiritual technology is described by Bradford Keeney in *The Bushman Way of Tracking God*, in which he describes the spiritual practice of trance dancing used by the Kalahari bushmen, a group of humans living in the same place and the same way that they have lived for 60,000 years.[41]

I myself recall sitting at sunset on the shore of a small tarn lake in the Yosemite high country, watching in fascination as a squirrel moved with great purpose from one pink flower to the next, eating the blossoms of only the pink flowers and standing periodically to look at the fading sun. It could well be that those pink flowers have some particularly attractive chemical compound, perhaps even medicinal, but the whole scene was so reminiscent of a humanly meaningful ritual. Who can say? What I can say with confidence is that the furry little Other pulled me out of myself in a way that is still meaningful for me as I recall her movements these many years later.

Heading for Home

I began this chapter with a personal account, rooted consciously in feeling, about my encounter with a whale, whose soul my soul recognized. I

39. Nelson, *Spiritual Doorway*, 258.

40. Goodall, *Primate Spirituality*.

41. Keeney, *Bushman Way of Tracking God*.

have shared that I have never accepted what seemed to me a self-serving bias in the elevation of human souls above all others. I have reviewed the science that provides factual and biological ways to think about soulfulness and morality in both humans and other animals. Now it is time to connect the dots. I have gone to this trouble because I think that the relationship of humans to other animals is changing and needs to change.

We, who have prided ourselves on our rationality and morality, reputedly so much greater than that of other species, routinely behave towards other animals in ways that would sicken us if we could feel ourselves. We are creative elaborators and story makers, and our imaginations and creativity have been used to justify and to elaborate methods of using others that do not take them into account as God's other children or as fellow beings, our own kin. In their otherness to us, we have cast them as dangerous and inferior, as competitors and as resources. Indeed we do this so deeply and routinely that is customary across human cultures to ascribe animal names to reprehensible human behavior: women who do not do what we want are bitches, greedy people are pigs, scoundrels are dogs, cheaters are snakes in the grass, those whom we wish to "cleanse" from the face of the earth are vermin. This verbal habit shows the depths of our negative imaginal othering of all animals. However, these others are also collaborators and companions; they always have been, and it is time to tell this side of the story.

I have been told all my life not to approach a strange animal, that animals are dangerous, especially wild animals. I have been told particularly that they are afraid of us and if we approach them they will react defensively and hurt us. Of course, it is possible in any instance that this would be true, depending on the given animal's history, but what I have learned is that wild animals want to know what we are feeling. If a human is afraid, they know he is dangerous. In other words, what I was taught is essentially a projection of our human fear and aggression onto wild animals.

More typically, approaching a wild animal with respectful curiosity elicits that animal's curiosity, and the conversation begins. So now I approach wild animals regularly and with greater confidence. I have looked many kinds of being in the eye, held many kinds of fur and feather and scales in my hands. This level of conversation, the level that happens beyond words, is what I think we need. Like Rosemary, the chimpanzee's sister, we need to learn what happens when we shut up, and then perhaps we can speak again from a truer place, to be ourselves *human beyond words*.

In their book on the necessity of human social connection, John Cacioppo and William Patrick say pointedly that people need people and that animals are poor substitutes: "One of the lessons of Hurricane Katrina was that pet owners were so committed to their pets that they were willing to risk their lives to remain in the city to care for their animals. Was it the sense of being left alone with the elements—in a sense, rejected by those who fled the storm—that made their attachment so strong? Studies show that rejection by other humans can increase the tendency to anthropomorphize one's pet. Perhaps many of these economically deprived people had felt rejected all along."[42] They then cite the passage of the Pets Evacuation and Transportation Standards Act, a bill that requires inclusion of animal companions in evacuation and disaster plans so that the humans who will not leave them can be saved.

Persisting in the modern humanist perspective, Cacioppo and Patrick go on to devalue other kinds of non-human encounters and relations, saying for example of monks and nuns that they "apply the intensifying effect of isolation when they remove themselves from other humans in order to 'feel the presence of God' more powerfully. Again, the feeling of isolation promotes not only the drive to connect, but the intensity of anthropomorphism."[43] I would say that there is anthropomorphism in their intellectual approach, the one that values only humans existentially. But ironically, assessing how social media performs to meet our social needs, they write in the next paragraph: "Studies have shown that the richer the medium—the more physicality it has—the more it fosters social cohesion." I might suggest they get a dog, or find another way to spend some time with other animals getting a real sense of physicality and social cohesion, the kind that lives strongly underneath mere words. To do so, I think, helps us to form again satisfying connections with each other, connections not lost in words.

Love Dogs

Molly Brown, that little brown and white Jack Russell terrier whom I met on her first day of life and whom I held on the day of her death, was my constant friend and teacher. In the weeks after her death, I clung to the idea that she would be reincarnated, soon and recognizably. I knew that

42. Cacioppo and Patrick, *Loneliness*, 257.
43. Ibid., 259.

such a thought is selfish if not silly, but I also learned in those weeks that there are worse dispositions than that of going through daily life asking of every living thing, "Are you my beloved? Are you my beloved?"

The most important, immediate, and shocking thing I learned when I met baby Molly was that I had a heart. At first and for several years, I thought this opening of my ossified heart was significant because Molly created a path to my heart for other humans. Soon after Molly arrived, I entered into a long and happy relationship, and I acknowledged her, calling her "Molly, the Baptist" because she prepared my heart for human habitation. When that relationship ended, many years later, it was Molly who comforted me, Molly who never left my side. Over the almost fifteen years in her company, I learned that the love of Anne and Molly is a real love; something of its own, and that my engaged heart supplies the pulse connecting me to the rhythms of everything; yes, everything. A fifteen pound dog with star-deep eyes had opened me to the universe, through my heart.

Let me say this clearly: Molly loved me. And being loved so intensely by Molly Brown simply compelled me to love her with equal fervor and, in that need to love her back, I had to learn to listen to her, to know who she was and what she needed from me. I had to learn about being a dog. Listening to Molly opened the entire non-human world to my awareness. Over the course of her life, that love completely transformed me into the whole person I once had been, related to a whole world. I stopped calling the world "it," and started seeing this one and this one and this one, each one as itself, I began to call each by name again.

Molly Brown was the doorway through which I walked from the mundane into the magical, out of the world and into the World. From Molly I learned that my thoughts about the world are not the world, that the world is real and out there, filtered for me through my thoughts, yes; but immediately available, direct, gazing, speaking, and dancing through my senses into my open heart. Perhaps the grandest thing I learned from Molly Brown slowly and over many years is that we cannot be human without the guidance and support of the non-human world, not merely as crass commodity for our consumption, as we are taught to see "it," but as companion, as friend, as teacher, as parent. Mother earth, indeed. Father sky. Grandfather and grandmother stars, not figuratively, but literally, all speaking to us continuously in the language of the body.

From practicing with Molly, I gained confidence to imitate the behavior of different creatures I came upon, to move as they moved, to make sounds like theirs, and to wait for their responses. I cawed at the crows and I still do. I cheeped with the squirrels. After a long courtship, I lay on the beach and hugged a wild elephant seal. I have observed, interpreted, imitated. And I have learned to respond to correction or initiation when I receive it. Crows for example will participate in your nonsense by repeating back to you the same number of caws that you make, then creating variations in number, pitch, and timbre. The conversations can become long and complex; the neighbors may grow weary. As for Molly, she got to the point where she dashed out, yapping her jealousy whenever she heard me start to say, "Oh sweetheart . . . mew, bark, caw, cheep, peep."

As I began to develop real and accurate empathy (you can tell that it is accurate when the other hops up and down saying, "Yes! Yes! That's it!" across species boundaries), I thought I saw other creatures doing so too. I recall the autumn day hiking in the high Sierra Mountains, alert for wildlife, trying not to crackle a leaf or break a twig, when I came upon a lone doe and saw that she was watching me with seemingly equal curiosity and interest. I suddenly understood the mutuality of being in the world; it is not just a setting for my life to play out. It is not a stage at all, but an elaborate choreography of relationships, a dance. And I recall, too, the stories I have heard of whales coming up to watch the people who are watching them. I, having apprenticed with Molly, graduated to other animals, but I have not yet stopped extending the lesson outward, deepening the lesson inward. I am learning that I can converse with the world, with the sun on my skin and the breezes in my face; yes, the dirt beneath my feet. They are all speaking, and it is all there for the receiving.

One quiet morning it was a bat. I had set out early for a trail walk, hoping to get some exercise for me and for the dogs and some mental focus before the day heated up. I had planned to write about having learned from Molly to love the non-human world. As I started out on the trail, I calmed my mind, stilled my thoughts and asked all the beings there to help me to stay awake and not drift into the lulling and dulling chatter of thoughts. After a few minutes of watching the woodpeckers and the cottontails, the rocks and the ragged cianothus and sage, I noticed a dead blossom lying in the middle of the trail. As I bent to look at it, I saw its fine and fragile wing-like structure. I picked it up and turned it over, still not knowing what it was. Then face-up in my hand, I could see that it was a dead bat. I observed that his little mouth was open, tongue out, and the tiny fragile fingers of both hands were clutching his throat. I thought he may have died of some poison, or gagged on contentious catch. I probably never would have picked up a dead bat intentionally, having heard terrible tales of bat-contamination. I carried the little corpse over and set it on a noteworthy rock, hoping that I would find it there for further study upon my return. As I turned to go, a wing fell open, or did he move it? I returned to investigate.

I understood then that he might have been one of the many flying creatures who have some kind of problem midflight that causes them to crash land, resulting in shock and dehydration, on top of any injury or illness. They frequently need water and safety more than any special care. I have learned that a lot of animals die just so of shock and dehydration, and I have also learned that they understand your intent in relation to them very quickly. I assured him in that soft hypnotic voice that creatures love that my intent was to do no harm and to do what good I might. I lifted him gently and watched him unfold and open entirely; beautiful wings made of a fine frame of bone and joint covered with translucent fabric that wrapped his body, webbing the entire back of his torso in an enclosure of fabric. I didn't have my glasses, and, at this point was interested to know if he had teeth. I peered at him closely and saw the soft petals of his pointed ears, but I never did ascertain the presence of teeth, in spite of his open mouth. His furry belly fluttered with uneven breath as his arm bent at the elbow and he reached for his mouth again. Then my mind's ear heard clearly the words, "I thirst." Ah, that. I do not know how to care for a bat and I know precious little about them, but I do know thirst. I decided I would carry him to the creek with me and see about arranging something between him and the moisture he so desperately craved.

I studied him as I walked, awed by the intricate beauty and the fragile toughness of him. He had tiny glass beads of eyes. Had I not heard that bats had no capacity to see? It was hard to tell exactly without my reading glasses. His body was about an inch and a half long with fine pointed little ears at the top and a webbed tail that he used to completely pull up the blanket of his fabric and enclose himself. His wings were about six inches in span, huge by comparison to his soft little body, graceful as a geisha's fan in their folding and unfolding. His arms were just like mine, bending at the elbow, with hands and fingers just like mine, except for the size, about an eighth of an inch. Again he brought his hand to his dry tongue. Do you doubt for a moment that he spoke to me about his thirst?

I set him down in the moist sand about two inches from the place where the water lapped the shore and I let my fingers dribble water down in front of him. He drank it; he gulped water down. Then he rested, then drank more, and more. Rested, more water. With no warning, he unfurled his wings, fanned out into the water as if he had a gentle breeze in his sails, and swam away from me. Have you ever seen a bat swim? Have you ever even seen a picture of a bat swimming? Oh glorious and graceful sight, oh human delight! He hauled himself with infinite grace onto the underside of a rock. I watched. He climbed, revived by mere water, climbed up under the rock and then over it and then up again. My work was done. On the definite underside of a rock, wedged well against other rocks, he hung upside down, asleep. So this is the dreaded bat.

Love one little thing and you love the entire universe that holds it, as well as the essence from which it pours forth, and the pulse that beats in it, and the breath that heaves it, and the awareness that connects it. Save one little thing and you save your soul entire.

That tiny desperate thirst is indeed your own, and you are quenched beyond measure, awakened in the water, merely for being there, responsive. This is what I learned from Molly Brown slowly over the many years of her patient instruction, that words hinder the communications of the heart, acting often as stoppers to the ears of empathy, which would otherwise hear every pulsing breathing body.

God speaks to us "secretly and in silence," said John of the Cross.[44] Perhaps the language of God is silence because only in silence can I deeply listen; and God is not shallow. The whole world is here, waiting to be heard, but I am too busy producing private words and thoughts to listen to it. I am so lulled by my word-making that I don't even know I am doing it most of the time. In silence, words are reborn and they become something expressive, something worthy of care. In silence, we learn love. You do not need information about bats to know a dry tongue and a hand reaching for a parched throat, but you are unlikely to see that reaching hand unless you are still inside.

Surprise! The whole world is a message under the words. What I learned by way of Molly Brown—she who would be understood and not just condescended to—is that the whole world is there, waiting to be known, interested in me, as I am interested in it, that we, multitudinous and embodied, are also inseparable and in Love.

---

44. John of the Cross, *Dark Night of the Soul*, 79.

CHAPTER 6

Spirit Unleashed: Becoming *Homo Sapiens*

For thousands of years, mankind considered itself the pinnacle of
life's creation on a planet sitting in the center of the universe. Science changed that perception.

—NEIL SHUBIN[1]

First there is the fall, and then we recover from the fall.
Both are the mercy of God.

—JULIAN OF NORWICH[2]

Homo sapiens

WE NAMED OURSELVES *HOMO* sapiens, but there is not a great deal of
evidence that we are wiser than the others. I wonder what they name
themselves? And I wonder whether we will ever grow into our name.
Though some of us seem to become *sapiens* individually, it is almost un-
imaginable to envision what it would take for us to get there collectively.
I do not think we can do it without the help of other animals, but we have
to want their help. I maintain that this is no private fantasy, but an idea
shared by many who have experienced transformation in the company
of animals.

1. Shubin, *Universe Within*, 24.
2. Julian of Norwich, *Showings*, cited in Rohr, *Falling Upward*, 58.

Roger Payne ends his book about his life with whales with a chapter about being saved by the whales, including these words:

> I want to ask now, in greater detail, just what it is we can learn from the brains of whales . . . [W]hales and humans seem to have an interesting kind of bond—call it a bond of mutual curiosity—which appears to form automatically and surprisingly whenever whales and people find themselves face to face. This bond also seems to occur when people hear the songs of whales for the first time. It is as though the two mammalian brains have more in common than we are aware and we really may have significant things to say to each other—despite our isolation for the last sixty-five million years—if only we could find a communication channel. . . . I have wondered, I say, whether the whales are trying to call us back from the edge, back from our lost and mesmerized state, or whether they, along with the rest of life on earth, are just relieved to see us self-destruct?[3]

Notice Payne's description of *Homo sapiens* as lost and mesmerized. He wrote those words in 1995, before the digital revolution and the radical change in public life brought about by pervasive hand-held devices.

Having successfully courted one particular whale, with the support of her mother, my small experience indicates to me that they like us. I think that they want us to become wise. I think that they want us to make it. But there is a limit. Moby Dick was a real whale, after all, and a whale who ferociously attacked whaling ships.[4]

When I say that we have to want their help, I recall listening to Guatemalan political activist Rigoberta Menchu as she described the human collective. She said that we humans need to come forward, one by one and group by group, and say, "Hi, we are So-and-So and we are alcoholics." She meant, of course, that there is a need for a massive recovery movement, recovery of our living soulful connection, and that it cannot happen until we stop numbing the pain and ask for help. Then, she implied, the whole world will come out to help us.

The Price of Kissing

Let me for a brief moment channel an imaginary reader. "OK, even if I accept all of this, I feel I need to remind you that we eat animals. It's

3. Payne, *Among Whales*, 346, 351.
4. Baird, *White as the Waves*, 274.

pervasive. Lots of animals eat other animals. Predator and prey and the food chain are scientifically demonstrated realities, more basic than all the social intelligence you have written about. It all depends on eating. Isn't that a kind of biological bottom line?"

Yes, perspicacious reader, you are right. But whether you choose to call it chance or grace, life is simply given to every animal. And as life is given, it is also taken away. The nature of any life is that it ends, and when it ends, its energy goes back into the whole where it is synergistically used to create new life. The great gift economy of life on earth is simultaneously the necessary sacrifice economy. Because each life is ultimately empty, Life is infinitely full. You may want some other scenario, but this one is reality. So while we strive to preserve our lives, we must also give them up. And perhaps our greatest wisdom lies in knowing the balance of these two things, knowing when to care for the self, receiving from the world, and when to nurture Other, giving of ourselves. Taking without giving only magnifies the pain in the system. Further, it cannot be done beyond the point at which the system as a whole would lose its integrity, climate change being the prime example.

There is no getting around the fact of our membership in something bigger. Perhaps equally importantly, we lose by failing to engage the otherness of life in caring and creative ways, for engaging the world is how we thrive. So attempts to unload the suffering onto other beings, taking all the goods for individual or collective self is a short-term strategy at best. We have to practice the art of pouring ourselves out, for that is what living is; and then one day, we must pour ourselves out completely, for that is what dying is. The poet Rumi said that "the price of kissing is your life."[5] He was right, and he was offering to us a carrot. What he did not mention is the stick: that the price of not kissing is your miserable un-kissed life. The price is the same, but the experience of what happens between being given life and being taken by death are radically different. And I think it essential that we gain more practice with the carrot, so that we can retire the stick, relatively speaking. I fear that by default we try to choose the carrot, referring the stick to the Other. But this is to misunderstand the nature of the carrot, that it grows by being shared and that life then feels good, kissed. Giving ourselves to life makes for happy living, and it also means giving ourselves to death. There is an unavoidable element of surrender in being here at all.

5. Rumi, *Essential Rumi*, 37.

Falling Gracefully

I picked the fledgling up from the cement where he had landed after falling from his nest. He was a ladder-backed woodpecker, black and white striped, with a red crown, and a bloodied wing. Looking at him in the palm of my hand, I understood that I had just made a commitment, and so I carried him home, washed his bloody wing, put some antiseptic cream on it and wondered whether the bones were broken. I knew that the good thing about immature bones is that they are flexible, and I hoped that his were merely dented. I fed him hummingbird food from a dropper and I made an old tee-shirt nest for him at the top of my bed. I have found that wild animals do better with a person around than they do left alone in a safe dark place, as is often advised; so I made him his own little nest in my nest.

Before dawn the next morning, some serious hammering on my forearm awakened me. Baby was hungry, and Baby got fed. Then I left Baby in the bedroom and went to my office across the hall to write. As I wrote, I heard scratching sounds, and then what sounded like bird laughter, little cheeps. When I went to look, I saw that Baby was climbing up the trellis of the French doors and flinging himself down, attempting to fly with his injured wing. There was little that resembled flight in his behavior; it looked like falling for most of that first day. Thereafter I named him Fling, and I called him by name frequently, crossing the hall to cheer him whenever I heard the happy cheeps.

This continued for three days, my waking each morning to having a bone hammered by a hungry woodpecker, then listening and watching as he set himself increasingly complex goals: from gliding instead of merely falling, to aiming for and landing in a pile of laundry. For Fling, falling was the route to flying, and he threw himself out with total abandon and concentrated effort at the same time. Achieving a goal elicited gleeful cheeps, and I would routinely get up to see what he had just mastered. Looking back, I wonder, was he building his self-esteem too, as he accomplished his goals?

On the fourth day I had to travel for business, so I took Fling to the local wild animal rescue nurse. She thought that the worst case was that he could live in my back yard because his climbing was very strong. If he succeeded in flying while I was away, she would release him. And release him she did, the best of all possible outcomes, though I would have liked to see him launch, having watched him learn from falling to fly. Even without witnessing it for myself, I was thrilled that he had gone back to wild.

The Postmodern Fall

If humans have held an especially high place in Western philosophical and religious explanations of reality, scientists, with their love of truth and fact searching, have necessarily taken us down a few pegs. We have fallen from the idea of ourselves as the most godlike of creatures in the gravitational center of creation to the understanding that we are mere specks on a dot of a planet somewhere on the edge of a galaxy that is one of 200 billion such galaxies, going back in time 13.7 billion years. This taking of humanity from glorious self-declared centrality to insignificance may be one reason that some people do not like science, which they are willing to reject wholesale, even as they take their medicine and expect it to work. Of this phenomenon, Neil Shubin says, in his book on the history of the evolution of the universe as it is expressed in humanity: "Discovery after discovery has confirmed the multibillion-year age of the earth, the sheer vastness of the cosmos, and our species' humble position in the tree of life on our planet. Against this backdrop, you could legitimately wonder if it is part of the job description of scientists to make people feel utterly puny and insignificant in the face of the enormity of space and time."[6]

With some irony, though, science as a subculture takes itself very seriously and bestows upon itself unprecedented human grandeur. Consider Stephen Hawking's suggestion that one day, as a result of cumulative scientific knowledge, humanity will grasp the mind of God through reason.[7] It seems at times as though the intent of some scientists still is to wrest the laurels away from childish religious voices and to claim it for adult scientists. However, what I notice is the similarities: both scientists and those who speak from religious perspectives may be understood to say clearly, if not centrally, that humans are members of something bigger upon which they necessarily depend. If we decide that it is somehow an insult to reason that our membership be meaningful, as Dawkins suggested with his "mustn't get mystical," then we decide in some sense to embrace futility, or meaninglessness, a strangely sad choice when we

6. Shubin, *Universe Within*, x.
7. Hawking, *Brief History of Time*, 191.

are equipped by evolution with the capacity to feel our connection to all that is and for that feeling to be meaningful. It is feeling that we need to reclaim because many things are, by evolutionary design, matters of the heart.

Describing both the scientific process whereby we have been diminished in our own eyes, and the possibility of a different kind of meaning, Shubin writes:

> For thousands of years, mankind considered itself the pinnacle of life's creation on a planet sitting in the center of the universe. Science changed that perception. Leavitt, Hubble, and others helped us see that we live near the margin of a vast galaxy, in a universe of galaxies, with our planet one of many worlds. Darwin and the biologists had their say, too. Our entire species is but one little twig on an enormous tree of life filled with all life on Earth. But each discovery that moves us from the center of creation to some obscure corner brings an entirely new relation between other species, the entire universe, and us. All the galaxies in the cosmos, like every creature on the planet, and every atom, molecule, and body on Earth are deeply connected. That connection begins at a single point 13.7 billion years ago.[8]

Shubin provides a good summary both of the diminution of humanity and of the possibility of constructing a bigger, truer, more flexible, and genuinely meaningful story within which we might live. It is a story of absolute kinship and belonging. And so it seems to me that we have to either choose to be delusional, clinging literally to religious stories that scientists have effectively reframed, or to take the chance that we might fall from our pedestal into something as good or better. Franciscan theologian Richard Rohr calls it "falling upward," this sensibility of surrender when life seems to go against us, and especially when events would redefine us, falling upward because it is the path of growth. "We get to the whole by falling *down* into the messy parts—so many times, in fact, that we long and thirst for the wholeness and fullness of all things, including ourselves."[9]

By changing the meaning of the word "nature" in scope and size and in sheer creative capacity, scientists have made the divide between natural and supernatural an anachronism. Nature is a 14 billion-year-old creative agent that has produced 200 billion galaxies and almost

8. Shubin, *Universe Within*, 24–25.
9. Rohr, *Falling Upward*, 150–51.

9 million (known) species of animals on our one little planet in our tiny corner of the cosmos.[10] This is very close to a description of the God of the prescientific supernatural category. Ironically, the feeling of being deeply connected and responsive is a traditionally religious sentiment, though the scientific validation seems somehow unorthodox to many religious people. And some religious traditions have taken the words of their scriptures for material facts of a kind that words can never be. It is a strange kind of humanism that emerges from religious resistance to humanism, the belief that literal divine authority is housed in mere human language: words, by definition, refer to some kind of reality, but they are symbols for things, representations of things, and not things in themselves. In fact, I think this belief that words can be facts—much less encapsulate divinity—is probably close to the essence of our collective "lost in thought" problem.

Homo sapiens does not exist in some abstract isolation from the rest of life, but we are living and dying in a living and dying world. The problem is that we have increasing difficulty knowing this simple truth because most of us live almost exclusively in relation to other humans and to human technologies, technologies that increasingly move us away even from our own bodies. This is perhaps why sick people find more comfort in the company of their pets than in their human spouses. Pets know what it is to be in a body, and that is where those who are sick have to be. Ironically, the very social and affective neuroscientists who most deeply understand our biology and evolutionary history also point to the acceleration in proliferation of technologies as potentially problematic. Recall Antonio Damasio's elegantly simple warning: "something may yet have to give." And Shubin ponders the way that our technology and biology together define us: "our history has been one of gizmos, medicines, and technologies to make our thoughts real and expand the possibilities of our lives. . . . Human creativity and biology are like different instruments in an orchestra."[11] I add to this that we have become really sophisticated players of the instrument of technology while at the same time becoming increasingly alienated from and rusty in the use of the instrument of biology that we *are*.

We seem to be on a trajectory of rapidly increased abstract and self-referential living as we wander through our days relating to handheld

10. Mora et al., *How Many Species*.

11. Shubin, *Universe Within*, 187.

interactive screens more than to anything flesh and blood, much less to anything earth, air, fire, and water, the context for which and in which we evolved, and the place in which the Others await us. And it is at this moment in our history that scientists can demonstrate the depths to which we are ourselves animal. We can come back down to earth and into our own bodies simply by stroking the cat, feeling the purr reverberating out the pleasure of divine eros, and so letting the world call us back home. In this simple way, we experience the biology of euphoria, evolved apparently for the purpose of giving us pleasure in belonging here.

Humanism, Scientific and Religious

Culture serves as a collective parallel to the self-story that we own as individuals, with the significant difference that it does not arise from the individual experience of life, but rather is given us from the experience of humans who have lived before us. It creates a collective hypnosis in which many useful and helpful memes are tossed about, along with damaging and misleading memes. When I say that we are lost in thought, it is probably even truer that we are lost in the unconscious givens of our culture than in our own false self-stories. Without effortful attention to our own minds, cumulative human culture flows through us; and because we do not notice, false "facts," unwholesome attitudes, and self-referential collective stories lead us into deeper ignorance. All the while, we point to our technological prowess that is indeed impressive as it is destructive, thinking ourselves wise, thinking that we know where we are going. Perhaps it is time for humanity to set aside the archetype of the hero and to take up the archetype of the jester, the wise fool, who sees the knower behind the knowing and whose pleasure is in laughter evoked.

Scientists and religious leaders alike have led us into a cultural conversation that is all and only about humans, though both claim otherwise. Of course, some religions claim to despise humanism and to correct it by asserting that it is God (or the gods) who put us at the center and gave us all the importance, the effect being that we are central, thank God. And many scientists, though sometimes sneering at religious grandiosity, elevate the human endeavor of science above all possible other activities, righteously focusing on progress for human concerns as if these could be treated independently from the rest of the world. The facts are that a great many tragedies have come by way of unintended "side effects" of scientific progress. Meanwhile, humanity is dying of humanism, of having taken ourselves out of our necessary context. In this, we hurt ourselves and impose a great deal of misery on all feeling creatures. Enter, of course, the dog, who is not lost in thought the way that we are, who still smells the world as it is, and who may yet help us to smell the truth.

The scientific affirmation that we are members of a continuous community of beings, comprised not only of every life form on earth but going back ancestrally to the beginning of the cosmos, matches the traditionally religious point of view that we are meaningfully and morally part of a bigger picture. But it is significant that those who believe that truth can come only from sacred texts consider such a perspective, when it is made available by way of science, suspect. I have often thought that, had the scientific worldview been communicated in these legitimately meaningful terms, in terms of Carl Sagan's "humans as stardust" rather than in that often-snide dismissal of everything perceived to be the other of science, religious resistance to it might have been minimized.[12] But who can blame scientists, whose cultural forebears were persecuted by the leaders of religious institutions in the collective youth of the scientific project? You see how we are?

Natural Spirituality

I recently read again a 1980 speech of Lakota patriot Russell Means entitled "For America to Live, Europe Must Die," the title being a reference to the fact that the Western world legitimizes the written word over the fluid and living oral tradition, and honors functions over relationships. In his speech he says that he is neither capitalist nor communist because both miss the point of Spirit, that the world is a place of Spirit and we cannot live rightly when we relate to the world as so much stuff for human use.[13] There is no stuff: there is only membership in the community of being. That is Spirit. Any other platform is delusional. And of course there are many indigenous traditions whose members never left the continuity of Being for some abstract other place. Though they are not the focus of this book, I have not forgotten them. Means' point that the only way that humans can be oriented correctly is to embrace the path of Spirit is central to my own thesis, and recalling it is one way of giving some recognition

12. Cf. Sagan, *Cosmos*; Benvenuti, "Science and Religion."
13. Means, "World to Live."

to those humans who never left the family of Life. Perhaps they are the carriers of the *sapiens* gene.

If we can emerge enough from the well worn grooves of the hypnosis that cultures provide, a universal understanding of essential humanity is readily accessible from scientific, religious, and indigenous perspectives, where essence is stripped down to basic facts about our history and context. These facts are far from trivial for being few and fundamental: that humans are creative members of a creative cosmos, and that we are ancestrally related to everything within that cosmos.[14] To have an integral sense of this as we journey through life is, I suggest, to open the way to the possibility of transformational gains in human well-being and also an existentially correct or truthful recognition of the others all the way up and down the great continuum of Being.

We need the company of animals in a direct and visceral way because we cannot tell the truth until we can smell the truth of our own animal natures and of the world beyond the human. To contemplate the souls of other animals and to take their company seriously and humbly is to return to our own souls in a significant way. Bad as humanism may be in removing us from our context, retrenching in dualistic religious orthodoxies is no solution but represents only a deepening of the problem. Rather, I suggest that we should embrace the imposed changes, fling ourselves out into the unknown, and discover what falling upward there may be for us.

Recovery Through the Fall

While writing this chapter, I woke one morning in awareness of three happy facts that had emerged in American popular culture. The first was that a 2013 Pew survey had reported a new category in its demographic profile of religious views in America. The emergent group is called the "Nones," people who reject ideological categorization.[15] The second fact that appeared to my waking mind was that, during the recession of 2008, while consumer spending dropped almost across the board, spending on pets increased. The third, and the best tickle of the lot, was the remembrance that the animals have started spontaneously talking back, in human languages. Or perhaps we have started to notice that they re-

14. Cf. Benvenuti, "Science and Religion."
15. Pew Forum, "'Nones' on the Rise."

late without instruction to human perspectives, and that some are even attempting to imitate human speech. Let me take these three facts in reverse order.

A Beluga whale named NOC and an Asian elephant named Koshik have each spontaneously, without having been taught or rewarded, altered their natural sound physiology to imitate human speech. Koshik inserts the tip of his trunk into his mouth to alter his vocal capacity from the deep and long distance rumble that is natural for him to a high squeaky pitch and timbre that is natural for us. Koshik consistently has a five-word vocabulary in Korean, reportedly validated by Korean people hearing the recordings without knowing that an elephant had produced the sounds. His somewhat predicable vocabulary includes "hello," "sit down," "lie down," "no," and "good."[16]

NOC, on the other flipper, has had to figure out how to lower his high chirping "canary of the sea" voice down a few octaves. To accomplish this, he overinflates his vestibular sac, an anatomical feature that allows him to close his blowhole to prevent drowning. There have been anecdotal reports for some time that whales imitate human speech, so when a research diver broke the surface asking, perplexedly, who had told him to get out of the water, the research team pursued the question.[17] My impression of the video recordings is that NOC speaks baby human language perfectly. He has mastered rhythm, timbre, pitch, and prosody.

Animal researchers have demonstrated too that African elephants spontaneously understand and respond to human gestures.[18] And dogs, no surprise, have been demonstrated to be able to take the perspective of humans, as evidenced by the fact that they steal in the dark, knowing that their humans cannot see what they are up to (and just as I have been propounding the cause of their sainthood).[19] I find these attempts on the part of other animals to understand and to commune with humans, seemingly coming from a range of motives, to be especially touching in the ways that they affirm that we are not alone, that we are not the only agents: that we may, in fact, be met and assisted as we struggle to understand both them and ourselves differently.

16. Morelle, "Elephant mimics Korean."
17. Ridgway et al., "Spontaneous human speech mimicry."
18. Smet and Byrne, "African Elephants can use Human Pointing."
19. Kaminski et al., "Dogs Steal in the Dark."

At the same time, we humans are reaching for animals and, by every account of the pet industry, spending more on them than ever, despite or perhaps because of the financial crisis. It is obvious that people experience animals as persons of significance. Now the very scientific project that started out with the proposition that animals are machines has corrected itself, as science routinely does, and, in this case, validated the experience of ordinary people. Indeed, by any definition of person that does not begin with the word "human," animals are persons. Chickens, for heaven's sake, have personal preferences!

People are choosing to be with animals, whether or not they can afford to do so, and whether or not they have a philosophy in place that explains their desire for the company of animals. This gives me hope that the divine eros, that capacity of animal affective SEEKING systems to be pulled into conscious relationship by others, is awakening again in postmodern humanity.

The denigration of this divine eros, by which I mean being drawn to other beings and the world, and the belittling of people who love God, and also the placement of human reason in the place where God once was, are surely the great egotistical follies of the cumulative culture of science, every bit as restrictive and destructive as the enforcement of religious doctrine and dogma were in past eras. The simplest and most direct way out of the painfully foolish and all too human aspects of both culture streams is to embrace the divine eros, letting "the soft animal of our bodies" love what they love, as Mary Oliver so elegantly expresses it in her poem telling how the wild geese invite us into the family of things.[20] Far from leaving our minds behind, we can allow ourselves to be aware and intellectually curious about this central and powerful feature of animal life, that we are attracted to each other and so drawn out of ourselves.

Changes in our ways of relating to animals are happening in both private and public spheres, in our homes and in the way we live, in our entertainment choices, and in our public laws and policies. In 2013, NBC cancelled a television show *Under Wild Skies*, produced with National Rifle Association funding, after the host, Tony Makris, shot an elephant for viewer entertainment with a gun that he declared was "made to shoot ivory." The Cable News Network report reads: "Makris and a guide got within around 20ft of the elephant before shooting it in the face. Both men posed with the dead animal before toasting the hunt with champagne. . . . The episode prompted an online petition, signed by more

20. Oliver, *Dream Work*, 14.

than 100,000 people, which called for NBC Sports Network to cancel the show." Makris compared his critics to Hitler, naming them "animal racists" who preferred elephants to pigeons.[21] If his point were that nothing should be shot in the face for mere entertainment, I would agree. But his unarticulated point appeared to be that all faces are fair game for the person with a big enough gun and limited access to feelings of empathy. The report concluded with the telling note that the hunting of elephants was not illegal in Botswana at the time of filming the episode, but would be from the beginning of 2014.

In the realm of American public policy, the Animal Welfare Act of 1966 was the first federal legislation related to animals. It both reinforced the notion that animals are objects legitimately owned by humans and also set mandatory requirements for the fair treatment of animals. The act has been revised and extended several times, including the Improved Standards for Laboratory Animals Act (1985). Additionally, the Endangered Species Act (1973) and the Pet Evacuation and Transportation Standards Act (2006) represent different lines of legislation related to animals in their own context on the one paw, and to animals as of central importance to human well-being on the other. The courts have also been busy with animal matters, including the decision by California courts to hold the United States Navy accountable for practices that harm cetaceans.[22] The fact that a slavery suit filed on behalf of captive orcas even got a hearing is groundbreaking, and the fact that the judge's decision was based upon their lack of personhood only opens the way for future cases, as personhood is scientifically determined to be a feature of animal life.

Policies related to animals continue to evolve in the direction of recognizing their personhood. The National Institutes of Health called for the cessation of most research using chimpanzees in the United States in 2013, and in his report on the policy change, director Francis Collins said: "Americans have benefited greatly from the chimpanzees' service to biomedical research, but new scientific methods and technologies have rendered their use in research largely unnecessary. . . . Their likeness to humans has made them uniquely valuable for certain types of research, but also demands greater justification for their use."[23] And I note that

21. Adam Gabbat, "NBC cancels NRA-funded hunting show after host compares critics to Hitler," *The Guardian,* September 30, 2013.

22. Center for Biological Diversity, "Federal Agency Failed to Protect."

23. National Institutes of Health, "NIH to reduce significantly the use of chimpanzees."

though scientists have demonstrated and continue to demonstrate that the similarities amongst mammals apply to mice and bats as well as humans and chimpanzees, it is still similarity to humanity that drives our natural interest. It is difficult for us to escape the fact that we are biologically wired to look for and at faces, and the greater the similarity to us, the stronger our empathy.

While mammals have much in common with each other, from whales to shrews, this is especially true of their emotional and social lives, dependent upon early attachment to form the emotional bonds that are the foundation for social living. But mammals also share brain systems that support the cognitive structures of general intelligence, as evidenced by ongoing studies comparing the structures and functions of mouse and human brains and intelligence.[24] Many of our animal similarities are vertebrate, hence the sharing of significant features that goes down to the level of all creatures with skulls and spines, and not only those with breasts, hair, skulls and spines.[25] As a side note, birds seem to have evolved many of the affective and cognitive features that mammals share, by convergent evolutionary processes. And of course we can make the similarity case all the way down the chain of evolution to the Big Bang. Physicist and evolutionary philosopher Brian Swimme refers to this divine eros as allurement, a mutual attraction of beings for one another that is for him an operating principle of the entire cosmos, gravity being a cosmic example of allurement.[26] We all share elements made in the stars. This completely natural feeling of belonging in the universe is a way of being pulled forward rather than driven; it is another level of the divine eros. But we human animals can easily feel our belonging in the likeness in other animals. We can feel that we belong together as a family to this planetary home.

Spirit Unleashed

And this brings me to my reason for happiness with the growing number of religious Nones, the fastest growing segment of religiously surveyed Americans. The Nones are people who were raised in religious homes but who no longer participate formally in religious institutions: "In just

24. Motzel et al., "Architecture of Intelligence," 342.
25. Shubin, *Inner Fish*, 182.
26. Swimme, *Powers of the Universe*, II.

the last five years, this group of willfully unaffiliated people has grown from 15% to 20% of the population. They are people who have no religious affiliation, and who don't want one. Yet only 5% of those surveyed call themselves atheists. In other words, the Nones include many people who, while they don't want a religious label also don't want the traditional secular-rationalist-humanist label."[27] They seem to be rejecting ideology.

The Nones refuse definition.

"Are you believers?"

"No."

"Are you atheists?"

"No."

"Agnostics then?"

"No."

"Are you, then, spiritual but not religious?"

"Go Away."

My sense is that they are deeply inclusive, not just religiously but in living, and that they do not want walls of words acting as artificial boundaries. I applaud them this twinned deep impulse, which I share. As I have said elsewhere, many of the Nones are "Alls," people who are interested in spirituality without borders, who are possibly more comfortable with the practice of many religious traditions than they would be with one.[28] Perhaps they have gone off leash in considering the whole world home.

This deep and broadly inclusive impulse points toward the limits of the old religious stories, stories in which there is always at least one great divide, between God and creation, between humans and animals, between saved and unsaved, truth and heresy. But the inclusivity of the Nones also points to the construction of a more flexible story. Allowing for a sense of spiritual connection, they are weary of being presented with preordained choices between secular rationality, including that of overly reductionist science, and religion of the kind that promises only rewards hereafter or religion that posits explanations dependent upon supernatural causation when natural causation is evident and sufficient. The assumption that religion has primarily to do with the supernatural is a false one in their eyes, and they reject an emphasis on the supernatural while craving the natural spirituality that is so necessary for embodied

27. Benvenuti, "Nones Are Off the Bus."
28. Ibid.

and relational life on earth. Sixty percent of the Nones say that they feel close to the natural world.

It should now be obvious to most thinking people that *Homo sapiens* is not the center of creation and also not the singular godlike being that inhabits Aristotle's lineage. Our relationship with animals is changing as we seek their help in coming down from the clouds of abstraction, as we rely upon them for companionship, as we learn collectively and individually to care for them as persons (even without a rigid and shared definition of personhood), as we increasingly choose to live without the false comfort of religious doctrines that separate us from them. I think that these facts in combination point to a movement toward healing. They indicate that our left hemispheres can pay attention to the stories we make and can evaluate their fit with reality. These trends also indicate that our unconscious and emotional right hemispheres are seeking the physical encounter and pleasant emotions of connecting that we are less able to achieve in human relations, heavily clad in concepts and symbols conveyed via electronic gadgets as they are.

The Fall and Recovery From the Fall

The articulation of a scientifically syntonic natural spirituality may well hold a key to the re-engaging of our SEEKING systems by allowing us to feel part of Life, called out of ourselves by a living world in which we belong and for which we are responsible, each animal according to its kind. Such a collective story may be the carrot that calls us forward, so much better for living happy and healthy lives than the stick that punishes transgressions.

An established principle of learning is that positive reinforcement is by far a more effective tool than punishment. Punishment works in a crisis to stop a behavior, but it does not produce effective learning so much as intense fear associations, and very often residual anger too. More pleasant, elegant, and effective is the process of being drawn into action by a sense of kinship and belonging rather than being driven to action with the stick of threats, be they the sticks of eternal damnation, of ecological collapse, or of nuclear disaster.

Yet we need to be cautious with stories, even with bigger, better, truer, and more flexible stories, because we know that we have a human tendency to delusional belief. We cannot get away from being story

makers, but perhaps we do better to stay close to facts and to actual beings, and to keep the stories spare. Feed the fish, gaze at the birdfeeder,
pet the dog, engage the world as it is wordlessly before us, a plethora of
faces looking into our faces, and let the experience be its own elaboration.

Soul is a quality of animal life, and we humans have not exactly lost
our souls, but we cannot feel them well enough to cooperate in life and
to have the happiness that comes from belonging to it. Animals, so far as
we can tell, have not lost contact with their souls; and this is why so many
people love them so deeply. And because they are sufficiently like us that
we can have the experience of empathy and direct biological communion
with them, they can help us connect to our own souls. Because they are
Other, they can call us out of ourselves, and they can help us get under
the words and back into the world.

Of course, it is obvious that I love animals and credit them as dearly
as any spiritual tradition or teacher for my own healing and homecom-
ing. The perspective that the fate of humanity matters above that of others
is fundamentally wrong and is causing enormous suffering to billions of
innocent creatures, debasing humanity in the process. Nine billion chickens a year live and die miserable factory-farmed lives because we choose
to ignore our shared soulfulness.[29] Again, it is the lack of feeling that is
the problem. Jane Goodall notes, in a recent assessment of progress in
relations between humans and animals during the course of her life, that
"the horror of factory farming is new."[30] The Dalai Lama acknowledges
that it was his having seen and felt the suffering of a chicken that finally
gave him the courage to become a vegetarian.[31] Of making this change he
said, "I have been particularly concerned with the sufferings of chickens
for many years. It was the death of a chicken that finally strengthened my
resolve to become vegetarian. These days, when I see a row of plucked
chickens hanging in meat shop it hurts. I find it unacceptable that violence is the basis of some of our food habits."[32]

I want to bring the issue of human imposed suffering on other animals down to one particular animal, no two—because all mammals are
essentially relational—so that we can feel it. I want to acknowledge the
wrong that we do by way of a true story about a particular animal, worthy

29. Encyclopedia Britannica, "Factory Farmed Chickens."

30. Goodall, in Bekoff, *Animals Matter*, xiv.

31. Dalai Lama, "Vegetarian Diet, Kindness to Animals."

32. Ibid.

of consideration in her own right. I invite and encourage you to feel the story, to grieve for her, and to lament for us. Consider this story of a mother bear who killed her infant son and herself rather than go on in a tortured existence in a bear farm.

In China, bears are farmed for their bile, which is considered medicinal for humans. These farmed bears are kept horizontal in coffin-like cages for their entire lives, with a metal catheter inserted into their abdomens to harvest their bile. They are allowed one unrestrained arm with which to feed themselves. It is a life so horrible that they sometimes simply go mad and beat their heads against the bars of their cages until they die.

So I offer the stark rendering of the story of a mother bear and her cub and the end of their lives on a bear farm, as told by anthropologist Barbara King in her book on animal grief: "The cub cried out in distress as a worker prepared to harvest his bile. The mother, distressed by her loved infant's pain, broke free and squeezed the life out of her baby so that he would no longer suffer. Overcome by her own emotional pain, she ran, purposefully, headfirst into a wall, killing herself."[33]

I pause to remember that every day of my life, I pray for caged animals, not because prayer will magically help those in cages but because it gives us the courage to be honest, and not to look away. It places us with them together in the context of the whole of Life, and calls on the one to whom we pray to witness, placing us all in the context of the whole. At the same time that I acknowledge our wrongs, I recognize that it is they, the animals, who are best positioned to help us. Because they do not share our compulsive story-making, and because they do have their mammalian social-emotional intelligence intact, they are perhaps likely to help us.

Let me say clearly and strongly, as a critical thinker and not as a softheaded sentimentalist, that Descartes had a motive, not a reason, for saying that other animals are machines. It allowed him and others to treat them as things, to use them as part of a project. Motive is an affective disposition to act, and I infer that his seeking system wanted to elaborate a story about a mechanical universe so much that he could override his own bodily information about his dog. Machine is one paradigm in which to see the universe, a paradigm that has proved valuable in our scientific explorations, but also morally debasing. Animals are not machines, as

33. King, *How Animals Grieve*, 117.

was always evident; they suffer. For those eschewing sentimentality, those who want cold and rational facts, this is a cold and rational fact: when we hurt them, they suffer.

Our own left-brain machinery makes reasons, explanations, and stories that justify our decisions and actions. This human foible, one of the engines that makes bugs in our programs, puts the whole earth, ourselves included, in danger. We need to recover from this notion of a mechanical universe, and we need to make a better story because we are animals of the story. Considering the souls of other animals may do a great deal to bring us back, more truthfully this time, to our own souls and to our own bodies, the only place I have ever found the word soul to make any sense at all. But we have to be willing to unleash Spirit in ourselves and in them, by recognizing other souls in a bigger story; and we have to allow them to catch us in our fall, giving to them the role of protagonist too.

Alternative Orthodoxies

I am convinced that a bare bones natural spirituality is foundational to a newer, truer, and better story. What I am suggesting is not a new religion, but recognition of something fundamental that underlies all religions, namely reality, the implicitly relational material universe. Such a natural spirituality is readily available to everyone, and I think it safe to say that every religion includes it. It is as self-evident as anything can be that words can never enclose God/Spirit, but only point our gaze in the direction of God/Spirit. Consequently, we are most foolish when we argue about definitions of God and Spirit. We cannot contain that which contains us.[34]

In various cultural lineages, there are continuous streams of philosophy and religion that give entree to a broad and inclusive alternative orthodoxy of natural spirituality, places in which animal souls can safely be unleashed, in which all being is Soul. In these systems of thought, God's first and foremost self-statement or revelation is the world itself, or "creation," to use the term of the Abrahamic religions. To exist at all is to be part of that greater Being, in which everything is impermanent, everything dies and rises, and in which living is pure grace that paradoxically requires complete sacrifice. Among these streams of culture and thought

34. Benvenuti and Davenport, "New Archaic," 231.

may be placed Spinoza's dual aspect monism, Buddhism in its essential teachings and practices, and the Franciscan theological tradition within Christianity. This is by no means an exhaustive list, but simply some lineages with which I have chosen to grow deeply familiar. I cannot hope to do any of them justice in a brief description, but I hope to say enough of each that they may be considered as roots of alternative orthodoxies converging upon a path by which we may emerge from being deeply lost in thought, an embodied path that leads us home.

Baruch Spinoza

Baruch (later Benedict de) Spinoza was born into Amsterdam's Portuguese-Jewish community during the middle years of the seventeenth century. He was seven years old and somewhere in the same city when Descartes sat by the fire that winter morning in his dressing gown, developing his method of doubt, and perhaps taking pleasure in the company of Monsieur Grat. Spinoza greatly admired Descartes's philosophical boldness, his willingness to question everything, his method of doubt. But he was equally disappointed with Descartes's dualism, the foundational formula that left minds and bodies distressingly dissociated, and left an even more anthropomorphic God than that of the scholastics still sitting in his distant sky.

Spinoza was actually the bolder philosopher, and by contemporary standards, by far the better of the two. He proposed a metaphysics that is referred to as dual aspect monism, by which he understood that the body and the mind are the same thing experienced in two different ways. He was a rationalist who wrote his *Ethics* in the style of a geometric treatise that is dense and difficult to read, which is perhaps one reason why he has been relatively neglected. His writing was even more geometric than that of the man he referred to as "the master," Descartes, and so followed in that rational lineage of seeking clarity and orderly relation of thoughts. It might also have appealed to him that only the sympathetic and determined reader would understand what he was saying. Religious persecution remained a threat hanging over most of Europe, and some of his friends had died in prison over ideas they espoused. Spinoza himself was expelled from the synagogue under the harshest terms when he was only twenty-four years old, long before his ideas were developed, much less disseminated. From that time on, though he had no regrets regarding the synagogue, he was cautious about the risks he took, while being extraordinarily bold in his thinking.

Spinoza wanted to accomplish what Descartes had failed to do—to create a philosophy that was rationally self-evident, that did not refer to scriptures nor require interpreters nor project human qualities on to a far away God, and that did not instruct people to abandon their lives on earth in order to gain another life for which there was no evidence. And he developed one of the most elegant philosophical works in human history, his *Ethics,* the final intent of which was to address how humans should live.

His ethics are grounded in his metaphysics, themselves beautifully syntonic with our contemporary scientific worldview. The first principle of his metaphysics was that there is only one substance, or self-existent reality, and that everything is part of this one. Another way to say this— and he was explicit—is to say that Nature is God and God is Nature. Every body is a mode or expression of the one God/Nature and every mind is the idea of that particular body, so there is no dualism, but only beings, experienced now as body and now as mind. And mind is simply the idea of a given body, the body knowing its own experience. Thus not only are God and nature united, but every body is an expression of God, and every mind is an expression of a particular body, and every mind is an idea in the mind of God.

Spinoza taught that self-interest, by which he meant ongoing self-organization, motivates the behavior of all organisms. He used the term *activity* to express the idea that agency, or capacity to act, is increased by consciously engaging a process of inquiry into the causes of oneself in one's actual circumstances. By actively inquiring about the causes and conditions of events in his own experience, a person comes to see that he exists only in relationship to multiple contexts, from family to the universe in scope, and also to an understanding that he himself is composed of many beings.

In following the natural path of self-love, a person, by actively engaging the internal and external conditions of his life, moves out from passive reception of cultural givens as a first developmental stage, and into a second stage of applying active reason in order to understand the causes of himself. In this second stage, he uses his human rational faculty (today, his capacity for left-brain conscious thought, or my metaphoric flashlight of reason) to pierce the illusions of living. And then this extended search to understand the causes of himself leads to a third stage in which the self arrives into an intellectual love of God.

This third stage is effectively the habitual placing of the self contextually in an all-inclusive continuity of Being that one has come to understand by way of engaging the particulars of one's own life, not superficially but deeply. In the culmination of his *Ethics*, Spinoza states explicitly, "The more we understand singular things, the more we understand God." And, he added, "The greatest striving of the mind, and its greatest virtue is understanding things by the third kind of knowledge."[35] While Spinoza does not name this third and highest function of mind, I would call it contemplation, and I would mean by that the active reception of one's own perceptions, thoughts, and feelings, along with one's sense of a great and inclusive reality, a constant and fluid "I belong to You."

In Spinoza's system, the human awakens through reason to belonging and can ultimately understand himself only as a particular creative point of view and a particular point of agency within the totality of being that is God. Philosopher Heidi Ravven says that Spinoza's person becomes increasingly agentic by waking up to the fact that love of self, biological self-interest, leads to an understanding of extended self, a self deeply integrated into the world and a self who has actively (consciously and intentionally) integrated the world into himself. Of this process, she says: "It was to love the world as oneself, and to realize that self and world survived together or not at all. . . . A harmonious relation between self and world, a sense of belonging in nature and being part of a nature working itself out in the self, was the moral posture that replaced that of an ongoing power struggle between body and mind and between the human person and nature."[36]

On the issue of Spinoza's conception of God, some scholars and interpreters have claimed that he was "really" an atheist: in the succinct conclusion of Steven Nadler, "Spinoza is, in substance, an atheist."[37] But Spinoza was also famously described as "the God intoxicated man."[38] I think that Spinoza would have been appalled at the notion of God-intoxication, since for him, love of God is active escape from passive dullness into a kind of bright intellectual clarity about one's state of belonging.

35. Spinoza, *Ethics*, 173.

36. Ravven, *Self Beyond Itself*, 235.

37. Nadler, *Spinoza's "Ethics,"* 121.

38. Leibniz, *Samtliche Schriften*, 553, quoting the German poet Novalis.

But however others might interpret him, I am inclined to take Spinoza at his word. He defended himself explicitly against the charge of atheism: "Does that man pray, renounce all religion, who declares that God must be acknowledged as the highest good, and that he must be loved as such in a free spirit? And that, in this alone does our supreme happiness and our highest freedom consist?"[39]

Perhaps the difficulty in accepting Spinoza's self-proclaimed love of God is that we are so entrenched in dualism that we cannot conceive of a God who is real and yet contains us, a God whom we genuinely and significantly know by participating directly in God's being. Unlike those transcendent traditions in which God is outside of creation, in Spinoza's metaphysics, "The human mind has an adequate knowledge of God's eternal and infinite essence."[40] What is impossible in a dualistic frame, for the limited human to grasp illimitable God, is necessary in Spinoza's monism: we humans know God because we are an expression of the divine life.

Before leaving Spinoza as a source of alternative orthodoxy, I want to address his treatment of the relationship between humans and other animals. Spinoza was intentional in putting humanity into the same analysis as the rest of nature, and he was critical of the self-indulgence by which philosophers assumed human exceptionalism. He said of this: "Most of those who have written about the affects and men's ways of living seem to treat, not of natural things, but of things which are outside of nature. Indeed, they seem to conceive man in nature as a dominion within a dominion. For they believe that man disturbs, rather than follows, the order of nature, that he has absolute power over his actions, and that he is determined only by himself."[41]

Because Spinoza considered every aspect of reality to be a mode of God, and minds and bodies to be two different experiences of the same thing, he granted to animals minds: "For the things we have shown so far are completely general and do not pertain more to man than to the other individuals, all of which though in different degrees, are nevertheless animate."[42] How touching that he uses the term "other individuals" rather than "beasts" or "brutes" when speaking of the ways in which all

39. Shirley, *Spinoza: The Letters*, 238.

40. Spinoza, *Ethics*, 61.

41. Ibid., 68.

42. Ibid., 40.

animals participate in divine life. For Spinoza, the human body "has" an idea, the body is the material object and the mind is the awareness of that material object, but I must emphasize that neither one "owns" the other; rather they are different ways of experiencing the same thing. And this is true of all animal bodies. So mind is nothing other than the experience of the particular body in the world. Of course, then, animals have minds that are in accordance with their bodies.

Spinoza goes on to make the case for human superiority on the basis of our complexity and independence of body: "in proportion as a body is more capable than others of doing many things at once, or being acted on in many ways at once, so its mind is more capable than others of perceiving many things at once. And in proportion as the actions of a body depend more on itself alone, and as other bodies concur with it less in acting, so its mind is more capable of understanding distinctly. And from these [truths] we can know the excellence of one mind over the others."[43] He assumed, then, on the basis of what could be observed and inferred, that humans have a more complex body producing greater clarity of mind, and that humans also have greater independence of action than do other animals. I think that this was a rare instance of his accepting a set of assumptions given him by culture. He inferred the central importance of reason from the fact that humans must engage active reason in order to make the transition from passive recipients of their own cultures, impulses, and environments to contemplative and free lovers of God. Humans must use reason to come to understand the causes of self in order to enter into contemplation. What he missed is that this may not be a necessary step for other animals. His placement of humans and other animals in relation to each other is not required of his system of thought, and, in fact, if it were shown to him that other animals have brains as complex as our own and undertake action independently also, he would, I think, easily welcome each according to its kind into the realm of contemplatives.

Spinoza would still, I believe, hold that it is necessary for humans to engage reason actively in order to move from passive recipient of culture to active participant in God/Nature. In fact, he was only a small gap of experience away from articulating evolutionary continuity of mind two centuries before Darwin formulated the theory of evolution and several centuries before Griffin's insistence on taking seriously continuity of mind. I am quite sure that, if Spinoza had had a pet whale with its great

43. Ibid.

complex brain and fantastic independence of being, he would have formulated the relationship between animal and human as one of continuity
of mind with particular bodies giving rise to correlative minds.

For Spinoza, there were no abstracts floating around without reference to bodies, and this, it seems to me, argues for the relative value of
any adaptive capacity, no matter how sophisticated. The burden of proof
would lie in acquiring facts about other animals for the purposes of com-
parisons. However, the very fact of differing bodies means that differing
minds and capacities for action are incomparable, such that humans can
only excel at being humans, and each species can only excel within its
particular niche so that excellence is a relative feature for each kind of being, and only absolute in relation to the whole of nature as one being. It is
in this relationship to the Whole that the Other offers such great value, as
he/she/it in all its own particularity pulls us out of our constructed selves
and back into Nature/God.

Stepping back from the details of my analysis, I wonder whether
Spinoza's philosophy offers fresh grounds for conceptualizing the relationship of human and animal. In broad strokes, he offers a view in which
everything is an expression or mode of God/Nature, and in which each
thing is provisional and impermanent in its membership in the whole
of reality. This is vastly different in tone and quality from the idea that
humans are separate from the rest of nature and should aspire to domi-
nate it, the view espoused in Western culture from biblical thinking. The
latter is a model that has been more than fully exploited, and the former
remains to be developed as a platform for shared animal life on earth.

Agreeing with Spinoza, I hold that when we strive to know reality,
we have to part with ideas that are inadequate or not in keeping with reality, and instead search for ideas that are in keeping with what we know
of the world with greater certainty. Doing so, we move to greater degrees
of perfection and blessedness. Consequently, I say with him: "By Reality
and Perfection I understand the same thing."[44] And, in this spirit, I applaud the affective animal sentience by which we recognize the Other and
also the science that challenges us to new ways of thinking about animal
Others.

44. Ibid., 32.

Alternative Orthodoxies: The Buddha

Another great stream of religious thought that supports reconsideration of animal-human relations is Buddhism. Indeed, the three central teachings, the Dharma Seals, all point to a great continuity of Being within which individual beings reside briefly. Buddhist master Thich Nhat Hanh names the Dharma Seals, "impermanence, no-self, and nirvana."[45] Impermanence refers to the fact not just that things change but that they are constantly in motion, never really a substantially separate "thing." And the practice of impermanence is more than an intellectual understanding that things change; it is the habit of looking deeply into the present moment of experience until the lack of absolute boundaries between beings is perceived and an understanding of impermanence deeply integrated into the psyche or soul of the practitioner.

The understanding of no-self is in many ways the same insight as impermanence, but where impermanence refers to the temporal dimension, no-self refers to the spatial. There is no separate self, but only "interbeing." To be is to be part of other beings and to have other beings as part of self. These two conceptual practices lead to a movement toward being beyond concepts. Thich Nhat Hanh says, "The word 'nirvana' literally means 'the extinction of all concepts.'"[46]

In Buddhism, there is always the Buddha's message to notice the difference between the moon, the light itself, and the finger pointing at the moon, the teachings that direct the practitioner's gaze. "Because impermanence contains within itself the nature of nirvana, you are safe from being caught in an idea. When you study and practice this teaching you free yourself from notions and concepts, including the concept of permanence and impermanence. This way, we arrive at freedom from suffering and fear. This is Nirvana, the Kingdom of God."[47] As Descartes suspected, thinking is one thing that defines us, but he was wrong in designating it godlike and superior; it is what causes most of our suffering. When engaged with awareness, however, as taught by both the Buddha and Spinoza, it is also the way that we can find our way out of the suffering that it causes. This thinking problem, and its thinking solution, is the heart of our utterly human dilemma.

45. Hanh, *No Fear, No Death*, 39–46.
46. Ibid., 39–40.
47. Hanh, "Practice of Looking Deeply."

Calling to mind the three-level structure of the brain, I might say that the practices of impermanence and no-self lead to going beneath concepts. And I would also suggest that this living in awareness that is beneath concepts is something that animals do more than we do, not because they are unable to think and also not because they have achieved enlightenment, but because in some way, they never left grounded and embodied sentience for a realm of abstraction. Though they think, they are not lost in thought, and because of this, they can be very significant Others for us. But they cannot be the "poor brutes" we have imagined them to be. There is a poor brute in the house, but he is the human who cannot feel himself over the din of thoughts.

Alternative Orthodoxies:
Practical and Franciscan Christianity

Christianity is the spiritual tradition in which I was raised, and it is the one I know best, both in terms of scholarship and in terms of integrative understanding. After a long sojourn, I returned to Christianity of a very different kind than the kind I left. I am now an Episcopal priest, but I have to confess that I have struggled long and hard to find language with which to speak of Christianity. I often feel as though all the relevant words have been taken and filled with meanings that are counter to my integrated and lived understanding. And so, it is for me nothing about words that has brought me back to this lineage, but the practices themselves, the fire and the water, the bread and the wine, the cycle of feasts that correspond (in the Northern hemisphere) to the seasons of the year. There is a natural spirituality here, underneath the geological layers of words upon words.

The fact that words are so tainted, that so many Christians think that affirming particular formulations of ideas is the essence of spiritual living, reflects a sad state of Christian theological affairs, and I am grateful to Richard Rohr, Franciscan Catholic priest, both for the expression *alternative orthodoxy*, and for articulating Franciscan theology in words that express an ancient stream of Christianity. But before I turn to the Franciscan tradition, I do want to speak directly from my own practical experience, which I have come to claim as infinitely more valuable than the theological tomes I studied so earnestly in my youth.

I acknowledge that many Christians (and any religious people who require a "literal" interpretation of scriptures) would be terribly upset by my notion of natural spirituality because they give to words a reality that words do not have, and these people hold the words of scripture to be "more real" than the world. They are attached to the concept that religion is from God and that this must mean it is transcendent and supernatural, as is their God. They might well choose a Bible verse (or several) to show me how I am wrong. They are also attached to the idea that the Bible (or other scripture) is revelation and that this must mean that the words are factual, conveniently ignoring that the words often contradict themselves. The real problem, as I see it, is that there is no such thing as a "literal" interpretation of any text, but such is their cultural inheritance and their conviction. There is nothing I can do about this, there is no response I can make because I do not share their attachment to those concepts and, further, I think those ideas have come to do more to hide God from view than to reveal God. I think such an approach to revelation is, in fact, idolatry; it is a looking away from the living God and worshipping instead a collection of words in a book. I often think of such religion as being like a marriage in which one partner refuses to look up into the face of the beloved spouse because he or she is too busy reading old love letters from that spouse.

Few Christians would deny though that Christianity has to do with the person of Jesus. What makes a Christian is love of Jesus, and wanting to follow him, and to be like him. I am a Christian and a priest because of a very particular love of a very particular human, and not because I endorse a set of ideas as beliefs. In fact, the idea that to be Christian is to endorse ideas would keep me away rather than draw me to it. I do care, though, that I am true to Jesus, and so I wonder, "What would Jesus say in response to my proposition that we humans should keep the company of animals as a spiritual practice?" I think that he would say something to the effect of this: "I thank you, Father, Lord of heaven and earth, because you have hidden these things from the wise and the intelligent and have revealed them to infants [and animals]; for such was your gracious will."[48]

Jesus, the lovable human, did not deem equality with God something to be grasped, though he was said to be in the form of God. Rather he emptied himself.[49] What is most meaningful to me is that Jesus is

48. Matt 11:25.
49. Phil 2:6.

humanity's gift to God, and the prototype of the gift we all must be. He accepted death, the fate of all animals, and made of his death an offering, something that may well be a particular grace of our human psyches. Jesus repeatedly taught that self-congratulating human efforts, religious, political, business, are not Source, but that everything comes from God. Just as he understood it all to be given by his Father, he understood that the 100 percent gift comes at the price of 100 percent sacrifice. Not only did he accept his death and make of it an offering but he encouraged us to eat his life, to take it for our own transformation and nourishment, and told us to do the same. Jesus died as a meal, but he refused to live as prey. This is a powerful food chain theology for living and dying on earth. It is indeed Christian orthodoxy to say that there is no separate self, for even God only exists in Trinitarian relationship. And for humans, there is only membership in the mystical body of Christ, God incarnate, the universe, and in this is the vehicle by which we can come home to truth that all life is family life.

Alternatively, we can close our eyes, stop our ears, and whistle in the dark the tune, "me, my god, my life and the things that are mine." That however is a delusion, a drug of choice. God incarnate did not start or end with the person of Jesus, but began, as far as we know, with the Big Bang, 13.7 billion years ago. If that sounds too radical an interpretation of Christian incarnation theology, too much God in the world, know that I am in line behind Rohr and the whole blessed Franciscan lineage.

The Franciscan Lineage

Some time ago now, I read historian Lynn White's groundbreaking 1967 essay in which he blames Christian ways of thinking and acting for the path to ecological destruction, and in which he suggests Christians urgently need to rediscover Franciscan theology. Francis is, of course, the cultural icon of love of animals and his love for them expresses the depths of his understanding that everything contains divinity, that everything is sacred, that every being expresses God. Bonaventure's thirteenth-century biography of St. Francis includes many stories of his kind-hearted and natural interactions with various animals, from crickets, to wolves, to his seeming favorites, the lambs and the hares, whom he saw as expressing the innocence of Christ. Commenting on Francis' love of animals, Bonaventure says: "When he considered the primordial source of all things, he was filled with even more abundant piety, calling creatures, no matter how small, by the name brother or sister, because he knew they had the same source as himself."[50] And he expressed this "mystical" knowledge several hundred years before Darwin expressed it in scientific terms and even longer before neuroscientists unveiled the mechanism of his knowing.

Francis was himself, however, pointedly particular rather than general in his affections, as the following story illustrates: "Another time at Greccio a live hare was offered to the man of God, which he placed on the ground and let it free to go where it wished. But when the kind father called, it ran and jumped into his arms. He fondled it with warm affection and seemed to pity it like a mother. After warning it gently not to let itself be caught again, he let it go free. But as often as he placed it on the ground to run away, it always came back to the father's arms, as if in some secret way it perceived the kind feeling he had for it."[51]

This feature of Francis' particularity in relating to each creature as its own unique self is no doubt the source of his seeming "animal magic." Who among us would not want to stay in the company of such a person! No doubt the hare used the same secret senses that all animals have to perceive the feeling and motivational state of another animal. The surprising part of the story is that Francis was able to get beneath culture and beneath words to the actual animal in his company. The St. Francis statue in the garden is a rare religious icon that affirms our natural love of God's own Others in their particularity. How sad that we should need it, but how good that we have it.

Imagine my relief as a "natural spirituality" priest, when I read of Franciscan theology in Richard Rohr's most recent book, "We were always a kind of *alternative orthodoxy* within Catholicism."[52] More good news, from my perspective, is the Franciscan emphasis on incarnation— God in the flesh. It is another way to emphasize particularity, or God in the details. This Franciscan particularity is what I intend to evoke when I call upon divine eros. The gospel might be good news for animals like us after all.

In keeping with the Franciscan style of particularity, I like Francis because I find him likable, and that is just how God made the world,

---

50. Bonaventure, *Life of St. Francis*, 254.

51. Ibid., 257.

52. Rohr, *Immortal Diamond*, 149.

according to Franciscan theology. It is not an exclusive club of any kind. Consider these words of Bonaventure: "God is the essence of everything, within all things, but not enclosed, outside all things but not excluded, above all things, but not aloof, below all things, but not debased, this God is all in all."[53] Bonaventure's reflection on the First Letter to the Corinthians is a statement of Franciscan univocity, a word for the way that all being speaks Spirit.[54]

When Francis blessed the sow, an old story retold by a contemporary poet, who could doubt the sow's soul, or the connection between her soul and the soul of Francis, not floaty and ephemeral cloud-like souls but souls that hold all bodies together in Soul?[55] And God is the Being in whom all things are held together; nothing is excluded. How very close this is to the creative almost 14 billion-year-old universe. How very close this is to Spinoza's Nature/God. How very close this is to Buddhism beyond concepts.

When we argue concepts, and especially when we argue them to point of harming one another and the world with them, we are fools. We simply must get beneath words again; we must find our way to the garden that the others likely never left. And the garden is here, and we are in it, as soon as we are still enough to perceive it.

Again, consider the words of Bonaventure:

> Whoever therefore is not enlightened by such splendor of the created world is blind, whoever is not awakened by such outcries is deaf, whoever does not praise God because of these effects is dumb. Whoever does not discover the First Principle from which all these clear signs come is a fool. Open your eyes, alert the ears of your spirit, open your lips, and apply your heart so that in all creatures, you may see, hear, praise, love, worship, glorify and honor God. If you do not do this, the whole world will rise up against you.[56]

It is no leap at all to see the contemporary global ecological crisis as the rising up against us that happens, as Bonaventure long ago suggested, when we fail to apply our hearts to all of creation. Pity us, though, in our great difficulty in feeling our hearts at all.

53. Bonaventure, *Soul's Journey into God*, 100–101.
54. Rohr, *Beyond the Bird Bath*.
55. Kinnell, *New Selected Poems*, 94.
56. Bonaventure, *Soul's Journey into God*, 67–68.

Awakening

William James described religious experience as feeling at home in the universe.[57] I have found that simply allowing myself to feel connected to animal others is a way of waking up from a vaguely dreadful dream to find myself safe at home in the company of Molly Brown, Fling, Barbilla, the unnamed bat who drank and swam and slept, and many more whose stories are yet to be told. Neil Shubin, the scientist writing as a scientist, almost enters the waters when he says of our connection to the entire history and material of the cosmos, that "there is something almost magical to the notion that our bodies, minds, and ideas have roots in the crust of the earth, water of the oceans, and atoms in celestial bodies."[58] How close to Bonaventure he is.

Bonaventure said that if we fail to see God, the whole world will rise up against us. Russell Means said that the path of Spirit is the only true path. By leaving our bodies, by refusing to surrender to the suffering and death they entail, we are deluded and we jeopardize ourselves. Yes, the proverbial stick. But by putting our eyes back into our faces, by facing into our experiences of living on earth with others, we are immediately saved. The question is, can we move into this way of being as our house of habitation? Individuals have always done so, but—because of our problems with depression and violence, and collapse of ecological systems—we will need to do so collectively. I think that the only way that this can happen for the long term is by the way of the carrot, by allowing our natural attractions and natural satisfactions to come into our awareness. Awaken to how the world attracts you and satisfies you, right here and now; go under the din of words so you can feel the sun on your skin and see the dog at your side, whose delight you are.

It is fairly easy to give this kind of advice to myself, and even to a reader or many readers, but it is quite another to imagine a mass turning away from fast food and towards the joys of belonging to, with, and in this world. Can we awaken as a species? Though it is the carrot of eros that can bring about change at deeper levels and for longer terms, it is the stick that gets immediate attention and interrupts the flow of behavior. So it is reasonable to guess that suffering of the kind that forces us to our knees will be required for collective change. Having said that, I recall John Cacioppo's explanation that the carrot and stick are each built into the

57. James, *Varieties of Religious Experience*.
58. Shubin, *Universe Within*, 190.

biology of our bodies—the rate of depression, the epidemic of violence, and the loss of natural systems on which we depend are evidence that we may already be on our knees, perhaps soon ready to ask for help. If we surrender to the fall that is already underway, we might yet fall upwards.

And so, insanely simple as it sounds, I do suggest that we turn to other animals for comfort and companionship and ask of them our own questions about living these lives, and listen to what they say and to how they say it. Shubin elegantly describes the importance of all that animals share, in these words: "There is order to what we share with the rest of the world. We have two ears, two eyes, one head, a pair of arms and a pair of legs. We do not have seven legs or two heads. Nor do we have wheels."[59] Looked at from this perspective, it is obvious that we belong. What we, *Homo sapiens*, seem to have lost is the energy of our hearts, and the sense of our bodies, and the connections amongst us. It is as though we are choked by the collars of our own devising, tethered by the very leashes we intended for others. Why not ask these others what it means to have hearts and to live in bodies?

Is That You?

One day, as I sat on my back deck grading papers, a ladder-backed wood-pecker was making a nest at the top of the telephone pole that anchors the corner of my property. He seemed to come frequently and boldly near to the area of the deck where I worked, so I noticed him. After a while I went to the corner of the deck, looked up the length of the telephone pole, and said for my own amusement, "Fling! Is that you?"

The bird opened his wings and dropped the length of the pole to the ground and landed cheepering in the leaves.

59. Shubin, *Inner Fish*, 178.

Bibliography

Alexander, R. McN. "Bipedal animals, and their differences from humans." *J Anat* 204:5 (2004) 321–30.

Allen, K., et al. "Cardiovascular reactivity and the presence of pets, friends, and spouses: The truth about cats and dogs." *Psychosom Med* 64 (2002) 727–39.

Anthony, Lawrence, with Graham Spence. *The Elephant Whisperer: My Life with the Herd in the African Wild.* New York: Thomas Dunne, 2009.

Aquinas, Thomas. *Summa contra Gentiles* II. c.1264. Excerpted in Matthew Fox, *Sheer Joy: Conversations with Thomas Aquinas on Creation Spirituality,* 75. New York: Tarcher/Putnam, 2003.

———. *Summa Theologiae* I-II. 1265–74. Translated by the Fathers of the English Dominican Province. Online: http://www.sacred-texts.com/chr/aquinas/summa/sum104.htm.

Aridjis, Homero. "The Eye of the Whale." In Dick Russell, *The Eye of the Whale,* 12. New York: Simon and Schuster, 2001.

Aristotle. *On the Soul.* c.350 BCE. Translated by J. A. Smith. Online: http://classics.mit.edu/Aristotle/soul.2.iihtml.

———. *Physics.* c.335 BCE. Translated with commentary by Daniel W. Graham. Oxford: Clarendon, 1999.

BBC News. "SeaWorld sued over 'enslaved' killer whales." Online: http://www.bbc.co.uk/news/world-us-canada-16920866.

Baird, Alison. *White as the Waves: A Novel of Moby Dick.* St. John's, NL: Tuckamore, 1999.

Balcombe, Jonathan. *Second Nature: The Inner Lives of Animals.* New York: Macmillan, 2010.

Bartal, Inbal Ben-Ami, et al. "Empathy and Prosocial Behavior in Rats." *Science* 334:6061 (2011) 1427–30.

Bekoff, Marc. *Animals Matter: A Biologist Explains Why We Should Treat Animals with Compassion and Respect.* Boston, MA: Shambhala, 2007.

———. *The Emotional Lives of Animals: A Leading Scientist Explores Animal Joy, Sorrow, and Empathy—and Why They Matter.* Novato, CA: New World Library, 2007.

———. "Observations of scent-marking and discriminating self from others by a domestic dog (Canis familiaris): Tales of displaced yellow snow." *Behavioural Processes* 55 (2001) 75–79.

Bekoff, Marc, and Jessica Pierce. *Wild Justice: The Moral Lives of Animals.* Chicago: University of Chicago Press, 2009.

Benvenuti, Anne. "A Beautiful Confluence: Science and Religion as Human Modes of Participation in the Cosmos." *Forum on Public Policy* (2007) 758–74.

———. *Gendered Forms of Depression,* Parallel Event Presentation for the UN NGO Committee on Mental Health, United Nations Commission on the Status of Women. New York, March 2013.

———. "The Nones Are Off the Bus and Many of Them Are Alls." *The Interfaith Observer* (May 2013). Online: http://theinterfaithobserver.org/journal-articles/2013/5/15/the-nones-are-off-the-bus-and-many-of-them-are-alls.html.

———. "Self Esteem and Self Protective Strategies of African American AFDC Recipients." PhD diss., University of California Los Angeles, 1992.

Benvenuti, Anne, and Elizabeth Davenport. "The New Archaic: A Neuro-phenomenological Approach to Religious Ways of Knowing." In *A Field Guide to a New Meta-Field: Bridging the Humanities-Neurosciences Divide,* edited by Barbara Maria Stafford, 204–38. Chicago: University of Chicago Press, 2011.

Beston, Henry. "The Outermost House." 1928. Edited by Robert Finch and John Elder. *Nature Writing.* New York: Norton, 1990.

Blackiston, D. J., et al. "Retention of Memory through Metamorphosis: Can a Moth Remember What It Learned As a Caterpillar?" *PLoS One* 3:3 (2008). Online: doi:10.1371/journal.pone.0001736.

Bonaventure. *The Life of St. Francis.* Thirteenth century. Mahwah, NJ: Paulist, 1978.

———. *The Soul's Journey into God.* Thirteenth century. Translated by Ewert Cousins. Mahwah, NJ: Paulist, 1978.

Bradshaw, G. A., et al. "Elephant Breakdown: Social Trauma: Early disruption of attachment can affect the physiology, behaviour, and culture of animals and humans over generations." *Nature* 433 (2005) 807.

Bruck, Jason. "Decades-long social memory in bottlenose dolphins." *Proc R Soc B* 280 (2013). Online: http://dx.doi.org/10.1098/rspb.2013.1726.

Cacioppo, John T., and Jean Decety. "What Are the Brain Mechanisms on Which Psychological Processes Are Based?" *PPS* 4:1 (2009) 10–18.

Cacioppo, John T., and William Patrick. *Loneliness: Human Nature and the Need for Social Connection.* New York: Norton, 2008.

Cacioppo, John T., et al. *Social Neuroscience: People Thinking about Thinking People.* Cambridge: MIT Press, 2006.

Call, Josep, and Michael Tomasello. "Does the Chimpanzee Have a Theory of Mind? 30 Years Later." *Trends in Cognitive Sciences* 12:5 (2008) 187–92.

Center for Biological Diversity. "Court Rules that Federal Agency Failed to Protect Thousands of Whales and Dolphins from Navy Sonar: West Coast Marine Mammals Continue to Be Harmed by Deafening Underwater Noise." Press release, 2013. Online: http://earthjustice.org/news/press/2013/court-rules-that-federal-agency-failed-to-protect-thousands-of-whales-and-dolphins-from-navy-sonar.

Cerroni-Long, E. L. *Diversity Matters: Anthropological Perspectives.* Trieste: COER, 2001.

Chardin, Pierre Teilhard de. *The Phenomenon of Man.* New York: Harper Perennial Classics, 2008.

Chomsky, Noam. *Syntactic Structures,* rev. ed. The Hague: Mouton, 2002.

Churchland, Patricia. *Braintrust: What Neuroscience Tells Us about Morality.* Princeton, NJ: Princeton University Press, 2011.

Collis, Helen. "The Moment a Brave Mouse Tried." *The Daily Mail,* August 19, 2013. Online: http://www.dailymail.co.uk/news/article-2397070.

Coren, Stanley. *The Intelligence of Dogs: A Guide to the Thoughts, Emotions, and Inner Lives of Our Canine Companions.* New York: Bantam, 1995.

Cottingham, John. "'A Brute to the Brutes?': Descartes' Treatment of Animals." *Philosophy* 53 (1978) 551–59.

Cozolino, Louis. *The Neuroscience of Psychotherapy: Healing the Social Brain.* New York: Norton, 2010.

Czech-Damal, Nicole U., et al. "Electroreception in the Guiana dolphin (*Sotalia guianensis*)." *Proc R Soc B (2011).* Online: rspb2011.1127.pdf.

Dalai Lama. "Dalai Lama Urges Vegetarian Diet, Kindness to Animals." *Art of Dharma,* 2009. Online: http://www.artofdharma.com/kfc-and-animal-experimentation -billions-die.

Damasio, Antonio. *Descartes' Error: Emotion, Reason, and the Human Brain.* New York: Harper Perennial, 1995.

———. *The Feeling of What Happens: Body, Emotion, and the Making of Consciousness.* London: Heinemann, 1999.

———. *Self Comes to Mind: Constructing the Conscious Brain.* New York: Pantheon, 2010.

Dawkins, Richard. *The Selfish Gene.* 1976. Oxford: Oxford University Press, 30th anniversary edition, 2006.

Decety, Jean, and Philip L. Jackson. "The Functional Architecture of Human Empathy." *Behav Cogn Neurosci Rev* 3:2 (2004) 71–100.

Descartes, René. *Discourse on Method.* 1637. Translated by John Veitch, 1901. Online: http://www.earlymoderntexts.com/pdf/descdisc.pdf.

———. *Meditation VI.* 1641. Translated by John Veitch, 1901. Online: http://evans-experientialism.freewebspace.com/descartesmeditations06.htm.

———. *Meditations on First Philosophy.* Translated by Jonathan Bennett, 2010–15. Online: http://www.earlymoderntexts.com/de.html.

Desjarlais, Robert, et al. *World Mental Health: Problems and Priorities in Low Income Countries.* Oxford: Oxford University Press, 1996.

Dickinson, Emily. *The Complete Poems of Emily Dickinson.* Edited by Thomas H. Johnson. New York: Back Bay, 1976.

The Economist. "Flea market: A newly discovered virus may be the most abundant organism on the planet." February 16, 2013. Online: http://www.economist.com/news/science.

Edelman, Gerald M., and Giulio Tononi. *A Universe of Consciousness: How Matter Becomes Imagination.* New York: Basic Books, 2000.

Encyclopedia Britannica. "Factory Farmed Chickens: Their Difficult Lives and Deaths." Animal Advocacy, 2007. Online: http://advocacy.britannica.com/blog/advocacy/2007/05/the-difficult-lives-and-deaths-of-factory-farmed-chickens.

Ferrari, Alize J., et al. "Burden of Depressive Disorders by Country, Sex, Age, and Year: Findings from the Global Burden of Disease Study 2010." *PLoS Med* 10:11 (2013). Online: doi:10.1371/journal.pmed.100154.

Fields, R. Douglas. "Are Whales Smarter Than We Are?" *Scientific American: Mind Matters* (2008). Online: http://www.scientificamerican.com/blog/post. cfm?id=are-whales-smarter-than-we-are.

Fisher, Helen. *Why We Love: The Nature and Chemistry of Romantic Love.* New York: Holt, 2004.

Fitch, W. Tecumseh. "The Evolution of Speech: a comparative review." *Trends in Cognitive Science* 4 (2000) 258–67.

———. "The Evolution of Language: a comparative review." *Biology and Philosophy* 20 (2005) 193–230.

Fowler, Karen Joy. *We Are All Completely Beside Ourselves.* New York: Putnam, 2013.

Freeman, Mark. "Thinking and Being Otherwise: Aesthetics, ethics, erotics." *Journal of Theoretical and Philosophical Psychology* 32 (2012) 196–208.

Freud, Sigmund. "The Unconscious." 1915. In *The Standard Edition of the Complete Works of Sigmund Freud,* vol. 14, edited by J. Strachey, 159–209. London: Hogarth, 1953.

Frost, Robert. *The Poetry of Robert Frost: The Collected Poems.* New York: Holt, 1969.

Gazzaniga, Michael. *The Ethical Brain.* New York: Dana, 2005.

Gentner, Timothy Q., et al. "Recursive syntactic pattern learning by songbirds." *Nature* 440 (2006) 1204–7.

Goodall Institute. *Toolmaking.* Online: http://www.janegoodall.org/chimp-central-toolmakers.

Goodall, Jane. "My Life Among Wild Chimpanzees." *National Geographic* (August 1963) 272–308.

———. "Primate Spirituality." In *The Encyclopedia of Religion and Nature,* edited by B. Taylor, 1303–6. New York: Thoemmes Continuum, 2005.

Goodman, David M., and Mark Freeman. "Editorial: Psychology and the Other Special Issue." *Journal of Theoretical and Philosophical Psychology* 32 (2012) 193–95.

Grey, Aubrey de, with Michael Rae. *Ending Aging: The Rejuvenation Breakthroughs that Could End Human Aging in our Lifetime.* London: St. Martin's, 2007.

Griffin, Donald. *The Question of Animal Awareness: Evolutionary Continuity of Mental Experience.* Los Altos, CA: Kaufmann, 1981.

The Guardian. "Whales not slaves because they are not people, judge in SeaWorld case rules." Online: http://www.guardian.co.uk/environment/2012/feb/09/whales-not-slaves-judge-seaworld.

Hanh, Thich Nhat. *No Fear, No Death: Comforting Wisdom for Life.* New York: Riverhead, 2002.

———. "The Practice of Looking Deeply." *Shambhala Sun,* September 2002. Online: http://www.shambhalasun.com/index.php?option=content&task=view&id=1647.

Harrison, Peter. "Descartes on Animals." *The Philosophical Quarterly* 42 (1992) 219–27.

Hauser, M., et al. "The language faculty: what it is, who has it, and how did it evolve?" *Science* 298 (2002) 1569–79.

Hawking, Stephen. *A Brief History of Time,* rev. ed. New York: Bantam, 1996.

Hume, David. *A Treatise on Human Nature.* 1739–40. Edited by David Fate Norton and Mary J. Norton. Oxford: Oxford University Press, 2000.

James, William. *Principles of Psychology.* Mineola, NY: Dover, 1890.

———. *Psychology.* 1892. Greenwich CT: Fawcett, 1963.

———. *The Varieties of Religious Experience.* 1901–02. New York: Macmillan, 1961.

John of the Cross. *Dark Night of the Soul.* 1584–85. Mineola, NY: Dover, 2003.

Joyce, James. "A Painful Case." 1914. In *Dubliners,* 70–77. Mineola, NY: Dover, 1991.

Kaminski, Juliane, et al. "Dogs Steal in the Dark." *Animal Cognition* 16 (2013) 385–94.

Keeney, Bradford. *The Bushman Way of Tracking God: The Original Spirituality of the Kalahari People.* New York: Atria, 2010.

Kinnell, Galway. *A New Selected Poems.* New York: Mariner, 2002.

King, Barbara J. *How Animals Grieve.* Chicago: University of Chicago Press, 2013.

King, Stephanie, and Vincent Janik. "Bottlenose dolphins can use learned vocal labels to address each other." *PNAS* (2013) 13216–21.

Kohut, Heinz. *Self Psychology and the Humanities.* New York: Norton, 1985.

Kuhn, Thomas. *The Structure of Scientific Revolutions.* Chicago: University of Chicago Press, 1970.

Landau, M. J., et al. "Defending a coherent autobiography: When past events appear incoherent, morality salience prompts compensatory bolstering of the past's significance and future's orderliness." *Personality and Social Psychology Bulletin* 35 (2009) 1012–20.

LeDoux, Joseph. *The Synaptic Self: How Our Brains Become Who We Are.* New York: Penguin, 2002.

Lee, Phyllis C., et al. "Enduring consequences of early experiences: 40 year effects on survival and success among African elephants." *Biol Lett* (2013). Online: http://dx.doi.org/10.1098/rsbl.2013.0011.

Leibniz, G.W. *Samtliche Schriften und Briefe.* Darmstadt: Otto Reichl, 1926.

Lieberman, Philip. "The Evolution of Human Speech: Its Anatomical and Neural Bases." *Current Anthropology* 48:1 (2007) 39–66.

Linden, Eugene. *The Parrot's Lament (and Other True Tales of Animal Intrigue, Intelligence, and Ingenuity).* New York: Dutton, 1999.

Loftus, Elizabeth, and Jacqueline E. Pickrell. "The Formation of False Memories." *Psychiatric Annals* 25/12 (1995) 720–25.

Low, Philip. *Cambridge Declaration on Consciousness.* Francis Crick Memorial Conference on Consciousness in Human and non-Human Animals, 2012. Online: http://fcmconference.org/img/CambridgeDeclarationOnConsciousness.pdf.

MacLean, Paul D. *The Triune Brain in Evolution: Role in Paleocerebral Functions.* New York: Plenum, 1990.

Maehle, A-H., and U. Trohler. "Animal experimentation from antiquity to the end of the eighteenth century: attitudes and arguments." In *Vivisection in Historical Perspective,* edited by N. A. Rupke, 14–47. London: Croom Helm, 1987.

Mallet, Marie-Louise. Preface to Jacques Derrida, *The Animal That Therefore I Am.* New York: Fordham University Press, 2008.

Marino, Lori, et al. "Cetaceans Have Complex Brains for Complex Cognition." *PLoS Biology* 5:5 (2007) 966–72.

Mayell, Hillary. "When did 'Modern' Behavior Emerge in Humans?" *National Geographic News.* February 20, 2003. Online: http://news.nationalgeographic.com/news/pf/38293939.html.

McAdams, Dan P. "The redemptive self: Narrative identity in America today." In *The Self and Memory,* edited by D. R. Beike, et al., 95–115. New York: Psychology Press, 2004.

———. "The Psychological Self as Actor, Agent, and Author." *Perspectives in Psychological Science* 8 (2013) 272–95.

McLean, K. C., and M. A. Fournier. "The content and processes of autobiographical reasoning in narrative identity." *Journal of Research in Personality* 42 (2008) 527–45.

Meaney, Michael J. "Maternal Care, Gene Expression, and the Transmission of Individual Differences in Stress Reactivity Across Generations." *Annual Review of Neuroscience* 24 (2001) 1161–92.

Means, Russell. "For the World to Live, Europe Must Die." *Mother Jones*, 1980. Online: http://www.motherjones.com/politics/2012/10/russell-means-mother-jones-interview-1980.

Milgram, Stanley. "Behavioral study of obedience." *Journal of Abnormal and Social Psychology* 67 (1963) 371–78.

Mithen, Steven. *The Singing Neanderthals: The Origins of Music, Language, Mind, and Body.* Cambridge, MA: Harvard University Press, 2006.

Mlot, Christine. "Unmasking the Emotional Unconscious." *Science* 280 (1998) 1006.

Mora, Camilo, et al. "How Many Species Are There on Earth and in the Ocean?" *PLoS Biology* 9:8 (2011). Online: e1001127. doi:10.1371/journal.pbio.1001127.

Morell, Virginia, *Animal Wise: The Thoughts and Emotions of Our Fellow Creatures.* New York: Crown, 2013.

Morelle, Rebecca. "Elephant mimics Korean with the help of his trunk." *BBC News*, November 1, 2012.

Motzel, Louis D., et al. "The Architecture of Intelligence: Converging Evidence from Studies of Humans and Animals." *Current Directions in Psychological Science* 22 (2013) 342–48.

Muller, Wayne. *Sabbath: Finding Rest, Renewal, and Delight in Our Busy Lives.* New York: Bantam, 2000.

Nadler, Steven. *Spinoza's "Ethics": An Introduction.* Cambridge: Cambridge University Press, 2006.

Nagel, Thomas. *Mortal Questions.* Cambridge: Cambridge University Press, 1991.

National Institutes of Health. "NIH to reduce significantly the use of chimpanzees in research." June, 2013. Online: nih.gov.

Neal, David T., and Tanya L. Chartrand. "Embodied Emotion Perception: Amplifying and Dampening Facial Feedback Modulates Emotion Perception Accuracy." *Social Psychological and Personality Science* (2011) 1–7.

Nelson, Kevin. *The Spiritual Doorway in the Brain: A Neurologist's Search for the God Experience.* New York: Plume, 2012.

Newberg, Andrew B. *Principles of Neurotheology.* Farnham: Ashgate, 2010.

O'Connell, Caitlin. *The Elephant's Secret Sense: The Hidden Life of the Wild Herds of Africa.* Chicago: University of Chicago Press, 2008.

O'Connell, Caitlin, and E. O. Rodwell. "Keeping an 'ear' to the ground: seismic communication in elephants." *Physiology* 22:4 (2007) 287–94.

O'Connell, Caitlin, et al. "Seismic properties of Asian elephant (*Elephas maximus*) vocalizations and locomotion." *Journal of the Acoustical Society of America* 108:6 (2000) 3066–72.

Oliver, Mary. *Dream Work.* New York: Atlantic Monthly Press, 1986.

Panksepp, Jaak. *Affective Neuroscience: The Foundations of Human and Animal Emotions.* Oxford: Oxford University Press, 1998.

Panksepp, Jaak, and Lucy Biven. *The Archaeology of Mind.* New York: Norton, 2012.

Panksepp, J., and G. Northoff, "The trans-species core SELF: The emergence of active cultural and neuro-ecological agents through self-related processing within subcortical-cortical midline networks." *Consciousness and Cognition* 18 (2009) 193–215.

Payne, Katy. "Listening to Elephants." The Elephant Listening Project, 2011. Online: http://www.birds.cornell.edu/brp/elephant.

Payne, Roger. *Among Whales.* New York: Delta, 1995.

Penn, Derek C. "How Folk Psychology Ruined Comparative Psychology and How Scrub Jays Can Save It." In *Animal Thinking: Contemporary Issues in Comparative Cognition*, edited by Randolph Menzel and Julia Fischer, 253–65. Cambridge: MIT Press, 2011.

Peterson, Dale. *Jane Goodall: The Woman Who Redefined Man.* New York: Mariner, 2008.

———. *The Moral Lives of Animals.* New York: Bloomsbury, 2011.

Pew Forum on Religion and Public Life. "'Nones' on the Rise: One-in-Five Adults have No Religious Affiliation." 2012. Online: http://www.pewforum.org/2012/10/09/nones-on-the-rise.

Poole, Joyce H., et al. "The social contexts of some very low frequency calls of African elephants." *Behavioral Ecology and Sociobiology* 22 (1988) 385–92.

Ravven, Heidi. *The Self Beyond Itself: An Alternative History of Ethics, the New Brain Sciences, and the Myth of Free Will.* New York: New Press, 2013.

Ridgway, Sam, et al. "Spontaneous human speech mimicry by a cetacean." *Current Biology* 22:20 (2012) 860–61.

Rizzolatti, Giacomo, and Laila Craighero. "The Mirror-Neuron System." *Annual Review of Neuroscience* 27 (2004) 169–92.

Rizzolatti, Giacomo, and Corrado Sinigaglia. *Mirrors in the Brain.* Oxford: Oxford University Press, 2008.

Rohr, Richard. *Beyond the Bird Bath.* Albuquerque, NM: Rohr Institute Online Education: Center for Action and Contemplation, 2013.

———. *Falling Upward: A Spirituality for the Two Halves of Life.* New York: Jossey Bass, 2011.

———. *Immortal Diamond: The Search for Our True Self.* New York: Jossey Bass, 2013.

———. *Oneing: An Alternative Orthodoxy.* Online: https://cac.org/oneing-announcement.

Rose-Walker, Sherri. "Wild Healing." In *We'Moon Desk Calendar.* Wolf Creek, OR: Mother Tongue Ink, 1999.

Royzman, E. B., et al. "I know you know: Epistemic egocentrism in children and adults." *Review of General Psychology* (2007) 38–65.

Rumi, Jalal al-Din. "I would love to kiss you." Thirteenth century. *The Essential Rumi.* Translated by Coleman Barks. New York: Harper Collins, 1995.

Russell, Dick. *The Eye of the Whale: Epic Passages from Baja to Siberia.* New York: Simon and Schuster, 2001.

Sagan, Carl. *Cosmos.* New York: Ballantine, 1985.

Schore, Allan N. "Effects of a Secure Attachment Relationship on Right Brain Development, Affect Regulation, and Infant Mental Health." *Infant Mental Health Journal* 22 (2001) 7–66.

———. *Affect Dysregulation and Disorders of the Self.* New York: Norton, 2003.

———. *Affect Regulation and the Repair of the Self.* New York: Norton, 2003.

————. "The Paradigm Shift: The Right Brain and the Relational Unconscious." Plenary Address, American Psychological Association, Toronto, Canada, 2009. Slides. Online: http://www.allanschore.com/articles.php.

Science Daily. "Can Dogs Smell Cancer?" Online: http://www.sciencedaily.com/releases/2006/01/060106002944.htm.

————. "Improving dogs' ability to detect explosives." Online: http://www.sciencedaily.com/releases/2013/07/130730091148.htm.

Schutz, Larry E. "Broad-Perspective Perceptual Disorder of the Right Hemisphere." Neuropsychology Review 15 (2005) 11–27.

Schwartz, A. "On narcissism: an (other) introduction." In Pleasure Beyond the Pleasure Principle, edited by R. A. Glick and S. Bone, 111–37. New Haven, CT: Yale University Press, 1990.

Seppala, Emma. "The Compassionate Mind: Science shows why it's healthy and how it spreads." Observer, Association for Psychological Science 26 (2013). Online: http://www.psychologicalscience.org/index.php/publications/observer/2013/may-june-13/the-compassionate-mind.html.

Shakespeare, William. The Tragedy of Hamlet, Prince of Denmark. 1623. The Oxford Shakespeare, 681–718. Edited by John Jowett, et al. Oxford: Oxford University Press, 1986.

Sheppard, James, et al. "Exploring Causes of the Self-serving Bias." Social and Personality Psychology Compass 2:2 (2008) 895–908.

Shirley, Samuel. Spinoza: The Letters. Indianapolis: Hackett, 1995.

Shubin, Neil. Your Inner Fish: A Journey into the 3.5-Billion-Year History of the Human Body. New York: Vintage, 2009.

————. The Universe Within: Discovering the Common History of Rocks, Planets, and People. New York: Pantheon, 2013.

Skinner, B. F. Beyond Freedom and Dignity. Indianapolis: Hackett, 1971.

————. Walden II. Indianapolis: Hackett, 1948.

Slobodchikoff, Con. Chasing Doctor Dolittle: Learning the Language of Animals. New York: St. Martin's, 2012.

Smet, Anna F., and Richard W. Byrne. "African Elephants can use Human Pointing Cues to Discover Hidden Food." Current Biology 23 (2013) 1–5.

Smith, Gregory Blake. "Hands." In The Company of Animals, edited by Michael Rosen, 121–30. New York: Doubleday, 1993.

Smithsonian Institute. "What Does It Mean to Be Human: Genetics." Online: http://humanorigins.si.edu/evidence/genetics.

Smithsonian National Museum of Natural History. "What Does It Mean To Be Human: Walking Upright." Online: s.si.edu/human-characteristics/walking.

Sorensen, Eric. "The Animal Mind Reader." Washington State Magazine (2013). Online: http://wsm.wsu.edu/s/index.php?id=1037#.UnP-HCQ1Z78.

Spinoza, Benedict De. Ethics. 1677. London: Penguin Classics, 1996.

Stanovich, Keith, et al. "Myside Bias, Rational Thinking, and Intelligence." Current Directions in Psychological Science 22(4) (2013) 259–64.

Susman, R. L. "Hand function and tool behavior in early hominids." J Hum Evol 35 (1998) 23–46.

Swimme, Brian. Powers of the Universe. DVD lectures. N.P.: Center for the Story of the Universe, 2004.

Tavris, Carol, and Elliot Aaronson. *Mistakes Were Made (But Not by Me): Why We Justify Foolish Beliefs, Bad Decisions, and Hurtful Acts.* New York: Mariner, 2008.

Taylor, Shelley E., and Marci Lobel. "Social Comparison Activity Under Threat: Downward Evaluation and Upward Contacts." *Psychological Review* 96:4 (1989) 569–75.

Vaillant, George. *Triumphs of Experience.* New York: Harvard University Press/Belknap, 2012.

Vitousek, P. M., et al. "Human domination of Earth's ecosystems." *Science* 277 (1997) 494–99.

Voltaire. *Voltaire's Philosophical Dictionary.* 1764. Project Gutenberg, produced by Juliet Sutherland, et al., 2006. Online: http://www.gutenberg.org/files/18569/18569-h/18569-h.htm.

Waal, Frans de. *Chimpanzee Politics: Power and Sex among Apes.* Baltimore: Johns Hopkins University Press, 2000.

Wechkin, Stanley, et al. "Shock to a conspecific as an aversive stimulus." *Psychosomatic Science* (1964) 17–18.

Weiss, Alexander, et al. "Evidence for a midlife crisis in great apes consistent with the U-shape in human well-being." *PNAS*, Early Edition (2012) 1–4.

Wexler, Bruce E. *Brain and Culture: Neurobiology, Ideology, and Social Change.* Boston: MIT Press, 2006.

White, Lynn. "The Historical Roots of Our Ecologic Crisis." *Science* 155 (1967) 1203–7.

Wiley, David, et al. "Underwater components of humpback whale bubble-net feeding behavior." *Behavior* 148 (2011) 575–602.

Wilson, Timothy D. *Strangers to Ourselves: Discovering the Adaptive Unconscious.* New York: Harvard University Press/Belknap, 2002.

Yeats, William Butler. *Collected Poems.* 1934. New York: Simon and Schuster, 1996.

Young, Richard W. "Evolution of the human hand: the role of throwing and clubbing." *J Anat* (2003) 165–74.

Zimbardo, Phillip. "Interpersonal Dynamics in a Simulated Prison." *Journal of Criminology and Penology* 1 (1973) 69–97.